THE BEST OF
SMASH HITS

EDITED BY MARK FRITH

'80s the

sphere

Neil Tennant in the *Smash Hits* office, 1987.

FOREWORD
BY NEIL TENNANT

I WAS LUCKY enough to work for *Smash Hits* in a golden age for British pop, between the end of punk and Live Aid. This was the period when young, intelligent pop stars had learnt the lessons and ideas of punk and decided to link them to the glamour of pop stardom and nightlife. A stylish, thoughtful, hedonistic pop era flourished, and *Smash Hits* was its house magazine.

To realise what made *Smash Hits* special, you have to be aware of the competition: *NME*, *Melody Maker* and *Sounds*; weekly newspapers whose styles ranged from the faux intellectual to leaden music criticism. In those days we used to call them "rockist", an ultimate term of abuse. Actually, from our Carnaby Street offices we could look right into those of the *NME* across the road and mock their falling circulation.

Unlike these black-and-white papers, *Smash Hits* came out every two weeks and was glossy, colourful, witty and part of the new pop culture. It also saw itself as providing a service to the readers: accurate song lyrics of all the latest hits, brilliant colour photographs and intimate access to pop stars. What are they like? What are their lives like? What is it like being with them?

Smash Hits was never afraid to puncture the pretensions of pop stars – indeed that was another of its functions – but nothing would have been possible without the enthusiastic cooperation of pop stars who wanted their brilliant moments captured in colour, preferably on the cover.

At the same time, *Smash Hits* covered emerging new types of music – hip hop, for instance – and put new stars on the cover as often as possible, wanting to encourage the latest talent and wary of repeating the same old faces, iconic though they might be. Pop music had to be fresh and exciting.

THE READERS RESPONDED with a matching wit and intelligence. Droves of letters arrived at the office every day, which were carefully sifted through and the best printed. Fearless readers' questions were posed to pop stars and answered. The demands and criticisms of the readers were continually discussed in the office, and the magazine developed and changed in response.

Working at *Smash Hits* was incredibly good fun. The staff had a warm camaraderie, all pretty much obsessed with music. Staff humour became part of the fabric of the magazine, with feature ideas, headlines, opinions and jokes ricocheting around the office. I sat next to the office stereo, from which new music played on cheap speakers all day long, unless it was being used for the meticulous checking of song lyrics. On Tuesday morning the new chart would be phoned through, with everyone gathered round alternately thrilled and appalled by the latest entries and positions. It was the best "proper" job I ever had.

In 1985 I quit being Assistant Editor with the somewhat ridiculous notion of becoming a pop star myself as half of the Pet Shop Boys. I secretly imagined that I'd have to return within the year, asking for my job back. But, amazingly, a year later we were on the cover of *Smash Hits*. We'd made it.

Neil Tennant

Contents

FEATURES

SONGS

POSTERS

Andre Csillag, Redferns, Smash Hits Archive, Eric Watson, Cover photos: LFI, Redferns, Smash Hits Archive

sphere

Brettenham House, Lancaster Place, London WC2E 7EN

Editor
Mark Frith

Editor-In-Chief
Mark Blake

Art Editor
Lora Findlay

Picture Editor
Dave Brolan

Production Editor
Michael Johnson

Designer
Isabel Cruz

Sub Editor
Justin Hood

Research
John Hindmarch

Publisher
Stuart Williams

Licensing Manager
Olivia Smales

Special Thanks
Nasarene Asghar, Ian Cranna, Mark Ellen, Chris Heath, David Hepworth, Tom Hibbert, Peter Martin, Barry McIlheney, Simon Mills, Sylvia Patterson, Maureen Rice, Dave Rimmer, William Shaw, Neil Tennant

The Sphere Team
Suzanne Fowler, Antonia Hodgson, Caroline Hogg, Marie Hrynczak and Alison Lindsay

First published in Great Britain in 2006 by Sphere

Copyright © Emap Consumer Media Ltd 2006

Smash Hits is a trademark of Emap Consumer Media Ltd and is used under licence. All rights reserved.

The moral right of the author has been asserted.

All rights reserved.

No part of this publication may be reproduced, stored in a retrieval system, or transmitted, in any form or by any means, without the prior permission in writing of the publisher, nor be otherwise circulated in any form of binding or cover other than that in which it is published and without a similar condition including this condition being imposed on the subsequent purchaser.

Every effort has been made to trace the copyright holders of the photographs in this book but one or two were unreachable. We would be grateful if the photographers concerned would contact us.

A CIP catalogue record for this book is available from the British Library.

ISBN-13: 978-0-316-02709-0
ISBN-10: 0-316-02709-X

Colour origination by Rival Colour.

Printed and bound in Great Britain by Butler and Tanner Limited, Frome and London.

Sphere
An imprint of Little, Brown Book Group

A member of the Hachette Livre Group of Companies

www.littlebrown.co.uk
www.smashhits.net

20

UTTERLY AMAZING FACTS ABOUT SMASH HITS

The famous funnyman's failed job application, the "coloured sock" question, the missing cans of jungle-themed fizzy pop… All these and 17 more snippets of vital Hits-related info.

3

A YOUNG CHAP named Jim Moir from Darlington made it down to the last three for the coveted *Smash Hits* Staff Writer position in 1987. Sadly for him, he was deemed to be "not funny enough for the *Hits*" and was "pipped" to the post by the officially more amusing Mike Soutar and Miranda Sawyer. Devastated, Moir went on to become a top comedian under his new name of Vic Reeves.

4

WHILE "LAYING OUT" the songwords to The Smiths' "Shoplifters Of The World Unite", the art "desk" thought it would be a top idea to superimpose the words on to a, er, Tesco bag. Cue panic phone calls from Tesco "bigwigs" re army of *Hits* viewers storming the tills and making off without paying. Luckily it didn't happen and Tesco profits remained unaffected.

5

ODD-ONE-OUT time: Strawberry Switchblade, Jimmy The Hoover, Michael Jackson and Department S. That's right. They were all on the cover of *Smash Hits* in the '80s *except* Michael Jackson. Fact!

6

JOHNNY POP STAR would come and go, but the *Hits* vernacular would remain largely intact. In this parallel universe, readers were "viewers", the word "please" became "pur-lease", and the highest form of praise was one louder than "ber-illiant", ie "swingorilliant" (see The *Smash Hits* Dictionary, page 24). At least one of these phrases was created by early-'80s Assistant Editor Neil Tennant, later to leave the magazine and become one-half of top pop "outfit" Erasure. (*Check this – Ed.*)

7

IN A SIMILAR "vein", certain pop types would mysteriously acquire a "new" name, which would stay with them forever more, eg "Dame" David Bowie, "Lord Frederick of Mercury", "Lord Clifford of Richard", etc. For reasons now lost in time, the members of top rock "combo" U2 would forever be known as Bobo, The Hedge, Adam "Clear Off!" Clayton and The Other One.

8

ON ENTERING *Hits*' Carnaby Street office in the late '80s, visitors would be "greeted" by the massive arch featured in the Lord Frederick Of Mercury video for top Olympics ditty "Barcelona". This had been donated by Lord Frederick's record company as the prize in a readers' competition, but was so huge that it would never fit into any normal house except in the unlikely event that the winner was literally a giant. It was also a fire hazard and was eventually removed by the London Fire Brigade.

1

1978, AND THE very first issue of what was to become The World's Greatest Pop Magazine™ is about to be launched. Ex-*NME* Editor Nick Logan had come up with the idea for a pop magazine with lots of posters and songwords, but he wasn't sure whether to call it *Disco Fever* or, er, *Smash Hits*. Luckily the "suits" at publishers Emap opted for the latter, and the rest, as "they" say, is hysteria. Belgian nut job Plastic Bertrand – he of "Ca Plain Pour Moi" "fame" – was the first cover star.

2

AFTER MANY YEARS of refusing to be in the magazine under any circumstances, David Bowie finally relented, "persuaded" perhaps by the bad smell surrounding his Glass Spider tour of 1987. Unfortunately for the Dame, the resulting three-page "interview" focused mainly on the mating habits of the chameleon, the reptilian creature the great man would often compare himself to, what with them both being keen on changing and that…

9 WITH SALES NUDGING towards the frankly astonishing one-million-per-issue mark during 1988, the great moment was fittingly reached around the time of the magazine's tenth anniversary, with the Kylie/Jason cover of November 1988 (see interview, page 168). Kylie would go on to become one of the only two popstrels to "grace" the cover of ver *Hits* in each of its three decades. The other is Madonna.

10 ONE OF THE magazine's biggest, if short-lived, cover stars was ex-Stock Aitken & Waterman teaboy-turned-warbler Rick Astley, best remembered for his debut smash hit "Never Gonna Give You Up". Unfortunately for Rick, he divulged in an early *Hits* interview that the first song he wrote as a boy had been called "A Ruddy Big Pig Came Down Our Street" – a piece of pure *Hits* gold that would be duly trotted out every time the words "Rick" and "Astley" appeared together in the mag.

11 DESPITE BEING THE biggest band in the world in the late '80s, U2 were never deemed quite right for the magazine, what with Bobo's tendency to waffle on about "where the streets have no roads", etc. This all changed at the Brit Awards in 1988, when the great man kindly agreed to draw a duck on a napkin and have said doodle analysed by a top head doctor. Conclusion? Whoever drew that duck is bonkers. (See more ducks on page 147.)

Photos: LFI, Retna, Rex, Smash Hits Archive

12 SHAM 69'S JIMMY PURSEY stormed into the office in 1981 and angrily demanded that the magazine never write anything about him – or his group – ever again. *Smash Hits* has kept its side of the "bargain" for 25 years now.

13 THE READERS' LETTERS in the magazine were "edited" by the mysterious Black Type, who would reward the sender of each issue's best letter with a case of most refreshing drink Um Bongo Um Bongo (They Drink It In The Congo…) – invariably lost in the post – while other readers whose mad ramblings made it into print would be sent a highly coveted Black Type Tea Towel. Prime Minister Margaret Thatcher was presented with the very same by writer Tom Hibbert on the occasion of their now legendary interview (see page 142), though it is unknown whether the PM declared this gift in the Parliamentary Register of Interests.

14 WHEN THE *HITS* ran a competition with the hip hop label Tommy Boy, the prize was a tall, knitted beanie hat with the record company logo on it. The office received just one measly entry – from Green Gartside of the band Scritti Politti – and the hat was duly mailed to him.

15 DESPITE OFTEN BEING referred to as "the magazine that asks pop stars what colour their socks are", this is in fact the one question that no pop star was ever asked by *Smash Hits*. Those that were, however, included "Do eggs make a queer whistling noise when you fry them?", "Have you ever thought you were a roundabout?" and, famously, "What colour is Tuesday?" (See page 116 for more classic questions).

16 OWING TO THE magazine's location in the heart of London's fashionable West End, minor pop stars would often turn up unannounced in reception and sit there for some time hoping to be interviewed. Eventually, anyone keen to be in the magazine rather than the other way round would be described as being "in reception". This could lead to confusion with new staff members who, on suggesting that, say, Toyah Wilcox should be in the magazine, would immediately be told that "Toyah's in reception". A thorough search of the cramped waiting area would then ensue…

17 AMONG THE MANY "celebrities" who have expressed their admiration for ver *Hits* over the years are *Little Britain*'s David Walliams and, er, the Prince of Brunei. The former once revealed a lifelong ambition to write for The World's Greatest Pop Magazine™, while the latter actually made a historic pilgrimage to the office and then presented the frankly confused staff with a cake he had baked for the visit.

18 A LAST-MINUTE add-on at most magazines, the Coming Next Issue or "trail" page in *Smash Hits* would be toiled over for many "moons", with staff members aiming to outdo one another in devising the most unlikely promised fare for viewers to enjoy in two weeks' time. The early-'80s trail for the next issue's feature on The Human Saucepans Of The Orinoco takes some beating.

19 A NUMBER OF *Smash Hits* alumni have moved on to allegedly bigger and better things. Long-serving staff members such as David Hepworth, Mark Ellen, Ian Birch, Barry McIlheney, David Bostock, Mark Frith and Mike Soutar have gone on to launch and edit magazines within *Smash Hits* publishers Emap and beyond. Ex-Editor Kate Thornton is rumoured to be on national TV, Ex-Assistant Editor Neil Tennant has written the Foreword to this very book, writer Chris Heath has retired on the proceeds of his Robbie Williams biography, *Feel*, and Tom Hibbert has simply retired. The whereabouts of Tom Moloney, Publisher and then MD of the magazine throughout the '80s, are "currently unknown".

20 2006, AND THE very last issue of what was still The World's Greatest Pop Magazine™ was created entirely on a mobile phone, using only a microchip, a monkey and a dwarf. The dwarf (*Stop it, this is meant to be serious – Ed.*). Sorry. The very last issue had as its cover star none other than Preston of Ordinary Boys "fame".

THE SUN KING

Mark Ellen flies to the south of France and finds Adam and his remade, remodelled Ants (battle cry: "Optimism and lots of drums!") basking in the sunshine of some long-awaited success.

WELCOME TO Aix-En-Provence. It's the kind of "leafy, tree-strewn township" that travel brochures always describe as "positively *dripping* with history".

Occasional cars hum past weed-encrusted fountains. The afternoon sunlight shines on café tables laden with the evidence of expensive meals. The murmur of contented voices is broken only by the soft chink of emptying wine glasses. France is putting its feet up.

Suddenly a hideous distorted wail erupts from the direction of the pavement. Rows of heads swivel to discover that a pair of deadbeat hippies with electric guitars have chosen this scenic spot for a painful rendition of "Black Sabbath's Greatest Soundchecks". The crowd aren't exactly thrilled. Least of all the table at the back.

"Oy, do you do requests?" enquires a muscular, pale-faced Englishman with a tattoo on his arm. They do. "Well, hop it then!" he grins. They're playing in the wrong key, someone observes.

"Wrong key? Wrong town, more like! Where's the tour manager? Get him to fix up an itinerary. South America. The Congo. Outer Mongolia… anywhere but HERE!"

Our musical friends seem to mistake this for encouragement and come shuffling over, cap in hand. Disguise, quick! "This calls for only one thing, men," the captain decides, "and that's hats!" He rises slowly to give the command, his three or four braids bound in red and gold ribbon catching the breeze. "Haaaats!!", and his three compadres promptly acquire table napkins and begin to fashion them into loosely constructed turbans.

"First afternoon off they've had in ages," explains their 'security man' gleefully. Time off for him too. "It's great here," he says, "they never get recognised."

I glance at the boys in question. Jeans, T-shirts, no make-up, napkins on their heads. Adam And The Ants? Know 'em anywhere!

WITH THEIR FIFTH Top Ten single, "Stand And Deliver", still

basking at Number One back on home turf, the Ants are moving through uncharted territory amid the kind of trappings that indicate freshly won Platinum status. A massive road crew, an articulated truckload of gear, wardrobe units, merchandise and make-up team, and a "minder" fresh from service with Led Zeppelin. There's even a trio of silky black limos hired to glide them to the evening's venue – the Krypton Ultra-Disco – and then whisk them back to the hotel at a carefully regulated "on-stage temperature".

It's what Adam's worked five hazardous years to achieve, what he now most definitely needs, and what – in my book – he also richly deserves.

As he's the first to admit, when we're staked out in the sun on the hotel patio awaiting the midnight gig, only last February he was being numbered by all and sundry as the "all-time loser". Working with no record company support, virtually no money and against a wall of public mistrust, along had come Malcolm McLaren, sifted

through his ideas, and then nicked the very band from under him to construct the suspiciously similar-sounding BowWowWow.

"If I learnt anything from him," Adam admits, succinct as ever, "it's that if you've got an idea, you've got to keep it to yourself. An idea shared," as he found to his cost, "is an idea halved."

At this point he'd enlisted the unmistakeable songwriting talents of Marco "The Big Man" Pirroni and, later, the twin drum support of Terry Lee Miall and Chris "Merrick" Hughes with, at that time, Kevin Mooney on bass. "It's all so simple," explains his replacement, Gary Tibbs, late of Roxy Music. "Kevin sacked the four of them then they all joined my band!"

Marco, incidentally, describes his living habits as "nocturnal". So nocturnal, in fact, that the rare moments he appears before dark are greeted by riotous applause. If he isn't eating, he's asleep in his hotel room escaping the "dreaded daylight". "France isn't bad," he scowls at the baking

Adam Ant: Preparing
to stand and deliver

9

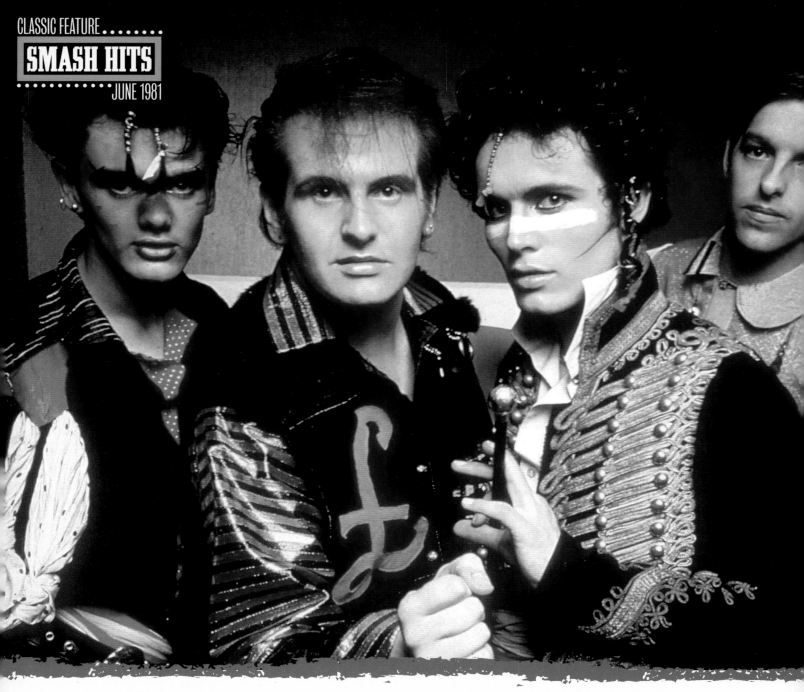

I.FI. Mark Ellen

sunshine, "it's just the weather that's so awful!"

Adam and Marco's compositional flair was first brought to life by Merrick's production. (You can tell he's a sound-man; he spends a happy afternoon listening to a tape of an industrial steam-hammer and recording Adam's digital watch, which plays on demand "The Yellow Rose of Texas"). The new Ants' sound and vision appeared last summer with "Kings Of The Wild Frontier" as its calling-card. As Adam recalls, it marked an official crossing of the threshold between "rock'n'roll" and "showbiz".

"It took me a long time to discover that they were two very different things and that one was more appealing to me than the

other. I felt rock'n'roll had lost all its colour, all its flair. Show-business has got more life to it. You have to be of a much higher calibre to survive.

"I realised that the most important thing was not to compete with any other groups. Not to feel jealous of anybody else. Just to get on with your own career. Also to be very colourful – and to push that to an extreme – and be very 'total' about what you do. Another really important thing, next to The Sound and The Look, was to *create* an audience, really, not to cater for one. And to *enjoy* life," he adds, simply. "I enjoy it more now than I did before."

What people needed was "entertainment", he'd decided at the time, and not yet another

band reflecting the gloominess of the period via a witless stage act and negative outlook. They needed something, he thought, that wasn't just willing to give up and drop dead. "And if it wasn't negative," Adam recalls, "it was esoteric and far too 'arty' for anyone's good. But then, I'm guilty of that as a writer, too. I think 'Dirk Wears White Sox' was 'arty', though a good album compared with what was coming out at the time. The topics on it were a little – shall we say – beyond the grasp of a lot of people that were listening to the group."

As he points out, it was that same grass-roots following who'd bought "Dirk", and sold out the Ants Invasion Tour prior to the CBS signing, who went straight

out and bought the "Kings" single. The combined force of 50,000 sales secured a *Top Of The Pops* slot and, once played, 250,000 more clapped eyes on something irresistibly Brand New and decided they'd better get themselves a copy, too.

And the rest, in the words of the prophet, is history…

ASKED TO EXPLAIN himself later, as he waits for a sound-check among crates of half-unpacked gear, Adam answers with the kind of clarity and sheer determined business sense that could almost put Stewart Copeland in the shade. "I've been in the clubs five years now," he'll remind you, "and I don't forget them. I don't forget what people

The Ants line-up that made the breakthrough: (left to right) Kevin Mooney, Marco Pirroni, Adam, Merrick and Terry Lee Miall.

due to television and the national press and to colour magazines like *Smash Hits* and *Flexipop*. And that represents, I think, a revolution in the music industry because we've been absolutely hated by the official music press and yet have still become the most popular group in the '80s. And that's an achievement because young people forming groups are absolutely at the mercy of some reviewers."

Even two years ago, the notion of an "artist" being a business-man was considered almost immoral and only associated with balding, middle-aged super-groups who spent more time making investments than albums. It's not hard to see why someone who's survived a succession of managers and record deals since '76 isn't about to fall into the same traps a second time. Interestingly, Adam admires Gary Numan – "the first non-airheaded rock star" – for the simple reason that, business-wise "he's one of the forerunners in being in control of your own destiny".

He's also suffered a lot of mud-slinging for his faith in his audience, but there's no denying success has proved him dead right all along. "The audience makes you. You don't bite the hand that feeds you. You respect them because they give you the respect. The reason I'm able to demand respect from promoters and people in the industry is because my records sell. And who buys the records? The kids. So they demand more respect and consideration than anybody.

"I think the music business is learning that because they went through a period in the '70s of pushing people to the limits, of saying: 'You're going to pay five

pounds for a piece of plastic that's worth 50p with no cover to speak of and no lyrics.' And the kids just turned around and said 'no'. And what happened? The music business nearly collapsed, and it brought it down to a harsh reality which I lived through, and I built on, because I'm aware of it.

"And I maintain," he says, scarcely drawing breath, "that the audience is the most important consideration… tonight, tomorrow, next year, next century. And once you think you're 'above' your audience, then I think that's the time to seriously re-consider your career."

THIS BEGS THE obvious question of whether the Ants' original diehard following have a right to feel "betrayed" by the current and sudden ascent. We get thousands – literally thousands – of letters on this, and other, Antopics at *Smash Hits*, I tell him. The postman's had to take a muscle-building course. "When a group's been very 'cult'," Adam considers, "and then gets 'acceptability', there is a feeling – initially – of betrayal. A feeling that it's got too big too fast. Really, it depends on how fast those fans are maturing. You see, somebody could have got into the Ants when they were 15 and they'd be 19 now! And I can't honestly look people in the face and say: 'I expect people to adhere to everything I do and say for five years.' I mean, I got into Roxy Music on their first album and I'm beginning to waver now. But I still buy Roxy albums because

I know that potentially Ferry can come up with songs like he did on the first two albums, and my heart's still there."

Most – if not all – of these letters, I mention, have that feminine touch about them. Adam smiles; the two teenage girls who've sneaked up behind us to listen in begin to quiver visibly. (One hitch-hiked from Manchester; the other from Stockholm.) "Well," comes the explanation, "I think rock'n'roll music – or *any* performance, entertainment, showbiz – revolves around sex in some gold belts."

I suggest to Adam that there's a growing similarity of dress among Ant fans that might threaten their individuality. He doesn't agree. "Imitation is the greatest compliment that any artist can ever hope for. I can remember imitating Bryan Ferry and the New York Dolls and T.Rex. Everybody goes through a stage of imitation and anybody who doesn't admit it is either a liar or a genius."

THE CARS DRIFT noiselessly on to the gravel drive outside. The Ants pile in and head back to the hotel. The next hour will transform Adam from this chap in baggy beige trousers, striped top and black buckled boots into the figure that's gradually replacing wallpaper in the bedrooms of Europe. "You know," he says, "I still think of England as a base.

'Cos that's where you're born, and that's where you launch, and that's where you get the most feed-back. British audiences are – without doubt – the most discerning and difficult to work to because they're the most choosy. I always worry when I put a record out that it's going to be a miss. 'Cos I've had misses. There's just no words to describe that feeling when a record doesn't make it. The fact that they

are like when you're supposedly 'a failure'. I know why this group is successful; because we work very hard and we're careful about who we work with now – we only work with professionals. Also," he prods the table-top for emphasis, "the success of the Ants has been

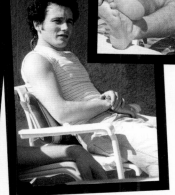

Paleskins in the pink: (left to right) Terry, Merrick, Adam and Gary Tibbs.

Dirk may wear white sox but Mr Ant opts for pirate/ dragoon guard/ native American/ glam chic...

good. He kept jumping about for absolutely no reason with this silly mask on."

They kept in touch on and off, and went their separate ways – Marco with The Models, The Banshees (with Sid Vicious on drums) and Rema Rema; Adam with the Ants, and nothing but the Ants.

THREE YEARS ELAPSED, and then a note was slipped under Marco's door. "Get In Touch", was the message – "Adam Ant". A phone call later and the pair were comparing notes. Neither had a band – McLaren having relieved Adam of his three former charges only the night before – and both wanted another one. Exactly what kind of band remained to be explored. One thing was established soon enough: their tastes were almost identical.

In sharp contrast to Adam's torpedo monologues, Marco takes up the story between long wistful pauses, still encamped in his hotel bed and hardly the healthier for a suntan. "We'd always liked the same things," he explains, "Roxy Music and the Sex Pistols. I loved all those early '70s groups – Slade, T.Rex, Gary Glitter, The Arrows, Hello, Alvin Stardust. And we both loved Alice Cooper [a performer considered so shocking at the time, his stage act was discussed in Parliament]. He was the sort of person who would scare your mum," Marco reveals fondly. "Very much a Sex Pistols sort of character. All that eating chickens and biting the heads off guitarists."

It's revealing that Marco's admiration continued even when Cooper became "this Beverly Hills showbiz-type character". For much the same reasons, he and Adam liked the New York Dolls (bisexual glam-rockers and McLaren's first protégés), particularly the women's shoes, the outlandish hairstyles, the satin shirts and the bassist with his wrist chained to his ankle. "Adam and I sat down in his front room and thought and thought. We had no idea what we wanted; we just knew what we didn't want. We didn't want keyboards, 'cos at that time there were all these bands like Throbbing Gristle and

became hits later didn't affect that at the time. Every element of what you do has to be thought about. You can't cut corners, 'cos if you do you just suffer in the end." So speaks the voice of experience. I like him, and admire him. Me and a few million others.

MARCO PIRRONI MET Stuart Goddard in '77 in Seditionaries, then the fashion/music nerve

centre of the Western World. Not the most eventful of occasions, but then not the easiest to forget. "This is Adam," said Vivienne Westwood, Malcolm McLaren's partner and co-founder of the King's Road shop. "He's in a band." "Who the hell isn't these days?" Marco had mused, it being a time when, if you hadn't switched line-ups at least twice by lunch-time, you weren't in the

race at all. "He seemed so enthusiastic and friendly," recalls Marco of Adam. "I thought, 'This must be an idiot.'"

He went along to see the Ants playing The Man in The Moon that night, to witness such crowd-pleasers as "Dirk", "B-Side Baby" and "Christian Dior". He'd expected the worst, so he wasn't disappointed. "They were *awful*," was the verdict, "but *he* was really

L.Fl. Redferns

The Human League. Morose, moronic synthesizer bands who were always moaning, so that was right out of the window. In fact," he decides, "we did want commerciality. Good songs, first and foremost, without having to rely on freeform instrumentation. And optimism," he adds, "and lots of drums."

The monster first peeled itself off the drawing-board in the shape of the "Kings Of The Wild Frontier" single, an unlikely marriage between "Burundi drums, Duane Eddy guitar and Gary Glitter shouting". This made its historic debut chez Marco with the help of two acoustic guitars, the rest being left to the imagination. Unsurprisingly, it "didn't sound like much at all".

Two weeks' recording followed in which to commit "Kings" to tape, along with new recruits Kevin Mooney on bass and drummers Terry Lee Miall and Merrick. The scene was a sardine-can of a studio near the British Museum. "Torture" is the way Marco remembers it. "It might just as well have been in the British Museum! But when we finished it, we loved it. Our manager at the time hated it. CBS said, 'What's this supposed to be?' Everybody hated it!"

Everybody except the public. As Adam points out, quite apart from their look, which set the charts alight on the strength of the first TOTP appearance, they'd achieved that crucial stamp of identity – the mark of Blondie, Talking Heads, Police, Abba – their own, unmistakable sound.

In his infinite wisdom (and honesty), Adam firmly insists it isn't "original". "I still maintain none of the ideas are mine. It's just the way Marco and I have moulded them together. The only people who are absolutely original are 'genius', and they're very rare." Asked for examples, he'll grudgingly betray his art school background and list four painters – the English visionary Stanley Spencer, the surrealist Salvador Dali, and the Italian futurists Marinetti and Boccioni. And the writer Joe Orton, whose biography "Prick Up Your Ears" may have a familiar ring to those well versed in the lyrics of "The Magnificent Five".

Musically, he says he's tapped the most obscure sources to arrive at the format he was looking for. "Off-the-wall stuff", he calls it: jazz, tribal music and "hours of listening to quite painfully dull vocal sounds. If you're not aware of the History of Art," it once fortunately dawned on him, "you're in great danger of repeating it."

THE PERIOD PRIOR to the TOTP debut found Adam Ant deep in research. "Getting some education" is the phrase in question. A vividly colourful romantic image was the requirement and – let's face it – both English and American history is rich in possible contenders. The Victorian novels of the former supplied plenty of ideas for the Highwaymen wardrobe that finally came together in the "Stand And Deliver" video (during the making

of which Adam knocked himself unconscious when leaping through a fake glass window). On the American side, the book of the somewhat tedious 1980 film "The Island" provided themes for the Pirate look, and three movies – "Soldier Blue", "Little Big Man" and the serial "Roots" – set the cogs in motion for the Red Indian image, all three having a strong emphasis on an ethnic culture oppressed by White Western Man.

These led him to discover more accurate accounts of Indian philosophy by reading "Black Elk Speaks", "Bury My Heart At Wounded Knee" and "Gospel Of The Red Man". Adam drew some parallels between the beliefs of the Redskin warrior and those of the equally threatened Ants.

He outlines a few details. "A chief becomes a chief solely by virtue of the amount of good he does for the tribe. A woman is Mother Earth, the only one who can produce children, and thus she demands – and gets – that respect. If a child is born out of wedlock, he belongs to the whole tribe. If somebody's born effeminate, he's not forced to become a warrior. And there's a respect for Nature – you give and you take".

There was also another contact. "The Indians had been misrepresented, and so had I. We (the Ants) were looked upon as the Last Store Of Punk. Our existence was being challenged, and that of the people who liked the group. So it helped me get out of a corner and stand up and be proud of my beliefs, because I believed in wearing make-up, and I believed in wearing certain clothes, and so did they. And that's why the lyrics on the "Kings" album are collective. WE ARE FAMILY!! Also," he adds, "the idea of the warrior ideal is that everyone is unique. I think there's an individuality in the way in which everybody dresses like Adam And The Ants. You get kids who've actually gone to books on pirates or books on Indians and found something that's theirs."

AND WHY NOT? It all sounds a bit far-fetched, but it's become the lifeblood that's resurrected the ailing Ants from what looked like a headlong dive into obscurity and, more to the point, given the charts a bold injection of Style, Class and Mystique. Pop music's been about "communication" since it first rattled out of a jukebox speaker nearly three decades ago, and we can rest assured that few – if any – have researched it with the depth and dedication of Adam Ant.

There's been a few misunderstandings, though. Some on the part of the Indians themselves. As Adam relates, the two heads of the North American Centre for Red Indian Culture – Rudi Martin and George Stonefish by name – wrote to him saying they thought the Ants' image was "a rip-off because it was promoting the sort of 'white' stereotype of the Indian as 'the mindless savage'" that the Centre was trying to discredit.

Adam wasted no time in putting things straight. He invited them to one of his US gigs, the agreement being that if they still believed that after seeing the show, he'd stop wearing the feathers and white line warpaint on stage. They came, they saw, and they thoroughly enjoyed themselves. So much so, they presented Adam with a Chief's bone necklace and a stack of Indian literature.

That moment, incidentally – along with meeting Liberace and a half-hour phone call from Michael Jackson – he considers one of the high points of his career to date.

ONE LAST QUESTION – the one that always tends to get lost in the rush: what's the point of it all? Adam: "I think pop music has to be fun, first and foremost. Any effort to dig any deeper into it has to come from the listener, not the band, otherwise you're preaching. And I'll leave the preaching to others." Marco: "There's no point in even picking up a guitar if you're not going to be Number One. There's no point in being Number Two, or Number Forty-Seven, or Number Three. You've got to be the best, the most successful, the most… popular."

Points taken. Over and out.

Adam sans stripe: you strum it, son, we'll sing it…

OUR FREE BADGES!

Whether it was Marilyn or Motörhead that floated your boat in the '80s, Smash Hits had a spiffy badge to suit. Here are the very best…

Are The Stars Out Tonight...

…or are they all round at Michael Jackson's place making platinum-selling records and movies? An everyday story of famous folk, starring Steven Spielberg, Adam Ant, Paul McCartney and Mark Ellen… (How'd he get in here? – Ed.)

MICHAEL JACKSON DOESN'T often do interviews. This is partly because he's very much happier expressing himself in music than words, and partly because a lot of the people who actually get to meet or talk with him are left with the distinct impression that he's just a little strange.

And he is. And seeing that – at the tender age of 23 – he's already chalked up some of the most colossal sales figures in recording history, he's got every right to be.

For much of the time, this faraway voice on the phone has the high-pitched, incredulous tone of a six-year-old at a perpetual firework party. The mention of particular films, books and songs that he likes are greeted with sudden gasps of wonder and delight as if this was the first time he's ever encountered them. Judging by the meagre portion of the 'real world' he's ever really exposed to these days, it's easy to believe that the youngest Jackson brother is actually a visitor from some distant planet.

He's calling from his home in The Valley of California, just outside Los Angeles, where he lives with his parents, Katherine and Joe, and his two sisters. The house resides in a luxurious belt of costly villas surrounded by orange and lemon groves, a little sodden, he says, following a recent rainstorm.

After a full 13 years of adulation from press, fans and record company magnates – The Jackson Five first hit the jackpot in '69 when he was just ten – Michael's become something of a recluse. He seems perfectly content to shut himself away in a curious fairy-tale world of science fiction and cartoon fantasy – or "magic" as he calls it – from which he draws the inspiration for his songwriting.

"I like things," as he puts it, "that when a person hears or sees them, they are just totally blown away."

The 'mod cons' around the house certainly bear this out. In one room there are rows of *Space Invader* machines; in another Walt Disney are busy installing a complete working set of their *Pirates Of The Caribbean* theme-park ride with fully automated Disneyland figures who launch into lifelike combat at the mere flick of a switch.

"When you step in this room," he says, spellbound, "there'll be this whole war going on, cannons shooting off and smoke puffing at one another…"

Down the hall there's a movie theatre, a fully blown 32-seater cinema for which he constantly orders up entertainment. The most regular visitor to the family screen is *E.T.*, which he likes so much that he collaborated with its director, Steven Spielberg, on the "E.T. Storybook" LP.

"I love E.T. 'cos it reminds me of me," he says mysteriously. "Someone from another world coming down and you becoming friends with them and this person is, like, 800 years old and he's filling you with all kinds of wisdom and he can teach you how to fly. That whole fantasy thing which I think is great. I mean, who don't wanna fly?"

HE AND SPIELBERG are about to embark on a couple more joint ventures, a financial pairing that will no doubt put even Paul McCartney and Stevie Wonder in the shade. One is a "futuristic fantasy type of film" with Michael in an acting role; the other is an animation for which he'll be supplying the storyline and has been "thinking like crazy!".

"I even gave Steven a present, a book on Walt Disney, as he's the only person who's inspired me in my music as much as Disney. He told me he loved it and gave me a big hug and everything."

Together with Quincy Jones, who was also the musical director for the "E.T. Storybook" project, he's just released a new LP, "Thriller" and a second single from it, "Billie Jean". The album is the eventual sequel to what Epic Records rightly describe as his "landmark LP", "Off The Wall", which was released in 1979 and went on to sell a staggering total of seven million copies worldwide. A hard act to follow.

"Yeah, well, I always like to improve," he says. "I don't like to take a step backwards, but it's a whole 'nother economy now. People aren't buying as many records, though that's no excuse."

What qualities does he look for when selecting material then? "For the music to be outstanding and, more than anything else, the

Corbis

melody. What's best for today's sound and today's market."

Asked who he admires, he lists early McCartney solo material, '60s Motown, Simon & Garfunkel, Elton John and "Adam Ant's drums". Adam, in fact, is one of a small but intimate circle of Michael Jackson's friends, despite the fact that they've never actually met in the flesh.

"We're phone-friends," he explains. "We talk about how to record that drum sound on 'Ant Music' and stuff. He talks about my dancing and I talk about his dressing. Could you say 'hi' to him for me?"

Other friends include the English actor Mark Lester, who played the starring role in the musical *Oliver!*, Elton John and Paul McCartney – "Say 'hi' to him, and Linda too." He's also acquainted with various film celebrities, among them 73-year-old Hollywood star Katharine Hepburn (who once saw a Jackson concert and promptly invited him to dinner) and Barbra Streisand, who he'll be recording a duet with fairly soon. His life, however, does seem a little isolated, I suggest. A little remote. Has he ever thought of moving away from the family home?

"I'd die of loneliness if I moved out." He says. "And plus, I wouldn't be able to control the fans and stuff. I'd be surrounded. But here there's guards and security, the whole set-up…"

He ventures outside "very rarely" and even then he's permanently flanked by body-guards and whisked straight off to the private jet. He talks about the hordes of admirers constantly watching his every move with extraordinary naivety.

"It's fun sometimes 'cos you get to run and dodge and hide. But once trapped it's not fun." As an example he relates a chilling tale about a fan he once met who opened up her purse to reveal a lock of his hair she'd painfully removed two years before. A note of resignation creeps into his voice. You can't say he leads a normal life.

"No, I can't say that…"

Do you ever wish you could?

"No," he says quietly. "I'm happy the way I am."

Michael Jackson in the Billie Jean video: people always told him, "Be careful what you do…"

BUS STOP

And You Can Take Them With You...

Cassette machines. Radios. Hi-fis. TVs. There are masses of them on the market – all shapes, sizes and prices. You can even get an all-four-in-one system. And best of all, they're portable. We asked nine pop stars to test drive some of the latest technology on the market.

Wham!

TIRED WITH AWAITING their four-wheeled transport, the **Wham!** quartet (above) play around with their various music-makers. Shirlie (far left) is plugged into a Sony Auto Reverse Walkman. It's the top of the range and plays either side of the tape without it having to be taken out and flipped. "I'd love one," she says, "if I could afford it."

George (second left) clutches a desirable JVC TV radio cassette. Want one? "Not really, no. I don't like watching television."

Dee (second right) has got a Sharp stereo radio cassette. The centre section slips out and converts to a mini cassette and radio for headphones. "I want one!" is her instant response.

And Andrew (far right) is tuning a Panasonic TV radio alarm. "It's a nice idea to have a miniature by your bed. In fact everything should be by your bed."

Eric Watson

18

Eurythmics

UNDETERRED BY THE climate, **Annie Lennox** is manning the Sony camera and video recorder pack, one of the smallest and lightest portable film-making units in the world. She and partner Dave have won prizes for their videos. "There are a lot of avenues for that sort of thing," she says. "This pack's marvellous. If you're inventive enough you could come up with some very good stuff. Maybe even make your own little feature story and then take it along to Channel 4. You shouldn't be too scared to try just because it's only you doing it."

Price Guide

Models and recommended retail prices at the time of printing.

JVC CX-5000 GB TV/Radio/Cassette: £299.00 (George)

Sony HVC 3000P Colour Video Camera: £1248.00 including recorder and timer (Annie)

Modern Romance

AFLOAT ON BOTH the waves and the wavebands is **Mick Mullins** of Modern Romance, rarely seen without his collection of soul cassettes, and here equipped with a Sony domestic hi-fi system. "It's really good," he claims. "A little bit heavy but the quality is good enough to reproduce home stereo, so if you're travelling around a lot it's great." But he's not keen on others having them in public: "It's a bit annoying when you're running around shopping and there's a guy wandering round Sainsbury's with one blaring away at top volume."

Sony FH7 Mini System: £299.95 (Mick)

Bananarama

LAUGHING IN THE face of traffic, **Bananarama** are toting a range of light but hardy hi-tech. Siobhan (left) handles a JVC stereo cassette recorder with a detachable centre that converts into a portable for headphones: "It's beautiful!"

Keren (centre) has a Panasonic stereo cassette with two pairs of headphones. "Perfect. Me and Sarah just plug in and groove down the road together. It's really like being in a film with a soundtrack."

And Sarah (right) has got a Panasonic cassette radio with a mini centre that also clicks out: "Great to carry around with you!"

JVC RCS55L Detachable Stereo Radio Cassette: £149.00 (Siobhan)

Jill Furmanovsky, Kobal

THE FAMOUS FiVE

IN THE NEW YORK High School for the Performing Arts, an end-of-term party is going on. In the hall a band is playing and Leroy dances with his teacher, Lydia. Over by the bar, crusty music teacher Professor Shorofsky chats to Coco over a drink…

But hang on, folks, it's just an illusion. Look up: there's no ceiling. Just racks of studio lights. For though it looks genuine, this isn't the real School for the Performing Arts on which the show is modelled. It's a set in the MGM studios in Los Angeles. And this isn't an end-of-term party. It's a "wrap party", held to celebrate the end of filming a second series of *Fame*. But the mood is uncertain. After they're shown the traditional "gag reel" – a collection of mistakes they made during filming – a few speeches are made. Although *Fame* is huge in Britain, in the US its ratings are low and it may be cancelled. There's a sad feeling in the air: these people aren't sure that they'll be working together again.

Whether it's cancelled or not, there's still plenty of work to be done. A nationwide *Fame* tour of Britain has just started. After here they're going all over Europe. In May there's an album and more singles.

After that, who knows? Lee Curreri, for one, is thinking of launching a solo career in England, and the others all have solo plans if the show folds.

In between the end of the filming and the beginning of rehearsals for the tour, we tracked down the show's five best-known actors at various locations in LA and New York. So here goes. Let's meet…

…better known as Danny, Lydia, Coco, Bruno and Leroy. Dave Rimmer travels the length and breadth of America in search of the Kids From *Fame*. Jill Furmanovsky takes the photos.

Carlo: *Fame* has been "easy" and he just wants "to be happy".

CARLO IMPERATO

ASK CARLO WHAT makes him laugh. He'll shrug and say, "Funny things." Ask what makes him angry. He'll reply, "The same sort of things that make you mad – just put them down." Ask him how he relaxes. He'll cry out, "Hey! We're getting personal over here."

Oh yes, he's a wag, this one. In fact he seems very like his character Danny.

"Well, they give me lines to say the way I'd say them. But they aren't necessarily the lines I'd say. People tell me I have a personality, but I don't want to be a comic. I don't want to act stupid in front of people all the time."

Carlo is smart, relaxed, talkative and owns an Alsatian dog called Major. He grew up and still lives in an Italian area of the Bronx. His mother is a secretary, his father a fruit-and-veg market trader. At the moment Carlo is helping them to move to California to open a restaurant.

"They're tired of the weather and their car being stolen all the time."

His first acting job was at the age of 13 in a play called *The Runaways*. It lasted two years. Before that he'd just been interested in basketball and other sports. "I just, er, hung out, you know." After that he had "a lotta calls", did some commercials and small parts on television and then, about a year and a half ago, ended up in *Fame*. So what's it been like?

"It's been fun. How else would a kid from the Bronx like me travel to England? It would be nice if it goes another series."

And if it doesn't? "Well, I'll just pick up and start again. *Fame* has been easy. There's nothing to it. As an actor I can go further."

The only problem with *Fame* is that his family and his dog ("he's too wild to take to LA with me") don't see too much of him.

As to the future, Carlo wistfully remarks that he'd like to do a movie with Robert De Niro, asserts that he really just wants "to be happy" and that he's got "other friends who aren't in the business and are just as happy", and then finally winds up with: "I'd like to win the lottery for a million dollars so I wouldn't have to worry about anything except keeping my mom and dad happy. If I win the lottery I'd quit *Fame* right now."

He chuckles.

"No, don't write that down… I'll get fired."

Debbie's relationship to her character Lydia is "very real".

DEBBIE ALLEN

DEBBIE IS A professional. She's been "in the business" for years, knows exactly how to handle interviews, has a lively sense of humour and is friendly. Somehow, though, as we chat in her neat little Hollywood "crash-pad", it feels that the very slickness of her interview technique prevents you from really getting to know her.

I dunno. Maybe statements like the following *are* the real Debbie Allen: "I've always thought of myself in relation to the universe. Not to the city of Houston, or the state of Texas, not America, but Earth and the universe."

Houston was where Debbie grew up. She traces her interest in showbiz back to visiting the circus when she was five.

Texas in those days was pretty racist. Debbie tried to get into ballet school when she was eight, but they wouldn't take her because she was black. She was eventually taken on at the age of 14. Later she went to the Duke Ellington High School of the Performing Arts in Washington DC

doing "much the same job" as her character Lydia in *Fame*.

Her relationship to Lydia is "very real", and she reckons the differences between her and the character would only show up if the programme went more closely into Lydia's social life.

"Lydia's OK. But I think Debbie Allen is a *lot* more fun!

Since working at the school, she's had all sorts of roles in plays and films. And when she's not working she sleeps, flies kites and goes roller-skating. "I find it very easy to relax, although I don't have much time to. I've learnt to disappear where my manager over there can't find me. And to-o-o-ough *titty!*" she laughs.

So far Debbie's answers have been confident and prompt. It's only right at the end, when I wonder what makes her angry, that she hesitates: "Self-indulgence... things that are unfair... erm... racism really makes me angry, racism of all kinds – against black people, Jewish people, women, gays. It's so dumb. Ain't it dumb?"

ERICA GIMPEL

ERICA SEEMS A very busy young woman. Tracking her down at first appears an impossible task, and when we finally do it's for a hasty interview in the lobby of her voice coach's apartment in Manhattan.

Although others in the cast went to the real Performing Arts School, Erica was the only one who graduated. "It was fantastic, but it was very different from the TV series. In the show they can't deal very much with the techniques that are taught, with people's day-to-day struggles with their abilities. The School is much more raw. People don't come all dressed up; they just wear regular cut-up T-shirts.

"I guess the producers feel that to show that would be boring. But I wish the show depicted the other, more depressing side of it."

As to her character: "I *love* Coco. I think she stands for what a lot of people in this day and age are trying to do – follow their dreams. I've learnt from her, but I think I'm a lot calmer than her."

Erica, a native New Yorker, began following her dreams at the age of seven. Her mother, also her manager, is a singer, and her father is a writer and actor, so she

had a lot of encouragement. One of her first jobs was touring in a musical with her mother at the age of 12. Despite her success in *Fame*, she still feels like she's "got a lot more studying to do".

Erica is very much the serious young *artiste*, dedicated to her work. This doesn't stop her laughing and smiling, but it certainly seems to guide her ambitions. "I'd like to work in theatre. I'd love to play Antigone or Joan Of Arc. Also parts that show the ideals that people are trying to hold on to in this day and age. I'd like to do a film or play that really said something about the world we're living in."

What makes you laugh? "Um... children. No, don't put that. A lot of things make me laugh."

OK, what makes you angry? "When people take a project that really could be something special and manipulate it to where it's only being commercial."

Are you talking about *Fame*? "Well, I don't think I should say anything about that. Wait 'til you see the new series, then you'll see what I'm saying."

And with that, she dashes off to her next appointment...

Remember her name: Erica has her sights set on serious drama.

Jill Furmanovsky

22

Lee can "get real crazy and put chopsticks up my nose". Thankfully he ate with a plastic fork when we met him.

LEE CURRERI

THE ONLY PLACE in LA where people actually get out of their cars seems to be the boardwalk at Venice Beach. Strangely, though, everybody is still on wheels: all manner of odd characters sweep up and down on roller skates. There are even dogs on skateboards! This is where Lee Curreri lives, in a wooden house just off the beach. As he strolls by the sea, lots of people recognise him. There's a busker with a piano. "Hey, come and play," he shouts. Lee sits down and obligingly bashes out a few chords. As he walks away, the pianist calls, "My sister watches your show every week!"

"Tell her to go read a book or something instead!" Lee replies.

He's serious. Lee has more reservations about the show than any of the characters we spoke to. "I like parts of it, but it *could* be a real celebration of music and dance." Lee feels that musically the show is "ten years behind the times" and clearly nurtures some frustration that they'll only let him write ballads. Really, he's more

interested in disco and R'n'B. Thomas Dolby, incidentally, is a big hero of his.

He doesn't much like his character Bruno either: "I'm not so serious. The similarity is that we're both composers. That's where it ends. I can get real crazy – go to a sophisticated restaurant and put chopsticks up my nose. Bruno wouldn't do that."

A native of Yonkers, just outside New York, Lee had his first music lessons when he was six. At 16 he moved to Manhattan and began freelancing as an arranger, pianist, singing coach and demo producer. Through that kind of work he "developed contacts", one of whom put him in touch with the *Fame* producers.

You get the impression that Lee wouldn't be too sorry if the show did end: he has plenty of ideas for solo work. He beavers away in his little home studio – packed full of drums and synthesizers – all the hours that God sends, and hopes to use his film and TV experience for future multi-media projects of his own.

GENE ANTHONY RAY

MOST PEOPLE SPEAK with gestures, expressions and tones of voice as well as words. Sometimes this is difficult to capture on paper. With the very animated Gene Anthony Ray, it's more difficult than most.

As we sit over cheeseburgers in a New York diner, Gene pleads with me to delete some of his more colourful language from the interview, jokingly covers up my mike and answers as many of my questions with looks as with words. A query about how he relaxes is met with a stare that means "Do you *really* want to know the answer to that?" before confessing a passion for – would you believe – backgammon.

When I ask what makes him angry, he fixes me with another look before admitting to "snobs, LA, the producers of our show and my cheques. There should be more zeroes on 'em".

By his own admission, Gene is "fickle". Though he "tries to be a good boy", he has a habit of disappearing for days on end.

Gene and his mother have just moved to the New York suburbs, but he grew up in the black ghetto of Harlem. He claims to have

begun dancing at the age of three and to have realised he was good at it when he began winning every competition entered. Sometimes he won trophies, sometimes cash – "my favourite prize".

Later, he ended up at the New York High School for the Performing Arts for six months. After developing a distaste for its "everything is beautiful" attitude, he had various shouting matches with teachers and was slung out – or, as the school put it, "recommended for a transfer" and told he "wouldn't make it" if he left. Gene was tickled that, after the success of *Fame*, he was asked back there to speak. He covers up the microphone before telling me what he would have said if he'd done it.

Despite superficial similarities, Gene carefully distances himself from Leroy. "I like him, he's fun to play, but he ain't Gene. He's way, way more arrogant than I've ever been." And as for the likelihood of being typecast as a Leroy: "With all the sense I got? I could play a doctor tomorrow. That's right. I'd love to do Broadway. Seriously. I'd love to play Othello on Broadway one day."

Gene: loves backgammon and "tries to be a good boy".

A SNIP (n): a bargain, cheap. As in, "Soap on a rope, £1.99 from Boots and all high-street chemist outlets. A snip!" The opposite of swizz.

AKCHEWERLERY (adv): similar to the English word 'actually', meaning 'in fact, really'. As in, "Madonna is her real name, akchewerlery." See also: ack 'chew' erly, akterchooerellement, akcheloi, atishoowerlerlee, etc.

BACK, BACK! BACK!!! (adv): what a pop star 'is' upon returning to the public eye after being away (often down the dumper) for any period longer than ten minutes. As in, "Adam Ant was down the dumper but now he's back, Back! BACK!!!"

BEN VOL-AU-VENT PIERROT (pers): lead singer of popular '80s beat combo Curiosity Killed The Cat, who couldn't even decide whether to spell his own name Ben Volpierre-

record token. Brutally murdered by a picnic table-wielding maniac in 1986, but the whole incident turned out to be (phew!) a dream ("Worra swizz!" – everyone).

BLEE (v): to eject matter from the stomach through the mouth, to be sick, possibly after too much Um Bongo, or getting up close and personal with a pair of pervgusting spewbreeks. See also bleeeugh, bleeoooer, groo, sper-yoo.

BLUB (v): to cry. As in, "We're sorry to confirm that Ken has left Bros. Blub!"

BORIS BECKER (pers): famous German tennis player who had a habit of popping up in the pages of Smash Hits chirping, "So do I, mate."

BOTTOM TOUCHING (v): what all fans would very much like to do to pop stars, and what some pop stars, especially uncle disgustings, would like fans to do to them. As in, "Duran Duran: 'Hello girlies, we're three devil-may-care guys from the wild

CORKY O'RORKY (excl): Lawks! By jiggins! Ruddy hell! etc. As in, "Corky O'Rorky, that's a particularly splendid blouse Holly Johnson's wearing."

DOWN THE DUMPER (adj): where pop stars go when no one wants them any more, the ultimate destination of 99 per cent of everyone in Smash Hits.

DAME DAVID BOWIE (pers): the chameleon of pop. Gawd bless yer, ma'am.

many clothes at all, or draped around an uncle disgusting. As in "Bananarama are a bunch of foxstresses and no mistake!" See also: saucestress, sexlicious saucepot.

FRIGHTWIG (n): a particularly imaginative or shocking 'do, often involving industrial quantities of hair-spray. As in, "Spagna: 'Is not, how you say, frighten wig. Is real hair.'"). See also: frightmask, Sigue Sigue Sputnik.

KEN FROM BROS (pers): 'twanged' the bass for Bros until he left the band in tragic circumstances (Matt and Luke picked on him) in 1989. Also known as Craig Logan, Ken is now a highly swanksome record company 'bigwig'. As in, "Ohmygod! It's Matt and Luke! And the other one, erm, Ken?"

LORD FREDERICK MERCURY OF LUCAN (pers): ex-singer and chief moustache wearer

The Smash Hits Utterly

Being a totally thumbs-aloft collection of made-up words, made-up names, mirth
(*sniiiiiIIIIP!!!*).

Pierrot or Ben Volpeliere-Pierrot, so what ruddy chance did we at ver Hits have? See also: Ben Parrotthing, Ben volleyballpingpong, Ben Preposterous-Surname.

BIRROVA (colloq): bit of a, rather. As in "that Ben Vol-au-vent Pierrot's got a birrova silly name, eh chaps?"

BLACK TYPE (pers): Smash Hits' long-suffering letters guru, named by virtue of the fact that he always wrote in, ahem, black type. Famous for his witty replies, highly desirable tea-towels and easy way with a £10

side of town. Would you like to touch our bottoms now please.'"

BULGARIA (n): a small republic in Eastern Europe formed when the Bulgars, a central Asian Turkic tribe, merged with local Slavs in the late 7th century. Modern Bulgaria threw off communist domination in 1990, joining NATO in 2004. Nowadays, the small country is known mainly because all pop stars' noses are shaped like it. As in, "Check out this swoonsome picture of Boy George and Mark Unpronounceablename from Big Country, both sporting noses shaped exactly like Bulgaria."

FAB MACCA WACKY THUMBS ALOFT (pers): ex-Beatle and happiest man in pop, Paul McCartney. As in, "Paul McCartney: 'Fab Macca Wacky Thumbs Aloft at your service! That's what you lot call me in Smash Hits isn't it? Love it!'" See also: "well thumbs aloft", a term of appreciation. As in, "Those Howard Jones threads are well thumbs aloft!"

FOXSTRESS (n): a not-particularly-ugly-at-all lady-type, often found prancing round a stage in not very

with rock 'legends' Queen. So named for his uncanny resemblance to missing peer Lord Lucan, who, spook-somely enough, has never once been seen at a Queen gig! See also: Lord Frederick Lucan of Lucan.

MARK 'HORRIBLE HEADBAND' KNOPFLER (pers): ex-singer and chief 'axe-merchant' with snoozesome rock grandads Dire Straits. So named for his horrible headband.

MARK UNPRONOUNCEABLE-NAME FROM BIG COUNTRY (pers): ex-'skinsman' with Scottish rock 'outfit' Big Country. Also known as Mark Brzezicki (pronounced 'Brzezicki').

MATEY 1 (n): a chum, pal or acquaintance. As in: "Luke: 'Love ya, matey!'; Matt: 'Love ya too, matey!' (blee!)." 2 (n): What no self-respecting megastar's bathtime would be complete without. As in, "Simon Le Bon: 'Pass the Matey,

Redferns, LFI, Rex

matey, my bubbles are disappearing faster than a yacht 'skippered' by yours truly!'"

MISS PRINGLE (*pers*): *Smash Hits'* publisher's secretary. The breadhead Publisher was forever butting into **Black Type**'s letters page, waffling on about "standards" before inevitably becoming distracted by Miss Pringle's awfully fetching thigh boots, or skirt or biro…

MORTEN 'SNORTEN FORTEN' HARKET (*pers*): singer with Norwegian goat's milk enthusiasts

Tempest. As in, "Why, Mr Tempest, that's a particularly tight pair of leather pervetrousers you're wearing! Blee!" See also: breeks, rumpo suit, pervgusting spewbreeks.

PUR-LEASE (*excl*): what a lot of rot, as if, pull the other one, matey. As in, "Neil Tennant's leaving *Smash Hits* to become a pop star. Oh, *pur*-lease!"

 **REG 'REG' SNIPTON** (*pers*): towering figure in the history of music, inventor of rawk'n'roll, fearless troubadour on rock's lost highway, colossus of (sniiiip!). Along with his band, The Useless Toadstools, Reg 'Reg' Snipton was responsible for such 'happeners' as "All I Want For Christmas Is A Parsnip In A Joshua Tree (And A Postman Pat Pencil Case If You're Feelin' Generous)". See also: Reg Snipton's kazoo quartet.

RUDDY BIG PIG (*n*): talented tunesmith Rick Astley's first musical

SIR BILLIAM OF IDOL (*pers*): leather-clad, bleached-blond rebel with the finest sneer in rock'n'roll, who sometimes answers to the name of Billy Idol (ex-Generation X singer, then LA-based solo 'artiste').

SNIIIIIIP!!!! (*v*): the fate of snoozesome pop stars who would drone on and on and on about the amazing live kettle drum sound on their new album and how hard it was finding a Rolls-Royce that matched the curtains and that fame was, like, a double-edged sword, y'know? and… sniiiiIIIIP!!!!

of calling himself Stephen "Tintin" Duffy. Now writing songs and doing the drying up for Robbie Williams.

SWINGORILLIANT (*adj*): Great! Brilliant! Fantabulous! As in, "We've been getting down to the utterly swingorilliant new platter from Hazel O'Connor!"

SWIZZ (*n*): a con, a rip-off, a big let-down. As in, "These new-fangled compact disc thingys cost a very un-sniplike £6 each! Worra swizz!" The opposite of snip.

Swingorilliant Dictionary

ome phrases, time-honoured in-jokes, blee-inducing 'gags', esoteric… (*sniiiiIIIIP!!!*).

A-Ha. As in, "Pål and Mags were annoyed that Morten 'Snorten Forten' Harket had polished off the goat's cheese roulade all by himself."

 PASS THE SICKBAG, MARCEL (*excl*): an exclamation oft heard in the pages of *Smash Hits*, usually when Bitz encountered something rather unpleasant. As in, "We spotted wrinkly grandad Keith Richards consorting with a foxstress a tenth his age! Pass the sickbag, Marcel!"

PATRICK SWIZZLE (*pers*): aka 'The Swizz', actor, star of such cinematic masterpieces as *Dirty Dancing*, who also dabbled with 'the charts' and had a 'hit' with "She's Got The Wind" ("*She's Like The Wind*", *actuellement*, a Number 17 'smash' in 1988 – Ed.).

PERVETROUSERS (*n*): trews of a particularly saucy nature, often seen decorating the lower halves of rockers such as Europe's Joey

offering, 'penned' when he was but seven years old. It goes: "A ruddy big pig came down our street / My mum said get it for something to eat / We had it with tea with apple pie / All mixed up with a dog." A song, we're sure you'll agree, dear reader, of staggering genius.

 SCOFFER (*pers*): 'hilarious' nickname of long-standing '*Hits* design-type David 'Scoffer' Bostock. So named for his habit of eating two lunches.

SNOOT- (*adj*) (*prefix*): posh, classy, not yer usual rubbish. As in, "Marilyn arrived wearing a snootcoat worth at least a squillion pounds." See also: swank.

SPOOK- (*adj*) (*prefix*): anything vaguely pertaining to the supernatural. As in, "Howard Jones claims to own a pair of haunted Y-fronts, but the 'so-called' spookpants looked pretty normal to us."

STEPHEN TEA-TOWEL DUFFY (*pers*): poor, put-upon popster who once sang for a pre-fame Duran Duran, then made the mistake

THE UNDISCUSSABLE (*n*): Band Aid, according to professional misery Morrissey. Later taken to mean anything not worth talking about, unworthy of comment. As in: "Big Fun are the undiscussable."

UM BONGO (*n*): popular '80s fruit concoction and the pop star's tipple of choice, drunk predominantly 'in the congo' and containing no less than nine – nine!! – varieties of fruit juice. As in: "Madonna celebrated her most fanciable female award with a magnum of Um Bongo and a spam bap." See also: Tizer, rock'n'roll mouthwash.

UNCLE DISGUSTING (*n*): any hideously old (ie, on the wrong side of 24) and wrinkly 'lothario', often seen sporting a pair of pervetrousers and with a foxstress or three in tow. As in, "Have you seen Tom 'bloody' Jones' new breeks? What an uncle disgusting!" See also: Rod Stewart.

THAT WAS THE WEEK THAT WAS

The week when Duran Duran got mobbed, met the Royals and hit the headlines every time they moved. Neil Tennant was never far behind.

IN LONDON

JULY AND AUGUST are known in the newspaper business as "the silly season". Parliament is in recess; all very important people are on holiday; there isn't as much news as usual. Consequently, the popular press have to go out and find it or even *make* it.

It must, then, have come as some relief to Fleet Street when Duran Duran flew into Heathrow from Montserrat via Miami the week before last to play two charity concerts: one at London's Dominion Theatre before the Prince and Princess of Wales for the Prince's Trust; the other at Aston Villa's football ground in Birmingham in aid of the charity Mencap. Here was a story blending pop stars with the Royal Family against a background of screaming fans. The silly season was about to get sillier. "It was mayhem at the airport," shrugged Nick Rhodes, "but I enjoy it when it's organised mayhem."

Estimates of the size of the crowd greeting Duran Duran on their arrival varied from 250 to 2000, depending on which paper you read. The jet-lagged group were then driven to the posh Grosvenor House Hotel on Park Lane, where they had to change and apply a little make-up before facing the motor-driven cameras of Fleet Street. Although they'd had only one hour's sleep on their transatlantic flight, Duran Duran coped professionally, standing in a semi-circle outside the hotel, all looking from left to right together so that each photographer would get pictures of the group staring into his camera.

"What's the name of the one in the middle?" a photographer asked me. Simon Le Bon's fame obviously hadn't percolated through to all of the camera corps.

Headlines the following Wednesday morning were predictable: "LOVE AND DURAN MANIA" (*Daily Star*); "DURANDE-MONIUM – IT'S JUST LIKE THE SCREAMING SIXTIES AS FANS MOB FAB FIVE" (*Daily Express*); "DURANTASTIC – BEATLE-STYLE MANIA AS PRINCESS DIANA'S FAVOURITE POP GROUP FLY IN"

(*Daily Mirror*). Much of the interest was focused on Simon's Canadian girlfriend, Claire, and whether the couple were planning marriage. Simon reacted in a down-to-earth way.

"We're just this week's story. Next week it'll be something else."

He's aware of the dangerous unpredictability of this kind of press attention.

"The papers are not loyal at all. They'll print wonderful things about you and then they'll get hold of some smut to print about you the next day. A lot of people now know our name because of the papers, but you can bore that kind of public – they can read too much about you and then you become no news. That's why we do it for a week and then scram before the backlash comes."

But the backlash was to come sooner than expected. The long-awaited Prince's Trust Concert turned out to be a bit of a disaster for the group.

"We had numerous technical problems," explained Nick. "Just about everything that could go wrong did go wrong. The bass

drum pedal broke twice. Andy snapped a string. Somebody threw a box of chocolates and knocked the bass out of tune."

Simon: "We had tuning problems during 'Save A Prayer' which were put right about halfway through the song. Everyone on stage was looking round saying, 'What the hell's going on?'"

The problem was that Duran Duran were really in the position of playing support to the concert headliners, Dire Straits. Unlike Dire Straits, Duran Duran weren't in the middle of a tour; they weren't working with a tightly knit and well-rehearsed crew; they were unlucky. Nevertheless they battled through and it *was* an extraordinary occasion.

Outside the theatre, crowds lined Tottenham Court Road to catch a glimpse of the group and the Royal couple. Inside, the atmosphere was excitable, to say the least. Girls trampled past legendary rock guitarist Eric Clapton to get to Steve Strange, who was sitting in the same row, and ask him for his autograph.

Eric Watson

Duran Duran, Grosvenor House Hotel, London, July 1983: (from left) Roger Taylor, Simon Le Bon, John Taylor, Nick Rhodes and Andy Taylor.

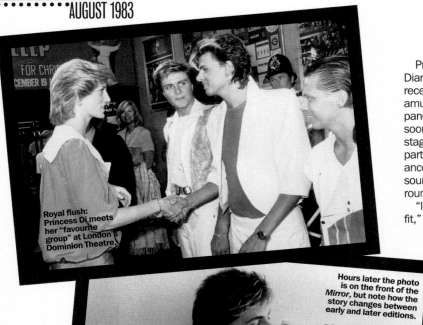

Royal flush: Princess Di meets her "favourite group" at London's Dominion Theatre.

Hours later the photo is on the front of the *Mirror*, but note how the story changes between early and later editions.

Claire and Alison's auntie knitted these Duranie sweaters – and went to the concert with them!

Backstage at Villa Park minutes before going onstage, with backing singers BJ Nelson and Michelle Cobbs and sax player Andy Hamilton.

Prince Charles and Princess Diana were given a rousing reception and then looked both amused and amazed at the pandemonium that broke out as soon as Duran Duran took the stage. Simon Le Bon gave a particularly energetic performance to compensate for the sound problems, hurling himself round the stage.

"I never knew you had to be so fit," commented Prince Charles drily in his speech after the interval. He was also greeted with a barrage of screams when he thanked Duran Duran for going to so much trouble to be present at the concert. And of course Duran Duran were introduced to the Prince and Princess.

Simon: "I think we've got a lot in common – we've both got a lot of fans! To begin with, we met them before the show, a very formal presentation, and answered a few questions – which was nice because it was like breaking you in very gently. They must know how nervous people like us would be. Then afterwards there was a reception upstairs. It was much less formal and much easier to talk. They were a very pleasant couple indeed."

Nick: "They were very nice, very human. Prince Charles liked our 'gear' – 'I rather like your gear… What do you call it?' They chatted about Montserrat. They seemed to know quite a lot about us – they'd obviously been briefed well. Everybody was impressed with them. She was chatting about the other gig we were doing and when we were coming back again. She looked great. Really pretty."

The group were panned in some of the papers the next morning. "DIANA'S LET-DOWN" was the *Daily Mirror*'s headline, although they'd clearly changed their minds. In earlier editions the headline was: "DIANA'S DELIGHT".

IN BIRMINGHAM

ON FRIDAY I travelled to Birmingham with photographer Virginia Turbett. We stayed in the Holiday Inn, the same hotel as the group. Outside, a crowd of about 30 girls had gathered, shouting in unison things like: "COME TO THE WINDOW, SIMON!" Inside the reception area, more fans were on guard – these girls had actually booked into the hotel (£32 per night, breakfast not included) in the hope of catching a glimpse of the group. Fleet Street's representatives were easily recognisable by their dusty clothes and grimly determined manner. A woman from the *News Of The World* was grilling some girls about Duran Duran's fan club. (Sunday's headline: "DURAN FANS RAGE: 'IT'S A RIP-OFF'".)

On Saturday morning a dismayed Duran Duran gazed at grey skies, drizzling rain and the Aston Villa pitch slowly being covered with groundsheets.

"But it's been sunny every day for the last month!" groaned Roger Taylor. "Nice weather – thank you, God!" Simon shouted at the thick clouds.

A biting run-through of "Is There Something I Should Know?", which put Wednesday night's version to shame completely, got everyone in better humour. "Never mind our gigs," joked John Taylor, "we play great soundchecks!"

By the afternoon the rain had stopped and the crowds had massed. Robert Palmer kept the audience entertained with a rugged set. Meanwhile, I'd been asking Nick if this massive stadium concert was the kind we can expect from Duran Duran in the future. Are they moving into a different league?

"Yeah – a more human league! No, we're not going to do a tour of these [stadiums]. If we do five nights at Wembley, we'll also do a few at Hammersmith."

He's a bit of a joker is Nick. How did you find Montserrat, I asked innocently.

"Turn left at Antigua."

Thank *you*.

"No. I didn't like it at all,

Corbis, Virginia Turbett

Plucky lad John Taylor wows the 20,000 fans at Villa Park.

Know?" begins with the group behind a black curtain that soon parts. Then screaming reaches such a pitch that it makes your teeth ache.

Unlike Wednesday's concert, this is a full-blooded show with few hitches. Simon dashes across the full length of the stage at such a speed that I expect him to trip over at any minute. A new song, "The Union Of The Snake" sounds pretty impressive: a big dance song with a "Let's Dance" backbeat. A tough version of Iggy Pop's "Funtime" is the show's biggest surprise. There are raised eyebrows backstage. It's all over by ten after two encores.

Later there's a party at the Rum Runner club and each of the group looks relaxed and happy, Simon and John proving to be the sort of people who are "always in the kitchen at parties".

Chatting to Simon the next morning, we glance at a couple of the Sunday papers – "SECRETS OF SEXY SIMON" (*Sunday Mirror*); "PRINCE OF HEART-THROBS – HOW DURAN STAR FOUND HIS OWN TRUE PRINCESS" (*Sunday People*). Downstairs photographers are prowling, anxious to snap some pictures of Claire.

From the pavement outside there are continual shouts. "JOHN! SIIIIMOOON! THROW SOMETHING OUT OF THE WINDOW!" Simon takes it all in his stride. He's not big-headed about it (like I thought he'd be after seeing him interviewed on *A Midsummer Night's Tube*) but I reckon he enjoys the attention.

"I expect it. It's part of my job. I'm staying here in the Holiday Inn, which is a totally public place. We've played a show. You've charged people money to come and see it. It's only fair that they can spend their Sunday morning standing outside and shake hands when we leave and go off.

"They're not going to get a two-hour interview each but they know that. They just want to see us when we're not on stage. If I wanted to have a bit of privacy, I'd go to Alaska."

Instead, he packs his bags and prepares to fly to Australia. Mission accomplished.

actually. I'd never go there again. All that's there is swimming pools, the studio and bad food. I got food poisoning, which didn't help. The studio kept falling to bits and the tape machines weren't running at the right speed. I thought the whole place was very shoddy."

However, he's very happy with the progress they've made on their third LP: "It comes up to the standard of some of my very favourite albums. I almost wish it was by somebody else and then I'd go out and buy it."

What will it be called? "I don't know yet. There's a possibility that it might be 'Seven And The Ragged Tiger' but we're not sure. I quite like that – it's about time we had one that was a bit of a mouthful."

Next the group will fly to Sydney to finish the LP. From Montserrat to London to Sydney all within the space of a week – don't they ever get fed up with this cosmopolitan existence?

Simon: "We've got to do it. If you choose this kind of living,

that's what you've got to do. It's like saying you want to be an accountant but you don't like doing maths. You can't do that. You have to find ways of enjoying it or it becomes very tedious. And you build up this nomadic sense of pride of being able to move from one place to another quickly. We're like a commando team: we move in and out very quickly."

AT 8.30 ON Saturday evening it's time for the group to perform. "Is There Something I Should

OUR WEIRDEST COVER STARS!

Not all Smash Hits' cover acts were destined for pop "super-stardom". For every Madonna or Wham! there was a Matt Fretton or a Hollywood Beyond. So let's hear it for the one-hit and "no-hit" wonders. What *were* we thinking?

THE PROFESSIONALS
JULY 10-23, 1980

They were the new rock supergroup, starring Paul Cook and Steve Jones from the 'orrible Sex Pistols plus, er, their heavy metal mate (actually, bassist Andy Allen). In its early days, *Smash Hits* boldly waved a flag for The Clash, Blondie, The Jam and more, yet this motley threesome would never make it into the same league or back on the cover of the *Hits* again.

SPLODGENESSABOUNDS
JULY 24 – AUGUST 6, 1980

Max Splodge was punk rock's court jester, becoming, briefly, a serious pop contender when his band Splodgenessabounds lucked out with a novelty Number 7 hit, "Two Pints Of Lager And A Packet Of Crisps". It would prove "last orders" for the band, though, when the follow-up, a cover of Rolf Harris's "Two Little Boys", stalled at Number 26.

35p USA $1·75
April 2·15 1981

HITS

FREE BADGE

**THE JAM
LANDSCAPE**

15 HIT LYRICS including
CEREMONY
IT'S A LOVE THING
ATTENTION TO ME
SPANDAU BALLET and
TEARDROP EXPLODES in colour

CLASSIX NOUVEAUX

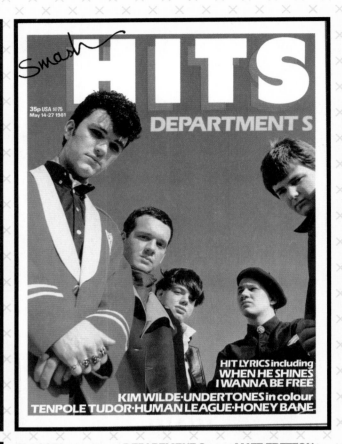

35p USA $1·75
May 14·27 1981

HITS
DEPARTMENT S

HIT LYRICS including
WHEN HE SHINES
I WANNA BE FREE

KIM WILDE·UNDERTONES in colour
TENPOLE TUDOR·HUMAN LEAGUE·HONEY BANE

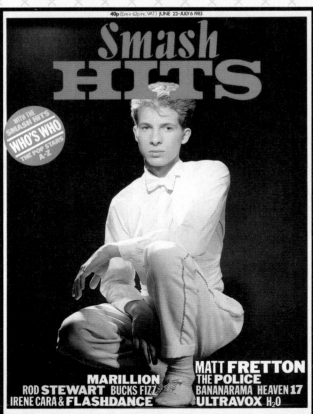

40p (Eire ir 62p inc. VAT) JUNE 23-JULY 6 1983

Smash HITS

WITH THE SMASH HITS WHO'S WHO THE POP STARS A-Z

MARILLION
ROD STEWART BUCKS FIZZ
IRENE CARA & FLASHDANCE

MATT FRETTON
THE POLICE
BANANARAMA HEAVEN 17
ULTRAVOX H₂O

**CLASSIX
NOUVEAUX**

APRIL 2-15, 1981

In the era of the New
Romantics, men in
make-up were welcomed
on to the cover of the *Hits*.
But ver Classix were no
Spandau Ballet or even
Visage. Baldy frontman
Sal Solo – and his black
lipgloss and shiny
necklace – must have
sneaked his way on when
we weren't looking!

DEPARTMENT S

MAY 14-27, 1981

A bunch of arty ex-punks
demanded to know "Is
Vic There?". Nope, like
everyone else in the
country, Vic was down the
road buying "Stand And
Deliver", the first of Adam
Ant's many Number 1s.
"Is Vic There?" was also
the Dept's first 'hit'.
Although in their case
it also turned out to be
their last.

MATT FRETTON

JUNE 23 – JULY 6, 1983

Eighteen-year-old Matt
Fretton ("a sensitive
young man with a haircut
occasionally reminiscent of
an ageing hedgehog," we
said) was this fortnight's
bright future of pop. But
even the white bow tie
and sequin-braided trews
couldn't bump his debut
single, "It's So High", any,
er, higher than Number 50
in the charts.

TRACIE

JULY 21 – AUGUST 3, 1983

Tracie Young was Paul Weller's young protégé, having hit the 'big time' after answering an ad in – where else?! – *Smash Hits*. Sadly, the 'big time' hit back and after one Top 10 hit, "The House That Jack Built", Tracie quickly sank without, erm, a trace, only to bob back up again as breakfast DJ on Essex's Dream 107 FM.

ROMAN HOLLIDAY

SEPTEMBER 15-28, 1983

"Foam sweet foam!" declared the *Hits* under a picture of Roman Holliday's elf-like frontbloke, Steve Lambert, in the bath. Ver Holliday all wore sailors' hats but by the end of the year even the nautical headgear couldn't save them from disappearing down pop's plughole.

JIMMY THE HOOVER

OCTOBER 13-26, 1983

Three months after Jimmy The Hoover's first hit, "Tantalise (Wo Wo Ee Yeh Yeh)", the *Hits* stuck broody frontman Derek – and his novel flying ace/chamois leather headgear – on the cover. And waited… and waited… for that second chart-sucking hit that never came.

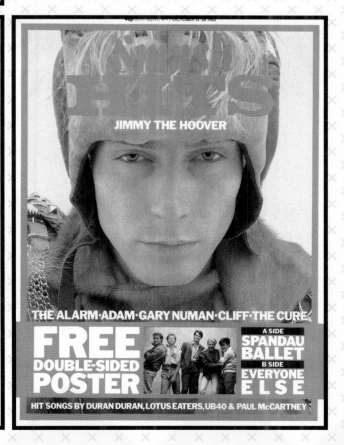

40p **6–19 DECEMBER 1984** (Eire ir 66p inc. VAT. Germany Dm 3 Singapore S $2.95)

Smash HITS

WIN A CHRISTMAS PARTY

STRAWBERRY SWITCHBLADE

NIK KERSHAW / CULTURE CLUB / WHAM! / FRANKIE

ANNIE LENNOX / SLADE / THOMPSON TWINS / BANANARAMA

THE BAND AID SINGLE: WE WERE THERE!

HOLLYWOOD BEYOND

JULY 30 – AUGUST 12, 1986

"What's the colour of money?" demanded dreadlocked Beyond man Mark Rogers. Whatever colour it was, the British public were willing to part with enough of theirs to give his group a Top 10 hit, before deciding to spend their hard-earned on something else next time they released a single.

NICK BERRY

JANUARY 14-27, 1987

He played pin-up barman Simon 'Wicksy' Wicks in *EastEnders* before, briefly, fancying himself as a pop star. After managing a Number 1 hit with the pass-the-sickbag smoochie "Every Loser Wins", it would be six more years before Nicholas troubled the charts again with the theme tune to *Heartbeat* – by which time we were looking the other way.

WE'VE GOT A FUZZBOX AND WE'RE GONNA USE IT

AUGUST 23 – SEPTEMBER 9, 1989

Former grubby indie types Fuzzbox scrubbed themselves up and had a proper hit with 1989's "International Rescue". Sadly, though, the girls couldn't save themselves from the pop dumper before the year was out.

STRAWBERRY SWITCHBLADE

6-19 DECEMBER, 1984

In defence of Scottish gothic hippies Rose and Jill, their distressed wedding dresses and eyeliner (as applied by Cleopatra after too much of the rock'n'roll mouthwash) guaranteed them a slot in *Smash Hits* – even if they only akchewerley managed one proper hit, "Since Yesterday". Bizarrely, the fortnight they landed the cover, the *Hits* had access to the biggest exclusive in the mag's history: the recording of the Band Aid single, which we dismissed with a single coverline. Hurrumph!

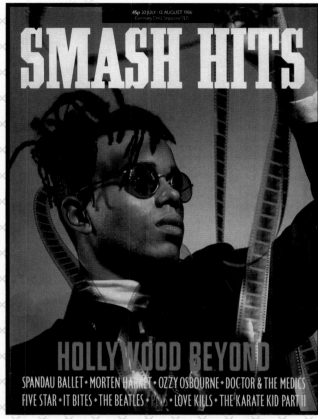

SMASH HITS

45p 30 JULY - 12 AUGUST 1986
(Germany Dm) Singapore S$3

HOLLYWOOD BEYOND

SPANDAU BALLET • MORTEN HARKET • OZZY OSBOURNE • DOCTOR & THE MEDICS
FIVE STAR • IT BITES • THE BEATLES • PWEI • LOVE KILLS • THE KARATE KID PART II

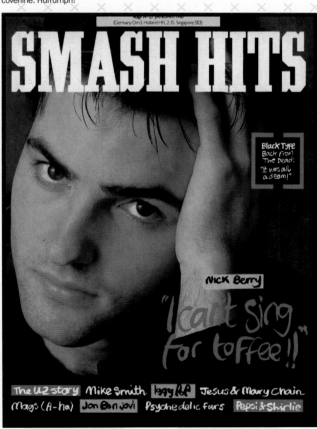

SMASH HITS

(Germany Dm 3; Holland HFL 2.35; Singapore S$3)

Black Type Back from The Dead: "It was all a dream!"

Nick Berry

"I can't sing for toffee!!"

The U2 story Mike Smith Iggy Pop Jesus & Mary Chain
Mags (A-ha) Jon Bon Jovi Psychedelic Furs Pepsi & Shirlie

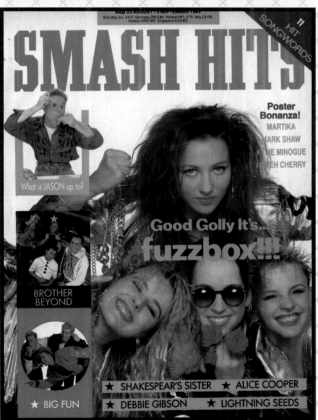

SMASH HITS

92p 23 AUGUST - 9 SEPTEMBER 1989
(Eire 80p inc. VAT) Germany DM 3.80 Holland HFL 2.75 Italy L2100
Greece DRS 300 Singapore S. $3.80)

11 HIT SONGWORDS

Poster Bonanza!
MARTIKA
MARK SHAW
KYLIE MINOGUE
NENEH CHERRY

What *is* JASON up to?

Good Golly It's...
fuzzbox!!!

BROTHER BEYOND

★ BIG FUN

★ SHAKESPEAR'S SISTER   ★ ALICE COOPER
★ DEBBIE GIBSON   ★ LIGHTNING SEEDS

Eric Watson

"YOUNG BOLD AND AGGRESSIVE"

That's Madonna's description of Madonna, who's just brought you "Holiday". "It's the kind of quality the more reserved British hate." So, how come Peter Martin (reserved, British) has ten copies of it?

AS SHE SWANS down the grand staircase of Manchester's lavish Britannia Hotel, Madonna looks every inch a *star*. A rare quality in this day and age when pop stars can get away with a daft haircut, a rather arty little video and very little else. In fact, a lot of people are labelling this 23-year-old from Detroit as some sort of female equivalent to Michael Jackson. Not surprising when you consider she can sing, dance and act, and once shared the same manager as Mr Jackson.

Madonna has just appeared on a "dance special" edition of *The Tube* that featured a live link-up between its home base of

Newcastle and the Haçienda club in Manchester. Outside, a long, black limo purrs in anticipation. The entire Madonna entourage – two dancers, one road manager-cum-minder, three record company executives, a chauffeur and me – pour through the hotel entrance and into the car.

WHY DO RECORD companies always seem convinced their American artists are going to be difficult? "I just play up to that image to keep them on their toes," she says cheekily.

Madonna constantly has a knowing look about her. Some people would call it an *aura*. This

is obviously part of the reason people are frightened to answer her back. For instance, tonight she's due to appear onstage at the Haçienda, but she's having none of it.

"I'm exhausted. I've had to cancel two phone interviews today already. I just haven't had a second. Last night it was *Top Of The Pops*, today it was *The Tube* and tomorrow I'm going to LA."

So she cancels. After a meal back at the hotel – salmon with generous helpings of Campari and orange juice – in which she laughs a lot, listens intently and makes more than her fair share of wisecracks, she slinks up to

36

her suite "to slip into something more comfortable".

Madonna's apartment is hardly run of the mill. It's on two tiers – a bed on the lower, a couch on the upper. In between answering the door and the phone, she runs through the day's events.

"People seeing me for the first time today must have thought I was a fruitcake. No, seriously, they probably thought I was sexy. A real *live wire*. But I can't come on and be sexy without humour."

DON'T GET THE wrong impression. Although she appears to be in the mould of the typical blonde female singer, she's certainly not dumb. Far from it. As she says, "There's a lot more to me than can possibly be perceived in the beginning." And, as I found out, she's extremely bright, with a sharp business sense – a valuable asset for someone so ambitious.

It seems this *ambition* derives from the "competitive environment" in which she was raised. She comes from a big Italian family – the Ciccones, Madonna's surname – of eight brothers and sisters. She also went to Catholic school, which "like all of America, gives you an incentive to win – to aim for the top rung of the ladder".

So she did and here she is: on the verge of success on both sides of the Atlantic. Not bad for a girl fresh from the streets of New York. She moved there when she was 17, starting out playing drums in a band called The Breakfast Club. But ambition took over again and she formed her own band, Emmy. She sang and played guitar. She lived in a studio and wasn't bothered by having to "wear the same clothes for three weeks". After hawking tapes around the hip local clubs, her persistence paid off, gaining her a deal with Sire. After she'd put out two 12in singles she felt the need for a manager.

"I thought, 'Who's the most successful person in the music industry and who's his manager? I want *him*.'" The answer was Michael Jackson, who at the time was managed by Freddie DeMann. She got him. Instantly, Madonna became hot property.

She can't resist telling the story about the time she met Boy George on her summer '82 jaunt.

"He came up to me at the Camden Palace. He had big high heels on and he had a big entourage of people all dressed the same. He kept going on about this group he had, but I wouldn't believe him. Six months later he was Number 1."

But it seems people aren't always as keen to impress her.

"When I laugh out loud here I'm made to feel as though I'm doing something wrong. You know, that sort of young, bold, aggressive quality the more reserved and sophisticated British people hate. Most times people aren't very nice to me here."

And that's not all. "I don't have many women friends either. It's because I haven't found many that are worldly wise and intelligent. Then again," she adds cheekily, "I just seem to get on better with boys."

I suggest this might have something to do with the way she looks. "I have mixed emotions about that. I wish I was taller [*she's 5ft 4*]. I probably look taller 'cos I've got such a big mouth. It's important to look larger than life if you're a performer."

She'll certainly be able to do that on the big screen. Madonna has just appeared in a film, *Vision Quest*. She plays a singer, also called Madonna. "The only difference is that I sing in front of a band in the film."

THE PHONE RINGS. It's New York. An "adviser" wants her to come home to appear in a video on Tuesday. Madonna agrees. She wakes up a record company person to change her flight from LA to NY. Her next project is a follow-up LP. It's to be produced by Trevor Horn, possibly Nile Rodgers and John "Jellybean" Benitez – her on-and-off boyfriend (off at the moment). In any case, it's bound to be absolutely massive. Madonna puts it all into perspective.

"Three to four years ago dancing was the most important thing – now it's music. That will lead on to something else… acting. Above all I want to be an all-round entertainer. And happy."

"We need a holiday," says Madonna – but let's hope she's not bringing that jumper with her…

おぜ

Culture Club in Japan are very big news INDEED. They fill massive stadiums. There are Girl Georges everywhere. Convoys of cars follow the group around. Some even say Boy George "has the power of magic". Dave Rimmer flew east to join their Japanese tour.

IN THE LAND OF THE RISING SUN

"GEORGE!" CALLS ROY Hay impatiently, "Hup, hup, hup, hup!" It's well past time to leave for the concert. Jon Moss, Mikey Craig, Helen Terry and the other session musicians have been at Nagoya's International Exhibition Hall for hours, but in his suite at the International Hotel, the Boy is still getting ready. In Japan, being late is an unpardonable rudeness. George, however, always seems to get away with it.

His door opens a crack. "Scisso-o-ors!" bellows George from within. Everyone laughs. The door slams. "Bill…" relays Culture Club manager Tony Gordon, "…scissors!" Seconds later, former butcher and mini-cab driver Bill Button, a kindly soul who is now George's assistant, zooms down the corridor with the desired implements. He knocks gently and passes them in.

"Bill!" George bellows again. "Bring the curling tongs as well!" "I've got 'em," Bill replies calmly.

He's well used to George shouting at him. "And he knows I don't mean it," George tells me later.

At last George appears and hurries into another room to have his picture taken with four local Girl Georges for the *Smash Hits* cover. They all have immaculate outfits copied from the "Miss Me Blind" sleeve and are all so consumed with excitement they can scarcely breathe. They cling to George for dear life and, one by one, burst into tears. George giggles: "I'm more nervous than they are, I'm telling you."

Then the various tour personnel move into the lift, go down to the basement, into the waiting cars and off to the concert. "He has the power of magic. Extraordinary power. Boy George is myself," Shinohiradayashi, one of the four girls, tells me.

JAPANDEMONIUM IS everywhere and, with the help of Japanese photographer Herbie

Yamaguchi, I'm interviewing some of the fans who mill about the hotels to figure out just how Japan sees Culture Club. The replies range from the boring – "Boy George is good singer" – to the frankly bizarre – "He has big face", "He is like dream" and "He has eyes of cat."

Surprisingly, most of the fans I talk to know about *Smash Hits*, or rather "*Smashitsu*". Keiko, a 22-year-old from Kobe, has been reading it since 1980. A group of about 20 fans outside the stadium in Osaka burst into applause at the mere mention of "*Smashitsu*" and begin chanting: "We want to go to Rondon! We want to go to Rondon!"

Several tell me that George has given them the courage to "be themselves". In a country where people are all apparently educated to be exactly the same, where an individualist is regarded as a "crazy", that's no mean feat, if true.

Another common comment was: "Boy George treats Japan well." That is to say, he is respectful of and interested in Japanese culture. "We appreciate that he likes Kyoto," one fan explains. As the old capital of Japan and the home of traditional culture amid the onslaught of technology and Westernisation, Kyoto is an important symbol for the Japanese.

For his part, George uses elements of traditional Japanese culture in the stage show – a Japanese bridal dress for the encore, a mask from the ancient kabuki theatre tradition for "Church Of The Poison Mind". In kabuki, I'm told, men wear make-up and dress as women. "It's funny," George muses on the way to the Nagoya concert, "I'm taking their own ideas and giving them back." He seems both proud and puzzled by the thought.

Sure enough, at that concert as at others, the audience contains

Andre Csillag

many girls in traditional geisha outfits. Girls who, without a Boy George to copy, would probably be wearing trendy Western clothes like everyone else. Your average Japanese youth seems as obsessed by Lacoste or Fila as any hardened British casual.

JAPAN HAS TWICE the population of Britain and a huge number of records are sold here. There are two charts: the domestic chart for local groups, which makes up 85 per cent of the sales; and the international chart, which counts for the rest. Only a handful of Western acts are capable of crossing over into the main chart, and Culture Club currently rank a close third after Michael Jackson and Billy Joel. As in this country, Duran sell a lot fewer records than Culture Club, but win a lot more polls. They appear regularly on TV, heads superimposed on silly bobbing dolls, advertising Suntory Whisky to the tune of "Is There Something I Should Know?". Culture Club, on the other hand, advertise Nissan cars to the tune of their current Japanese single "Miss Me Blind".

The railway line from Tokyo to Osaka, Japan's second city, is about 300 miles long. On the Bullet train, 300 miles takes about three hours. Time enough for Channel 4's *The Tube* to do a lengthy interview with George. Further up the carriage, which has been mostly overtaken by the Culture Club entourage, Jon and I sit chatting about Japanese politeness. "I like the air of respect around here. You don't have to shout your head off to be noticed. I might even come and live here…"

That "respect" is something appreciated by the group, although the main thing they all hate is the Japanese attitude to women, who are expected to be servile. "I think it's disgusting," comments George.

Culture Club are like a family. And like every family (and most groups) they have their arguments. Mikey feels it all keenly: "I'd like to think of Culture Club as an example to the world. I'm black, Jon is Jewish, George

is Irish, Roy is English. I'd like the world to look at that and say, 'This is how it should be.' But even with us it gets difficult sometimes. Each of us has an ego. We all want to be the leader and we all want to be first. It keeps us thriving, because that's the way the Western world works, but it frightens me a lot."

AFTER THAT NIGHT'S show, the convoy snakes its way through the back streets of Nagoya. At the International Exhibition Hall the cheering hasn't even died down yet, but already Culture Club are halfway back to the hotel.

The manoeuvre's been organised with almost military precision – offstage, straight into the transport and out; a mini-van for George, Roy, Jon and Mikey,

(Top) Boy George onstage with Helen Terry – and that troublesome kabuki mask; posing (surely not!); and with a gaggle of "Girl Georges".

cars for everyone else, all the drivers conferring with walkie-talkies. But even this wasn't quick enough to stop at least 20 cabs full of fans who'd been lying in wait from following in our wake. As we skid around corners and zoom down straights, they urge their drivers on, trying to catch up and catch a glimpse.

In a car with trumpeter Ron Williams, I'm right behind the group's van. It's exciting – probably the nearest to a Hollywood car chase sequence I'll ever get. Suddenly, out of nowhere, a cab swerves dangerously out in front and matches speed with the van. Several fans lean out of the windows, shouting and waving. George laughs and waves back, throwing them towels as the convoy bumps up

and over a bridge and back into town. "I can't possibly see what anyone could get out of sitting there trying to be the Queen," George tells me later. "If I see fans screaming I just want to give them something. You've got to respond and they love it when you do. How can you not be excited by it?"

That night's concert was the first time the show really seemed to click. Although, as Jon said, they'd played this set – essentially the same as that from the Kiss Across The Ocean concerts – "Oh, maybe 400 times", the opening concert was, by Culture Club's high standard, rusty. Not that the fans seemed to mind. They clapped in time right from the opening bars of "Take Control" through to the dying chords of "Melting Pot". Bizarrely, they even clapped through ballads "Black Money" and "Victims". George unveiled his new outfit – a Japanese bridal dress by designer Kenzo (rumoured cost: two million yen or about £6500) – and ripped the outer garments off Jon and Mikey to reveal matching shorts and singlets beneath, all of which gave Fleet Street something to write about.

The second show, at Osaka, was better but the group still clearly weren't in peak condition. George didn't rip the clothes off Jon and Mikey, but did remember to finish with "Miss Me Blind", the Japanese single. The first night, after "Time", the usual closer, he'd started offstage and had to come running back.

And then at Nagoya it all came together: a brisk, uplifting show in front of 10,000 fans who, needless to say, clapped through everything. The only hitch was George's kabuki mask. In the long intro to "Church Of The Poison Mind", while Helen takes centre stage, he rushed off to change as usual. Coming back, he found the mask wasn't on properly and he couldn't sing through it. He paused in the wings, pushed it back, composed himself and dashed on. After "Church…" he ducked side-stage and angrily ripped the mask off. Worried that he'd smudged his eyebrows, he

The concert at Nagoya, with Mikey in fetching beachwear and George in the bridal dress (a snip at two million yen).

bellowed at Bill Button to go and fetch a mirror. After the next song he looked at himself, saw his make-up was OK and calmed down. He won't wear the mask again. At The Budokan in Tokyo, the old "Colour By Numbers" bedspread outfit comes out of mothballs to take its place.

MID-MORNING IN THE lobby of the Keio Plaza Hotel, the usual crowd of fans are milling about and at the front desk Bill Button is posting George's letters. Some are going to fans in Britain and the USA, others to Japan. George has had all these translated. "He spends about £20 or £30 a day on postage," reckons Bill. He should know. He has to lick all the stamps.

Writing letters is one of George's main pastimes during the long hours he spends in the hotel suite he shares with Jon. Sometimes he'll make clothes, or go to the restaurant for a meal with manager Tony Gordon and his wife Avi and usually the rest of the group. It's almost impossible

for him to get out, but he doesn't mind. "I do have a social life. Our floor in the hotel is like a little street in suburbia. We all pop in to see each other and have a cup of tea," he giggles. "It's just like when I was living in a squat, only now I make a lot more money."

Although Jon tends to stay in and keep George company, I get the impression he finds the containment harder to deal with. He and I get out together a couple of times, sneaking down service elevators and out back doors, once for a walk and a chat with some local punks, another time to an arcade for an hour playing a currently popular game, *Nagora Tatake* – in which plastic moles pop up out of holes and you beat them back down with a mallet. You can see Japanese businessmen working out their frustration on these machines, and the game becomes a popular joke on tour: "Who's coming out mole-bashing tonight then?"

TOKYO'S BUDOKAN, BUILT for the 1964 Tokyo Olympics and

meaning "house of martial arts", is a vast place with a huge domed ceiling. Nevertheless, on this third and final night the roar of the 12,000 crowd more than fills the place well before the group have appeared. Backstage there isn't the slightest trace of nervousness. George dances in front of me and hitches up his skirt. "Look! Freshly Immac-ed legs," he grins. "Come on," bawls tour manager Gary Lee. "The quicker we get on stage, the quicker we can all get out mole-bashing."

"Here-we-go-again-Oh-my-God-it's-so-boring," Jon grins over at me and does a silly, stiff march on the stage. George waits behind and, as he does each night before going on, yelps into his radio mike: "This is my favourite bit – YELP! – it's brilliant – YELP! YELP!" The audience answers again and George runs on stage too.

The concert is smooth and exciting, the audience loud and excitable – but not so much so that they get up on their seats. That isn't allowed. But by the time it gets to "Karma Chameleon"

there is hysteria in the ranks, with every move of George's being screamed at, and loads of bouncy balls being, for some reason, flung on to the stage. They run back on, do "Melting Pot", bow and then belt out the back. We pad up an iron staircase and leap into the waiting cars.

Outside the hotel there are loads of fans. There are even some inside as we twist and turn down the narrow tunnels of its underground car park.

Two girls are waiting near the lift in near hysterics, held at bay by two security guards. "Calm, down, calm down!" shouts George as he gets out of the van, although it's impossible to tell whether he means the two fans or the over-zealous guards who are pushing them back. "Let them through, I'll sign."

The girls run up and cling on to George, sobbing their hearts out. "Calm down," he says more softly, signing their programmes, kissing their cheeks and shaking their hands. And then he slips into the lift and is gone.

"Hmmnnng… Er, how many 't's in 'lentil' again?"

"Hea-veee! Even this yellow paper is trying to hassle me."

"OH NOOOOO... WHAT A BUMMER!"

Poor old Neil from *The Young Ones*. Just when he thought he was dead, ver Hits' Mark Ellen came along to tell him he's a pop star! "Heavy", etc.

IF YOU SAW the last episode of *The Young Ones*, you'll know that Rick, Vyv, Mike and Neil are all dead. They were in a double-decker bus and it suddenly fell over the edge of a cliff and then sort of blew up. Shame, really. Amazingly enough, Neil has still managed to release a record – it's called "Hole In My Shoe".

Perhaps even more amazingly, *Smash Hits* managed to get an interview with him (just before that tragic event) *and* get him into a photographic studio (though he didn't seem terribly sure what was going on most of the time). The whole thing wasn't, er… how can we put this?… a great success.

HERE'S WHAT HAPPENED…
Neil: "Well, listen, before we start, you will remember to tell them that I'm dead, right, and this was recorded before I died. Otherwise I'll get into real trouble."

So how come you're actually putting out a record?
"Well, I just went along to this studio to, like, do some of my poetry and sing some of my songs and have a really mellow experience, and then they got this really heavy producer in who said, you know, that we had to use tape recorders and things and then, you know, the whole thing kind of escalated from there and just became, like, a real hassle."

Mike Putland

"Oh wow, it's really dark in here. And really horrible too."

"Look, guys, I'll pay for it, OK, but I spent my last 10p on the bus getting here…"

So you didn't really want to put out a record at all?
"No, no. I think it's all a sell-out. And all the films and books and everything and the T-shirts and all the little mugs and everything that are going to come out to promote the single, the jingles on the radio and everything, all the "sell-out" stuff, right, was all done, like, before we died, and we're all supposed to be going off to a special island that's a tax haven… Oh no we're not. Oh no. I've blown it already… a special tax exile island where we can rest up and watch the royalties come in."

What will Rick and Mike and Vyv think when they hear your record on the radio?
"Well hopefully they won't hear it 'cos, well, like, they're all dead, aren't they? But if they *do* happen to switch on the radio then it'll be like really heavy for me, man, so the main thing is, like, please don't anyone play it on the radio, right, and don't do any publicity about it!"

So you wouldn't want anyone to buy it, really?
"WHAT! They're selling it! Oh no. Oh no! Why don't people just give records away? Like, just go up to people on the street and say, you know, like, 'Would you like a record, right? 'Cos it's got some really good chanting on it and everything.'"

What if it was a hit? Could you, you know, *handle* it?
"What, like people throwing their underwear away at you? No, no. I'm not into all that being hassled by the media but I wouldn't get any of that anyway because I'm dead, right?"

You *sure*?
"Yeah. I've got to be dead as otherwise this whole thing won't work. Mike *said*."

OUR FAVE SONG LYRICS

Grab a hairbrush, strike a pose in front of the bedroom mirror and warble along to your fave '80s pop tune – full of sexual innuendo, the odd swear word and plenty of complete gibberish. NB: accuracy of lyrics cannot be guaranteed!

JOE JACKSON'S

Boys (what ya gotta say down there?)
Oh boys (what ya gotta say down there?)
Palamar shalomar swanee shore
Let me dig that jive once more
Boys (take it right on down to the gator)
Oh boys (gotta take the side elevator)
Can't you hear those hep cats call
Come on boys, let's have a ball

The jim jam jump is the jumpin' jive
Makes you dig your jive on the mellow side
Hep hep hep hep
The jim jam jump is a solid jive
Makes you nine foot tall
When you're four foot five
Hep hep hep hep

Now don't you be that ickaroo
Get hep, come on and follow too
When you get your steady foo
You make the joint jump like the gators do
The jim jam jump is the jumpin' jive
Makes you like your eggs on the Jersey side
Hep hep hep hep
The jim jam jumpin' jive makes you
Hep hep on the mellow side

The jim jam jump is the jumpin' jive
Makes you nine foot tall
When you're four foot five
The jim jam jump is the jumpin' jive
Makes you dig your jive on the mellow side

Now don't you be that ickaroo
Get hip, come on and follow through
When you get your steady foo
You make the joint jump like the gators do
The jim jam jump is the jumpin' jive
Makes you like your eggs on the Jersey side
Hep hep hep hep
The jim jam jumpin' jive makes you
Hep hep on the mellow side
Skiddleydoo, skiddley-diddley-diddley-diddley
Diddley-going-going-going-going-gedadda
Now I told you bout the jumpin' jive
Jim jam jumpin' jumpin' jive
I know you dug this mellow jive
Cause you dig it on the mellow side

Words & music Calloway/Froeba/Palmer.

*Reproduced by permission|
Lawrence Wright Music Co. Ltd.*

JUMPIN' JIVE
on A&M Records

Haysi FANTAYZEE

Pic: Joe Bangay

John Wayne is BIG LEGGY

Shot gun gimme gimme low down fun boy
O.K. yeah showdown
Shot gun gimme gimme low down fun boy
O.K. yeah showdown
Shot gun gimme gimme low down fun boy
O.K. yeah showdown
Showdown

Take me away
He's as big as a ranch
Take me away
He's as tough as they come
J, J, J, J, J, John Wayne
Take me away
He's so long
Take me away
You know he's never wrong
J, J, J, J, J, John Wayne

Chorus
He stands so high it's enough to make any redskin cry
He knows what's right
And he knows that God is with him 'cause he's white
Big Leggy lives
J, J, J, J, J, John Wayne

John Wayne in lover's lane
Making whoopee with his squaw
But his bullet belt, it starts getting in the way
It's making his life a bore
So she says to him take off that thing
It's getting right between us
Now listen honey I can't do that
Not even for you my sweetness
Now big John if that's a fact
Then how do you propose we do our act
If that's the way it's gonna be
Get the hell out of my tepee
Now speckled hen just stop this squawking
Big bad roosters doing the talking
I know a trick we ought to try
Turn right over, you'll know why

Repeat chorus

If you're wondering why he stands so high
It's just the space between him and the sky
If you're wondering why he stands so high
It's just the space between him and the sky

Repeat last verse

Take me away
John Wayne is big leggy
Take me away
John Wayne is big leggy
Take me away
John Wayne is big leggy
Take me away
Somewhere.

Repeat chorus

Shot gun gimme gimme low down fun boy
O.K. yeah showdown
Shot gun gimme gimme low down fun boy
O.K. yeah showdown
Shot gun gimme gimme low down fun boy
O.K. yeah showdown
Showdown
Showdown

2

M♥DERN R♥MANCE

Ay Ay Ay Ay Moosey

You gotta Bossa Nova gotta Samba too
You gotta dig the Cha-Cha like your Papa do
You gotta take a chance
You gotta learn to dance
Modern Romance on the road to Rio

Now when I hear those trumpets
And congas start to play
My heart it starts a dancing
Down that Argentina way
I see Carmen Miranda
A shuffling on her feet
She's just another lover of that saucy salsa beat

Chorus
Ay ay ay ay moosey
Ay ay ay ay moosey
Ay ay ay ay moosey to help me through the day (everybody)
Ay ay ay ay moosey
Ay ay ay ay moosey
Ay ay ay ay moosey to help me through the day

Moose, moose, moose

We're flying down to Rio
Havana bound are we
We're gonna dance the Mambo
We're a happy family
My best girl's dressing latin
From her head down to her feet
She's just another lover of that saucy salsa beat

And I'm singing

Repeat chorus
Hello
So why not be like moosey
When the band begins to play
The conga's getting longer
As we dance the night away
So hit those old timbales
And shake that tambourine
Become another lover of that saucy salsa scene

Repeat chorus and ad lib to fade

Words and music by Geoffrey Deane/David Jaymes
Reproduced by permission Copyright Control
On WEA Records

happy birthday

by Altered Images

Chorus
Happy birthday, happy birthday
Happy birthday, happy birthday
Happy birthday, happy birthday

Happy happy birthday
In a hot bath
To those nice nice nights
I remember always always
I got such a fright
Seeing them in my dark cupboard
With my great big cake

If they were me
If they were me
And I was you
And I was you
If they were me
If they were me
And I was you
And I was you
I they were me
And I was you
Would you have liked a present too

Repeat verses

Happy birthday, happy birthday
Happy birthday, happy birthday
Repeat to fade

Words and music by Altered Images
Reproduced by permission Beam Down Ltd.
/Warner Bros. Music Ltd.
On Epic Records

TOTO COELO

I EAT CANNIBALS

Chorus
I eat cannibal
Feed on animal
Your love is so edible to me
I eat cannibals
I eat cannibal
It's incredible
You bring out the animal in me
I eat cannibals

What can you do
You're in a stew
Hot pot cook it up
I'm never gonna stop
Fancy a bite
My appetite
Yum yum gee it's fun
Banging on a different drum

Repeat chorus

I like a spice
Tasty and nice
Roasting vitamin
Forget the dieting
Mmmmn such a dish
I can't resist
Healthy recipe
What you got is good for me

All I want to do
Is make a meal of you
We are what we eat
You're my kind of meat
Gotta hunger for your love (hot pot cook it up, I'm never gonna stop)
That's all I'm thinking of (yum yum gee it's fun)
Give the world a bone (I'm banging on the drum)
I've got a steak at home (roasting vitamin, forget the dieting)
I eat cannibal

Repeat chorus

Roasting toasting
You're the one I'm boasting
Eat me eat you
Incredibly delicious too
Gourmet flambé
Serve you up an entrée
In take home bake
You're the icing on the cake
Eat you eat me

Repeat chorus and ad lib to fade

Words and music by B. Blue/P. Greedus/R. Nicolson
Reproduced by permission Magic Frog/Heath Levy/Copyright Control
On Radialchoice Records

Here they are! Possibly the most profound set of lyrics since Paul McCartney & The Frog Chorus . . .

CLOSE (to the edit)
the art of noise

Play hey

Verse
**Dum Dum
Da-dum dum dum dum dum
Dum dum dum
Tra la la**

Chorus
**Dum Dum
Da-dum dum dum dum
Dum dum dum dum
Dum dum dum**

Tra-la tra-la tra-la-la

Repeat verse

Repeat chorus

**Tra-la tra-la tra-la-la-la
C-c-c-close to the to the to the edge
To-to-to the edge
To be in England in the summertime
(hey)
With my love (hey)
Close to the edge**

Hey hey h-hey

**Close close
Close to the edge (hey)
Yeh yeh hey**

*Words and music Dudley/Horn/
Jeczalik/Langan/Morley
Reproduced by gentle permission Perfect
Songs Ltd/Unforgettable Songs
On Zang Tuum Tumb Records*

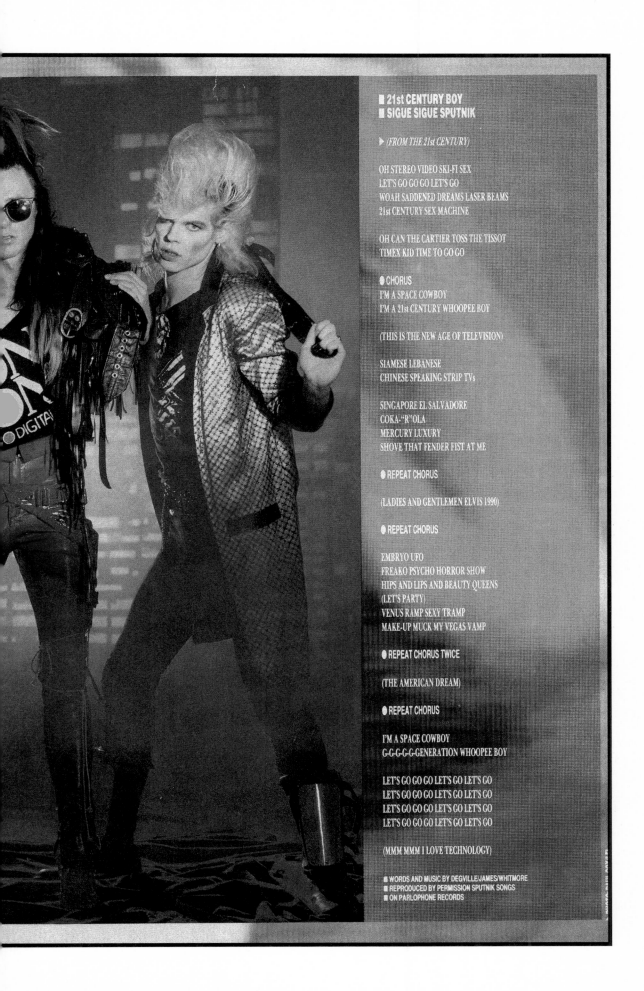

■ 21st CENTURY BOY
■ SIGUE SIGUE SPUTNIK

▶ *(FROM THE 21st CENTURY)*

OH STEREO VIDEO SKI-FI SEX
LET'S GO GO GO LET'S GO
WOAH SADDENED DREAMS LASER BEAMS
21st CENTURY SEX MACHINE

OH CAN THE CARTIER TOSS THE TISSOT
TIMEX KID TIME TO GO GO

● CHORUS
I'M A SPACE COWBOY
I'M A 21st CENTURY WHOOPEE BOY

(THIS IS THE NEW AGE OF TELEVISION)

SIAMESE LEBANESE
CHINESE SPEAKING STRIP TVs

SINGAPORE EL SALVADORE
COKA-"R"OLA
MERCURY LUXURY
SHOVE THAT FENDER FIST AT ME

● REPEAT CHORUS

(LADIES AND GENTLEMEN ELVIS 1990)

● REPEAT CHORUS

EMBRYO UFO
FREAKO PSYCHO HORROR SHOW
HIPS AND LIPS AND BEAUTY QUEENS
(LET'S PARTY)
VENUS RAMP SEXY TRAMP
MAKE-UP MUCK MY VEGAS VAMP

● REPEAT CHORUS TWICE

(THE AMERICAN DREAM)

● REPEAT CHORUS

I'M A SPACE COWBOY
G-G-G-G-GENERATION WHOOPEE BOY

LET'S GO GO GO LET'S GO LET'S GO
LET'S GO GO GO LET'S GO LET'S GO
LET'S GO GO GO LET'S GO LET'S GO
LET'S GO GO GO LET'S GO LET'S GO

(MMM MMM I LOVE TECHNOLOGY)

■ WORDS AND MUSIC BY DEGVILLE/JAMES/WHITMORE
■ REPRODUCED BY PERMISSION SPUTNIK SONGS
■ ON PARLOPHONE RECORDS

Salt 'n' Pepa

push it

Aah push it aah push it (hit it)
Ooh baby baby baby baby
Ooh baby baby ba-baby baby
Pick up on this
Aah push it (high)
Pick up on this aah push it
Pick up on this aah
Ow baby
Salt-n-Pepa's here
Salt Salt Salt Salt-n-Pepa's here
Salt Salt Salt Salt Salt-n-Pepa's here
Salt-n-Pepa Salt-n-Pepa's here
Salt Salt Salt Salt-n-Pepa's here
(Now wait a minute y'all)
(This dance ain't for everybody)
(Only the sexy people)
(So all you fly mothers out there)
(Get on out there and dance)
(Dance I say)
Salt-n-Pepa's here and we're in effect
Want you to push it back
Cooling by day
And at night working up a sweat
Come on girls let's go
Show the guys that we know

How to become number one in a hot body show
Now push it
Aah push it push it good
Aah push it push it real good
Aah push it push it good
Aah push it pu-push it real good (pow) ow
Ooh baby baby baby baby
Ooh baby baby ba-aby baby
Yo yo yo yo baby pop
Yeah you come here gimme a kiss
Better make it fast or else I'm gonna get pissed
Can't you hear the music pumping hard
Like I wish you would
Now push it push it good pu-push it real good
Aah push it pick up on this
(Aah) pick up on this (aah) pick up on this
(Take it) boy you really got me goin'
You got me so I don't know what I'm doin'
Aah push it aah push it
Boy you really got me goin'
You got me so I don't know what I'm doin'
Aah push it aah push it aah push it
Push push push push it push

Words and music by Azor ● Reproduced by permission
Intersong ● On London Records

D-MOB

D-MOB

(Acieeed acieeed acieeed acieeed acieeed acieeed)
(Acieeed acieeed acieeed acieeed acieeed)

Acieeed the musical phenomenon
Only for the headstrong
Makes you want to dance
Move groove beat
Puts you in a trance
Keeps you on your feet
We call it acieeed (acieeed) acieeed
(Acieeed acieeed acieeed acieeed)

You turn on you tune in you drop out
Acieeed has that effect
Bassline be pumping bodies rocking
People in the crowd you hear them shout

(Acieeed ac-ac-ac-ac-ac-acieeed)
(Acac-acac-ac-ac-ac-acieeed)
(Acieeed acieeed acieeed)
(Acac-acac-ac-ac-ac-acieeed)
(Acieeed acieeed acieeed acieeed)

If you thought it was a drug
Now you know you're wrong
You hear it in Future Schoom and Spectrum
And we call it acieeed

(Acieeed ac-ac-ac-acieeed acieeed acieeed)

(Psycho attack psycho attack)
(Psy-psy-psycho attack psycho psycho psycho)
(Psycho attack psycho attack)
(Psy-psy-psycho attack psycho psycho attack)

(G-g-g-g-g-g-g-g-g g-g-get right on one matey)
(Get right on one matey)

(Psycho attack psycho attack)
(Psy-psy-psycho attack psycho psycho attack)

You turn on you tune in you drop out
Acieeed has that effect
Bassline be pumping bodies rocking
People in the crowd you hear them shout

(Acieeed ac-ac-ac-ac-acieeed)
(Acac-acac-acieeed acieeed)
(Ac-ac ac-ac-ac)

(Get get get get right on one) alright
(Get get get get get right on one matey) alright

(Acieeed ac-ac-ac-ac-ac-acieeed)
(Acieeed aci-acieeed aci-acieeed)

Alright alright alright

(Acieeed acieeed acieeed acieeed acieeed acieeed)

We call it acieeed

Words and music by Danny D ● Reproduced by permission SBK Songs ● On FFRR Records

S-EXPRESS
SUPERFLY GUY

Michelé	Superfly guy superfly guy
	CHORUS
Michelé:	Superfly guy gonna take you higher Superfly guy gonna take you high
	REPEAT CHORUS
Steam:	He is bad he is smooth He's the man that'll make you move REPEAT ABOVE THREE LINES
Steam:	Get on the right track Yeah yeah yeah yeah yeah superfly Get on the right track Yeah yeah yeah yeah yeah superfly express (Woo woo)
Michelé:	Gonna take you higher Gonna take you high Superfly guy
Steam:	Like a train
Michelé:	Superfly guy (OK weirdos) (Ain't this a mother) REPEAT THREE TIMES
Michelé:	Superfly guy gonna take you higher
Adrian:	Yeah yeah get on the right track
Michelé:	Superfly guy gonna take you high
Adrian:	Express yourself oh oh
Michelé:	Superfly guy Gonna take you higher
Adrian:	Superfly express
Michelé:	Superfly guy Gonna take you high

REPEAT CHORUS TWICE

(Hey you what you say come on)
(Let's play)

REPEAT THREE TIMES
REPEAT THIRD VERSE

(Woo woo)
REPEAT CHORUS TO FADE

Words and music by M. Moore/P. Gabriel
Reproduced by permission Rhythm King Music
On Rhythm King Records

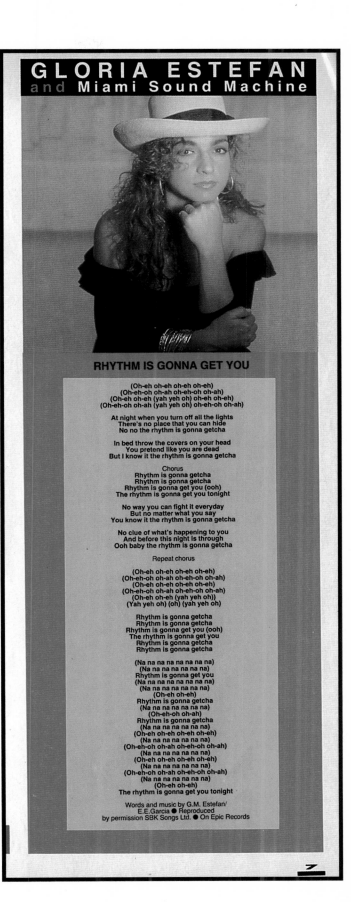

GLORIA ESTEFAN
and Miami Sound Machine

RHYTHM IS GONNA GET YOU

(Oh-eh oh-eh oh-eh oh-eh)
(Oh-eh-oh oh-ah oh-eh-oh oh-ah)
(Oh-eh oh-eh (yah yeh oh) oh-eh oh-eh)
(Oh-eh-oh oh-ah (yah yeh oh) oh-eh-oh oh-ah)

At night when you turn off all the lights
There's no place that you can hide
No no the rhythm is gonna getcha

In bed throw the covers on your head
You pretend like you are dead
But I know it the rhythm is gonna getcha

Chorus
Rhythm is gonna getcha
Rhythm is gonna getcha
Rhythm is gonna get you (ooh)
The rhythm is gonna get you tonight

No way you can fight it everyday
But no matter what you say
You know it the rhythm is gonna getcha

No clue of what's happening to you
And before this night is through
Ooh baby the rhythm is gonna getcha

Repeat chorus

(Oh-eh oh-eh oh-eh oh-eh)
(Oh-eh-oh oh-ah oh-eh-oh oh-ah)
(Oh-eh oh-eh oh-eh oh-eh)
(Oh-eh-oh oh-ah oh-eh-oh oh-ah)
(Oh-eh oh-eh (yah yeh oh))
(Yah yeh oh) (oh) (yah yeh oh)

Rhythm is gonna getcha
Rhythm is gonna getcha
Rhythm is gonna get you (ooh)
The rhythm is gonna get you
Rhythm is gonna getcha
Rhythm is gonna getcha

(Na na na na na na na na)
(Na na na na na na na na)
Rhythm is gonna get you
(Na na na na na na na na)
(Na na na na na na na na)
(Oh-eh oh-eh)
Rhythm is gonna getcha
(Na na na na na na na na)
(Oh-eh-oh oh-ah)
Rhythm is gonna getcha
(Na na na na na na na na)
(Oh-eh oh-eh oh-eh oh-eh)
(Na na na na na na na na)
(Oh-eh-oh oh-ah oh-eh-oh oh-ah)
(Na na na na na na na na)
(Oh-eh oh-eh oh-eh oh-eh)
(Na na na na na na na na)
(Oh-eh-oh oh-ah oh-eh-oh oh-ah)
(Na na na na na na na na)
(Oh-eh oh-eh)
The rhythm is gonna get you tonight

Words and music by G.M. Estefan/
E.E.Garcia ● Reproduced
by permission SBK Songs Ltd. ● On Epic Records

"WE THOUGHT THERE MUST BE SOMETHING MORE WE CAN DO"

One chilly Sunday in November 1984, 38 pop stars gathered in a studio in Notting Hill to record the historic Band Aid single. Peter Martin saw it happen.

THREE WEEKS AGO, Bob Geldof saw a television report on the famine in Ethiopia and felt "outraged". He rang Midge Ure and suggested they make a record to raise money. Midge agreed. Then he rang Sting, Gary Kemp and Simon Le Bon. They agreed too. Then he rang a lot of other people – more pop stars, record producers, record shop owners, designers, photographers, film crews and T-shirt manufacturers – and they all offered to help as well. The Band Aid project was underway…

IT'S 9.15AM SUNDAY, November 25 and something's stirring outside Sarm West Studios. The road's being blocked off, police are everywhere. Passers-by stroll up to see what's going on. Local residents lean out of windows just in case they're missing anything. The air's heavy with anticipation.

A clutch of rather chilly looking photographers mill around the doors of what's come to be known as the ZTT building – it houses the studio where Trevor Horn helped Frankie make "Relax". Clearly something of a big deal is about to take place.

Inside the speckledy-blue building there's even more commotion. No less than seven camera crews are setting up cameras and lights. There are five British crews, ranging from *The Tube* to the BBC News team, and two American crews. They rush into action as a lanky, unshaven, bleary-eyed bloke arrives. It's Bob Geldof, showing signs of strain from ten days of organising today's events. So what's it in aid of and why has he done it?

"I was outraged after seeing the first shots from Ethiopia, but rather than just put my hand in my pocket I thought there must be something more I can do. So I just phoned up everyone I knew, starting with friends like Midge Ure, Sting, Gary Kemp and Simon Le Bon, and they all agreed to help.

"Hopefully this event will raise a substantial amount of money.

And then, to cut out the administrative costs, I'll just phone Addis Ababa direct and ask them what they want, buy it, charter a cargo ship and try and get various sections of the music industry to sponsor jeeps to take the stuff out there. That way everything will get through and no money will be wasted.

"Also, all the people involved today are doing it for free, from

Brian Aris

the musicians to the technicians and even down to the people in the factory who are going to press the record."

Out of every £1.35 spent on the single, £1's worth of food should reach the starving people of Ethiopia.

Next through the door is Midge Ure, who'll be producing "Do They Know It's Christmas?" (which he wrote, along with Bob). In fact

he's already recorded the synthesized backing track ready for the musicians and singers to do their bits over.

"It's just like my bedroom," he quips, pointing at the large Roman pillars inside the recording room. Behind him is Jon Moss, assuring all and sundry that Boy George will be arriving later (the pair of them have specially flown back from their American tour by

Back row (left-right): Adam Clayton (U2), Phil Collins (Genesis), Bob Geldof (Boomtown Rats), Steve Norman (Spandau Ballet), Chris Cross (Ultravox), John Taylor (Duran Duran), Paul Young, Tony Hadley (Spandau), Glenn Gregory (Heaven 17), Simon Le Bon (Duran), Simon Crowe (Boomtown Rats), Marilyn, Keren Woodward (Bananarama), Martin Kemp (Spandau), Jody Watley (ex-Shalamar)

Middle row (left-right): Bono (U2), Paul Weller (Style Council), James Taylor (Kool & The Gang), Peter Blake (the artist who designed the record sleeve), George Michael (Wham!), Midge Ure (Ultravox), Martyn Ware (Heaven 17), John Keeble (Spandau), Gary Kemp (Spandau), Roger Taylor (Duran), Sara Dallin (Bananarama), Siobhan Fahey (Bananarama), Francis Rossi (Status Quo)

Front row (left-right): Robert 'Kool' Bell (Kool & The Gang), Dennis Thomas (Kool & The Gang), Andy Taylor (Duran), Jon Moss (Culture Club), Sting (The Police), Rick Parfitt (Status Quo), Nick Rhodes (Duran), Johnny Fingers (Boomtown Rats), Pete Briquette (Boomtown Rats)

THE SINGLE FOR ETHIOPIA

Concorde). He seems thrilled to bits to be working on the record with his "hero" Phil Collins.

Now, it appears, the floodgates are open. For the next two hours a constant stream of the world's most famous pop stars stream into the building, ready to be filmed, photographed and recorded. Sting's just arrived in his jet black Range Rover. He looks very much the family man these days with his comfy, casual clothes and straggly centre-parted hair. Paul Weller's turned up on foot and spends most of the time in the corner, minding his own business: "I'm hardly everybody's favourite person. They just seem to ignore me – I don't blame them." Next in are Spandau Ballet. Up they roll in two chauffeur-driven limousines along with no less than four minders. "I get it," cracks Gary Kemp on entering the start-studded coffee bar, "it's all a ploy by Island Records. Get every pop star except Frankie in one room and blow the whole place up!"

NEXT ARE DURAN Duran, who, like Spandau, have just got off the 6.30am plane from Dortmund, Germany. Nick is fully made up and sporting ski goggles while John, quite frankly, looks a bit of a wreck: "Actually I'm on another planet." Suddenly the place is choc-a-block. You can't move for pop stars. You can't even go into the toilet without bumping into someone like Simon Le Bon.

Trevor Horn arrives and offers to mix a 12in version. The offer is accepted immediately. Then he asks for three weeks to do it in. "You've got a night," smiles Geldof. After all, the 7in will be recorded today, mixed tonight, mastered tomorrow (when it will receive its first radio play from a tape), pressed in the factory on Wednesday and will be in the shops on Saturday, on its way to raising the hoped-for £1.5million for the Ethiopian Famine Trust. And, owing to Geldof's persist-ence, the record company Phonogram and main stores like WH Smith and John Menzies have agreed to forgo profits.

By noon all but Boy George have arrived and been ushered upstairs for a grand photo

The photo shoot: "*Simon*! Eyes to the camera! Midge, stop talking…"

Rick Parfitt (left): "What's that funny smell?" Neil (right): "There's a hole in my shoe, man."

Simon Le Bon finds something amusing. Not George's 'kerazy' new 'do, surely…

session. Like any good school assembly picture, the tall ones stand at the back, trying their best to conceal fags and cans of lager, the middle-sized stay in the middle and the smaller ones perch down the front. A Kop-style football chant breaks out in the John Taylor/Paul Young/Steve Norman area accompanied by much swaying of the arms. "Eyes to the camera," yells official photographer Brian Aris. "Simon! Eyes to the camera! Midge, stop talking." Bono and Paul Weller are then asked to stop nattering. Marilyn puts on his best pout and Francis Rossi even manages a

Weller: "How about a bit of flamenco?" Geldof: "Er…"

Retna, Steve Hurell/Redferns

slug from his hip flask in between each click of the shutter.

Then it's time to sing. Lyric sheets are handed round, choirboy positions are assumed and the backing track is set in motion. "One, two, three, four. Let them know it's Christmas time again/Feed the world," is the message that reels over and over. The general consensus is that the song is quite good and all agree that "it's the idea and feeling behind it that counts".

"Calling Mr Michael... we're ready for your 'solo bit' now."

Wake up, Midge! Only another six hours' mixing to go.

After an hour's worth of takes Trevor Horn moves in. Setting up one main microphone, he gets the throng – or Band Aid as they're collectively called – to form a semi-circle. Then, in true headmasterly form, he raises his arms and gives instructions on how to sing in a relatively complex 'cascading' motion, with one line swerving into another. After an hour he's off. "Thanks a lot, I'm sure we can make something out of it." Class dismissed.

All disperse into little groups. The naughty ones like Status Quo and John and Andy Taylor sneak around the toilets for a smoke.

Paul Weller, Marilyn and Bananarama plonk themselves in front of the telly (with the sound off). Spandau and Heaven 17 go for a cup of tea. Nick Rhodes has a go on the *Asteroids* machine. And people like Paul Young, Bono and George Michael keep shooting upstairs to do their 'solo bits'.

"Female vocals upstairs now," is the call. Bananarama trot off but not before Keren shouts, "Coming, Marilyn?"

A nucleus of people starts to congregate in the small studio console for the evening's recording. Jon Moss is there, impatiently waiting to do his bit of percussion with Phil Collins. Bono's chatting to Simon Le Bon while they wait to do their vocals. Then in comes Sting with his girlfriend Trudi, his baby daughter, and two small dogs that keep sniffing around in every nook and cranny. Downstairs, John Taylor is scoffing some chili con carne when Neil from *The Young Ones* meanders through with the unit from *The Tube*. "Typical," splutters John, "I wait all day to have something to eat and then *they* turn up." Neil stops for a minute, asks if anyone knows how to make herbal tea, and then slides off to hear an acoustic rendition of the song by Paul Weller, Bob Geldof and Gary Kemp.

IT'S ABOUT TIME

to shoot the video. Everyone is gathered round and put into position. John Taylor (who did his bass part on Wednesday because he thought "playing in front of all these posers would be a bit unnerving") and Sting sit next to each other, both with basses (Sting doesn't actually play on the record). Midge stands behind the keyboards. Phil Collins sits behind his huge drumkit (he's also just "laid down" his part) while Jon Moss coolly stands behind his drum and cymbal. Then in the background stand Bob Geldof, Paul Weller and Gary Kemp, all with acoustic guitars. They do it in two takes. It strikes everyone that, combined, the total sales behind

a "supergroup" would amount to a staggering 200 million records.

Then who should walk in but Boy George? Strangely for him, he looks quite fazed and waves his arms in the air shrieking: "My god, it's so trippy seeing all these faces in one tiny room!" He sits on the arm of the couch next to Jon Moss, who's chatting to Simon Le Bon. On his left are Trudi (plus baby), who's talking to Paula Yates (plus baby Fifi Trixibelle) and Bono, who's talking to Sting. George just sits there and smiles in mild disbelief. Being there all day, it seems quite natural the way everyone has got together, "working for the cause". But to someone who's just come in from the cold the scene must appear rather odd. I mean, Simon Le Bon sharing experiences about life on the road with Bono? Paul Weller getting on famously with Marilyn? Dogs and babies in a studio? Surely some mistake?

Understandably in the circumstances, George asks for some brandy before he does his vocal. Within minutes it arrives, as does Marilyn. "Hello Doris!" yowls George and gets up to give him a hug. And then he's off in the studio to do his bit. After about six takes – with George making little alterations here and there – it's finished. Midge announces that it's been a pleasure to work with everybody and "everything that needs to be recorded is finished. You can go home now." Gradually everyone makes their way downstairs, farewells are said and "good lucks" exchanged.

"It was very important that people were here and seen to be here," reckons Sting. "We all go round making records and touring the world and we never meet – it's isolated. So to get the industry behaving as a unit is a tribute to Bob Geldof."

NOW ALL THAT'S left is a night of mixing for Bob and Midge. "They all did their parts incredibly well," smiles the extremely weary-looking Midge Ure. "With all those potential prima donnas out there it was surprising but there were no ego problems. It made a pleasant change."

Bob, meanwhile, peers at the television screen and sees a

playback of events that took place earlier today. "You know, when you see it like that it looks like ancient history. In fact it looks like you weren't even there at all." And with that he rubs his eyes and strolls off back to the studio.

No matter what you think of the song or the feelings behind it, it struck home that there is more to pop music than total insincerity, naked ambition, blind profit, a lot of hot air about all things 'positive' and useless social comments made through crummy 'post apocalyptic' videos.

Today proved once and for all that pop music can still be a force.

"WANTED: WHAM! FANS (NO DURANIES!!!)"

For ten years Smash Hits offered to set you up with your perfect penpals. And *these* are the letters you sent in. The mind boggles…

● **White-faced flyingsuit-clad type** wants to correspond with any madmen, S.U.'s or U.D.'s. Must be into Numan, synthesizers, science, cybernetics and other synth groups, e.g. OMD, Human League, Ultravox, Kraftwerk, etc. Preferably Intergalactic correspondents but Universal ones not refused, any age… (I'm 15). Write to: Rebekah Rednal, Birmingham.

● **White Rasta**, 17, wants to write to Rastafarians anywhere. Contact: Angie, Ballymoney, N Ireland.

● **We're two very lonely, fun-loving girls,** into Motörhead, A.N.L., Saxon, and many other punk and heavy metal groups. Likes: orange Smarties, knobbly knees and hairy shoulders. Dislikes: normal people and intelligence. Please write to: Sharon and Claire, Ystradgynlais, Nr Swansea, S Wales.

● **Amazing, I'm in RSVP!** Hi, world! I'm a 14-year-old female Brussel Sprout with a weird sense of humour who hates home-work, HM and Duran and loves Nik Kershaw and canoeing. Anyone in the entire universe write to: The Brussel Sprout, Haverhill, Suffolk.

● **I am a 16-year-old boy** interested in Animal Rights and peace. Likes include UB40, U2, The Undertones and The Smiths. Dislikes racists and swimming. All females 13-16 write to: Alistair, Dundonald, Belfast.

● **Hi! We're two female OK Ya's!** Both aged 12 ¾ requiring freaky penpals aged between 11-13 ¾ into DD, Wham!, and *Playschool*. Write to: "Piglet" and "Jelly Bean", Aberdeen, Scotland.

● **Calling all Goober-smootchers**, Bean-Bones and Jelly Heads! If you're into FGTH, Graffiti, Devilled Eggs, Japan, Billy Idol or any other two-legged organisms, sketch out a note to: Eden (Professional Scribe), Houston, Texas.

● **Hi geezers!** Sixteen-plus, write to us: Lara if you're hunky, write to Lizzie if you're punky, write to 'H' if you're funky. 'H', Lizzie, Lara, St Giles Hill, Winchester, Hants.

● **Nutters of the world unite** (or write!) to 'Loooweez' at: Roundhay, Leeds. Luvs: Garfield, Steve Wright and any 2-Tone. I am allergic to skool, politics and Marilyn. Pleez rite – I'm really ultra kool.

● **Hello there! I'm a self-confessed ugly person** who wishes to get in touch with people who also think they're no threat to George Michael or Madonna in the 'looks' category. I'm 18 and into Yes, Marillion, ELP, The Incredible String Band (*What!? – Ed*) and The Beatles. Get scribbling to: Kevin Bignell, Rubery, Birmingham.

● **I'm a weird 17-year-old male** (so weird I actually like Culture Club) who is deeply into pop, CB radio and the werewolves. Anyone crazy enough to want to write to me, contact: Hobgoblin, Solihull, West Midlands.

● **OK ya!** My name is Jordon Blair McKenzie and I'm heavily into Art, especially Van Gogh and Leonardo. I also do ballet and am a great fan of Paul McCartney's Frog Chorus (especially the three on the lilypad). JB McKenzie, Newmilns, Ayrshire.

● **I used to be a Skin**, then a Mod, then a Biker, then a Mod again. Now I've moved to Bristol and buy lots of Frankie records. Write to: Carl, Shirehampton, Bristol.

● **We are two boys**, Mark and Simon. We are 15 years old and about 5 foot 5. We like UB40, Big Country, The Smiths, etc. We would like girls aged about 15 from anywhere (no Duranies). Send a pic if poss. Write to: Simon, Halstead, Essex.

● **Name: Paul.** Fave music: Status Quo, TT, etc. Hobbies: wrestling, computers. Age 17½. Paul Empsey, Middleton, Manchester.

● **My name's Jacky Latter / I'm truly getting fatter** / When I eat my fish and chips in batter / I think I'm pretty funky / But I just look like a monkey / And my hair's pink and punky! I'm interested in Nik Kershaw so write to: Jacky Latter, Upper Hasfield, Glos.

● **Hi, I'm Omar,** 16, and he's Gavin, 15. He's good looking blond with blue eyes and a stunning personality and I'm envious. Likes include: Ultravox, Madonna, Frankie and squash. Write to us at: Woodford Green, Essex.

● **I like Showaddywaddy** and disco music. I am 19 years old and enjoy swimming, pool, and weight-lifting. My name is Cliff and I live at: Ramsgate, Kent.

● **Hi! Interested in writing to a 16-year-old Northern Irish "bloke"** who is very much an existentialist nihilist? (Phew!) I'm also into The Smiths, U2, The Mighty Lemon Drops, Echo and New Order. Get writing to Schmerk, Dundonald, Belfast.

● **Hi to all you Madonna fans!** I'm a 12-year-old girl who wants a penpal aged 10-14. If you like Betty Boop, Minnie Mouse, Madonna, Kim Wilde, Whitney, french fries, Philip Schofield, organs, cycling and kittens, write to me and I will try to reply to all letters: Vanessa, Cock Clarks, Chelmsford, Essex.

● **Hi, my name's Ray and I'm 17**. I love Echo, Aztec Camera and The Smiths but hate Ford Capris and breakdancing. If you're female, interesting and different, write to me at: Sidmouth, Devon.

● **Calling all *Brookside* fans!** I'm Barry Grant's girlfriend and my friend goes out with Damon! Contact us in Darwen, Lancs.

● **Hello, we're two squares who are totally into Mozart and Beethoven!** Ackcheloi, we're two Madonna freaks who are into Sigue "Sigue" Sputnik, FGTH, Five Star, Pet Shop Boys and most other chart music. If you are female aged 14-16 and like parties and having a good time write to: Nik and Rik, Brimscombe, Gloucester.

● **Hi there. I'm a 13-year-old boy hunting for any Sam Fox lookalikes** (or near enough). I'm into Sigue "Sigue" Sputnik, Madonna, The Housemartins, etc. If you're interested, please write to: Roy Peeka, Purbrook, Portsmouth.

● **Hello. We are two English boys living in Paris.** We are both tall and hunky (6 foot 2+), into Lou Reed, Scott Walker (*Hurrah! – Dep. Ed*) The Fall and Jim Morrison. Please write immediately to: Rue De L'Abbée Patureau, France. P.S. Really into spaghetti bolognaise and Lenny Bruce.

● **Hi, my name is Marc and I'm a zealous fusion jazz devotee** desperately seeking female jazz fusion fanatics from all over the world. I love aquatic sports and sun-bathing, so get scribbling to me at: Bedok Reservoir Road, Singapore.

● **If you wanna be startin' somethin' and are a bit of a thriller**, it would be human nature for you to beat it along to a post-box with a letter in which you can say, say, say anything about yourself. Contact: Melanie George (12), Towcester, Northants.

● **I always dress like Boy George, even when I'm at school or just at work.** I'm just mad about Culture Club. Contact me at: Boy, Wolfschlugen, West Germany.

● **Don't miss this unique opportunity to write to two 15-year-old Janet Street-Porter lookalikes**. Into: Journey, Peter Gabriel, Plastic Bertrand and Chris de Burgh. We want to get in touch with boys aged 15-18. However, this offer does not apply to Duranies or Greeboes! Contact: Debbie and Clare, Oakham, Leicestershire.

● **I'm a 16-year-old Finnish boy and I like writing letters,** Duran Duran and Andrew Landers. If you enclose any pictures of *Dallas* actors and actresses, I'll reply to you quicker! Contact: Timo Paulamäki, Halikko, Finland.

● **My name is Peter, I'm 19** and looking for Talk Talk fans. I dislike most other groups and will only reply to Talk Talk fans, so send your pictures to Peter Doyle, Wembley, Middx.

● **Here sit I, in my cage** (my bedroom), looking forward to yet another boring day in prison (school). I wonder if there are any other beings like me? But at last there is a beacon in the darkness… I think Duran Duran, Spandau

Ballet and Culture Club are mint, so if you would like to share stories of tragedy and light, write to me! Contact: Donna Boyd, Parmelia, Western Australia.

● **Hey, the party was rough!** Could you send me some aspirin and a few words of consolation? I'm a 14-year-old female and just gorgeous! Write to: Froggy, Savannah, Georgia, USA.

● **I'll write this slowly so you don't have to read fast!** I represent the Daily Pinta news letter and desperately need readers. If you want to read about the Low Forehead Bridge Auntie Social and more (inc. me), scribble to: Wells Fargo (that's my stage name), Lakeside, Cardiff.

● **Grunt, grunt, male, grunt, 14, grunt, likes Queen.** Grunt, grunt, wants male or female penpals, grunt. Grunt: Dermot Fogarty, Upper Woolhampton, Berks.

● **Hello!** If you say "Goodnight" to a Duran Duran poster every night before you go to sleep, if you think Duran Duran are the best in the world, if you dream about Duran Duran every night and think of Duran Duran every day, and if you would like to have such a crazy Duran Duran fan to correspond with, please write to: Simon(a) Ricci, Rome, Italy.

● **Calling all hip-hoppers!** If you've got juice, you'll get on down and listen to the meanest breaker in town. Afrika Bambaataa And Soul Sonic Force are BAD (that's good!) so don't be wack or have a heart attack, drop a line (or two!) to: 'Crazy Legs', Newport, Gwent.

● **Orange-haired poseur** (female) would like to write to make or female poseurs. Likes: Doris Day, Cilla Black,

● **Blimey! At nearly 30, I must be the oldest regular reader of *Smash Hits*.** If any girls fancy writing to a music-crazy, sports lovin' dinosaur, contact: 'Musky', Ermine East, Lincoln.

● **Jeff's the name, music's the game…** I'm into Gary Numan, Art Of Noise, Rah Band, Rush, Devo, Tubes, Helen Of Troy, Rick Wakeman and so on. Write to me at: Greatfield Estate, Hull.

● **My name is Nigel and I'm a real hunk into Wham!,** The Spands, Nik Kershaw, etc. Hobbies include origami, hang-gliding and posing on my mean 250cc bike. All you chicks aged 16-20, write to: Nigel Carr, Shipley, W Yorks.

● **Female Herbivore, 17, enjoys '60s music.** Fave group are the Stones, Buddy Holly, The Beach Boys, etc. I also love sunsets, puddles, cornflowers, beanshoots, eyes, *Solo*, and talking to trees and twiglets. Write to me in Cleeve, Bristol.

Julie Andrews, Dusty Springfield, Aztec Camera, Virgin Dance, The Mystery Girls and loads more. Also enjoys clubbing, *The Sound Of Music* and spaghetti. If you like the sound of me, write to: Polly, Brighton.

● **Breaker on 11 for male/female penpals from any 20 in the universe.** I'm an 18-year-old CB fanatic and I like Rod Stewart, The Rolling Stones, Howard Jones, Billy Idol and Meat Loaf. Pics if possible to: Mary Hughes, Foxford, Co Mayo, Ireland.

● **I'm a 13-year-old female who loves Nik Kershaw,** Howard Jones, and Limahl. I collect soaps of all sizes and every shape possible. Dislikes include heavy metal and hippies (but not Neil from *The Young Ones*). Write to Veronica Sterland, Leicester.

● **Peace man!** We're two male hippies in search of females. Interests include blackberry-picking, lentil soup and making curtains. We're aged 17 and 18. Write to: Winston and Jerald, Washington, Tyne & Wear.

● **We're two 15-year-old casuals (females)** who like Wham!, Nik Kershaw, Shalamar and *Playschool*. Any Big Ted, Little Ted, Humpty, Jemima and Hamble fans, scribble a line to Jo and Tani in Sanderstead, Surrey.

● **Life is like a Duran Duran record** – repetitive and thoroughly boring. If you're female and aged 16+, please cheer me up (too much Genesis!). Write enclosing photo to: Tony Cook (18), Gosport, Hants.

● **I enjoy listening to Rush, Richard Clayderman,** Bucks Fizz and Shakin' Stevens. Write to: Leonard Low, Upper Largo, Fife, Scotland.

● **Hello out there!** I'm no George Michael but, then again, who'd want to be? I'm 15 and into Howard Jones, Madonna, DD, and some Prince. My nickname's Cheese, so if you want to know why, pick up a pen and write to: 'Mature Cheddar', Westgate-on-Sea, Kent.

● **Two extremely kool female dudes, aged 15** and into Frankie, Duran, Howard Jones and Nik Kershaw, wish to hear from all kool male bleached-jeans wearers. We dislike heavy metal, lemon-curd sandwiches and CND. Gunge and Kool Cat, Beverley, N. Humberside.

● **Does anybody want to write to a French girl?** I'm into U2 and FGTH and anyone, anywhere on earth or from any other planets are welcomed into my pleasure-dome… (*Pardon?! – Ed*). M Cirou, Asnières, France.

● **Please write to me because I'm sick of getting French penpals** and free Abbey National magazines through the post. I'm Kate and I'm into soul and just about everything else. Write to me in Cottingham, North Humberside.

● **Imaginary boys/girls into The Cure,** A.F.O.S. and anything "new" to help a 14-year-old female who is trapped in the normal world. I dislike Reagan, heavy metal, and stereotypes. All Love Cats send me some messages: Andrea Lagno, Berea, Ohio.

● **Tall tanned blonde wants tall tanned male,** urgently! Must tolerate Eurythmics and rubber plants. Anyone 15-plus welcome. Write to: Louise, Doha, Qatar.

● **If you don't write to me you're a Neo-Nazi!** I'm twice as left-wing as Paul Weller and I'm into Duran, Grace Jones, Japan, The Power Station and Nile Rodgers. Julian, Bookham, Surrey.

● **Hello, is it us you're looking for?** If all you wanna do is funk and have no more lonely nites, why not call us? We're two girls who just wanna have fun. Guys between sweet sixteen and n-n-n-nineteen get into the groove and write to: Kristen and Trisha, Norwich, Norfolk.

PET PROJECT

"Meat Is Murder" is both the title of The Smiths' new album and a message Morrissey is "madly serious" about. But when the vegetarian singer turns up looking "terrible", Tom Hibbert wonders whether a burger wouldn't sort him out…

What's the matter with you?
Oh, just a general mental decay – so many things… Don't I *look* ill?

Yes, you look terrible, actually. Are you under the doctor?
I don't believe in doctors, I believe in self-cure. I find that doctors are all relatively useless.

How long have you not been eating meat?
For almost a decade.

Can you remember the last time you ate meat?
I can't really. I'm quite sure it was bacon because I had a moderate bacon fetish. And I can remember as it came to the end of my bacon period, I thought, "Oh, I don't like the taste of this any more." It was simply the realisation of the horrific treatment of animals – I had never been aware of it before. I suppose I knew vaguely that animals died, but I didn't know how and why. I think generally that people think that meat doesn't have anything to do with animals. It's like potatoes or something – it hasn't got a cow's face and it doesn't moo, so people don't think it's animals. But of course it is – as I'm sure you've recently realised.

Yes, I did twig. Did you approve of the Animal Liberation Front's Mars Bars hoax?
I totally believe in hoaxes.

But would you approve if it weren't a hoax?
Oh, yes. Completely. Yes, I would because I think we have to take these measures now because polite demonstration is pointless. You have to get angry, you have to be violent, otherwise what's the point? There's no point in demonstrating if you don't get any national press, or nobody listens to you or you get beaten up by the police. So I do believe in these animal groups but I think they should be more forceful and I think what they need now is a national figure, a national face – I think they need some very forthright figurehead.

Veggie pop musicians don't tend to be very militant types – Paul McCartney, Limahl, etc…
Yes, very effete figures, non-political figures who would never raise their voices, which of course is pointless. Whenever vegetarianism has been covered in the press, it's been whispered, nothing very forceful. Nobody concentrates on the reasons why people don't eat meat – it's "this person doesn't eat meat, instead this person eats blah blah blah".

Yes. Brown rice and here's how to cook a nut cutlet in your Habitat kitchen…
Yes, so the brown rice becomes the centrepiece of this person's stand – when of course it isn't.

Why do you think being vegetarian is almost considered effeminate? Ozzy Osbourne, Ted Nugent, so-called 'macho' people like that have to be real red-blooded meat-eaters.
Yes, I've never really thought about that. I can't think of any reason why veggies should be considered effeminate. Why? Because you care about animals? Is that effeminate? Is that a weak trait? It shouldn't be, and I think it's a sad reflection on the human race that it often is.

What about your heroes? I'm sure Oscar Wilde enjoyed a nice leg of mutton.
Or a big rump steak. Yes. He was a hideously fat person, so I'm sure he did indulge quite often – but he is forgiven.

And James Dean probably enjoyed a tasty hamburger.
I'm sure he did. But we all have our weaknesses.

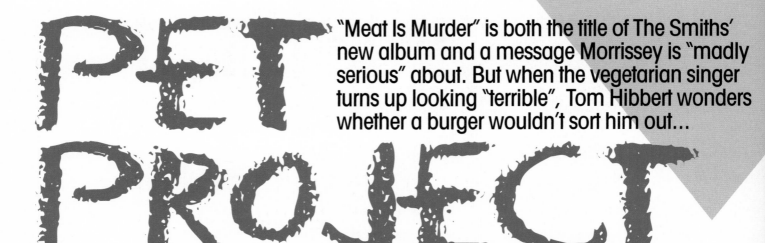

So it's alright, is it?
No, it isn't. Certainly not.

How far can you take this? What do you want to achieve?
Well, I'm very nervous about it because I'm deadly serious. It isn't, you know, catchphrase of the month. It isn't just this year's hysteria. I'm madly serious about it.

Did you have any pets when you were young?
Yes, I had a pet, which I still have in fact. I have a cat that is 23 years old – 23 human years old, I might add, which makes him something like a thousand in cat years. He's actually older than other members of The Smiths, which is remarkable.

What's his name?
His name – and I'm not responsible – is Tibby. It could be worse but I think that was a very popular cat name in the early '60s. It's quite extraordinary because we have family photographs of me when I was a day old and I'm clutching this cat, and there he is today still hobbling around.

What do you feed him on?
Regrettably, cat meat. Sad as it is, he eats meat, but nothing can be done now because he won't eat anything else. Certainly if I bought a pet today, I'd feed it on non-meat products like Smarties and baked beans. It's a shame that Tibby is glued to meat, as it were, because – in effect – he's eating other cats.

Sheila Rock

Morrissey: "If I bought a pet today, I'd feed it on non-meat products like Smarties and baked beans."

But cats are carnivores. Wouldn't it be a bit selfish to impose *your* beliefs on a cat and turn it into a vegetarian?
No, because cat food is an animal. It's a horse or it's a dog or whatever. So how can I be selfish by not allowing an animal to eat another animal? I'm simply looking after it. Animals can live without meat. We get violently upset when animals eat human beings, it's horrific, it's dreadful. So why shouldn't we feel horror when human beings eat animals?

I do.
You do what? Eat humans?

***No*, eat animals. Which human would you most like to eat?**
Well, now. This is tricky because I spent the last 18 months criticising people, putting them down, destroying them, and I've reached the point where I realise there's not any point. Because you meet these people and you realise that some of them are really quite affable. Some of them are quite nauseating.

Is Limahl affable?
No, he's certainly not in that category. But I've got a new policy. I'm not going to drag people down any more. Everybody within this curious profession has to do their own thing, however obnoxious that may be. And nothing I can say is going to change them. Besides, I've too many enemies. And it's a bit of a strain because one is welcome almost nowhere. I don't want to go to parties or go skiing with Spandau Ballet or anything but still it's become quite tiresome, this constant barrier of hate. Silence is the safest thing.

What do you eat?
I have a daily intake of yoghurt and bread.

Do you think this might be responsible for your present state of ill health? A good McDonald's quarter-pounder would put you back on your feet in no time.
I sincerely doubt it.

If you died tomorrow, went up to heaven and met Colonel Sanders of KFC fame, what would you say to him?
Words would just be useless. I think I'd just resort to the old knee in the groin – 'This is on behalf of all those poor animals who died simply because of you.'

That was a trick question. You should have said he wouldn't *be* in heaven.
Oh.

OK. That's the end.
Of what?

Of the interview.
Thank heavens for that. You didn't ask me about Band Aid.

What about Band Aid?
Band Aid is the undiscussable, I'm afraid.

***You* brought it up!**
Yes, and *I* finished the sentence. Full stop.

Shopping Lists

What do pop stars stock up with at the supermarket? Is it cordon bleu or should it be cordoned off? We conducted this special survey to nose through their baskets...

Rose & Jill
(Strawberry Switchblade)

1 20 cans of cat food, 'cos we've got three cats.
2 Vegetable juice, 'cos we're vegetarian and we like it.
3 Instant mash potato.
4 Baked beans.
5 Lentil soup.
6 Chocolate.
7 Lots of Mr Kipling cakes (especially French Fancies).
8 Lots of tangerines.
9 Frozen brussel sprouts (got to be Birds Eye's).
10 Hairspray – the cheapest, stickiest and horriblest.

Holly Johnson

Nothing at all. We've just eaten the last of the food because we're about to go away. The fridge is empty, so I guess we need everything and nothing.

Howard Jones

1 Avocados. They're my favourite vegetable. [*It's a fruit!* – *Ed.*]
2 Milk, because I've never got enough of it. We don't have a milkman.
3 Films for my Polaroid camera.

The Art Of Noise

1 An elephant.
2 A Burton's suit for Kenneth Williams.
3 12 floppy disks.
4 A clarinet.
5 Three tickets on a slow boat to Sydney.
6 A volume of *Art Rainbow* (published by Oxford University Press).
7 A large boat.
8 A pair of bales.
9 Yehudi Menuhin (world-famous classical violinist) for the Fairlight.
10 A crate of Carlsberg 69 lager.

Kirsty McColl

1 The (London) *Standard*.
2 Perrier water.
3 Bog-rolls.

Sade

Goat's cheese. I had some goat's cheese yesterday for the first time. I was very impressed.

Marilyn

1 I like those kind of biscuits – I can't remember what they're called, but they've got wheat and raisins and stuff in.
2 Farmhouse muesli.
3 Orange juice and things that look healthy.
Shopping is one of my favourite occasions. I pick anything up and buy it.

John Taylor

1 I always buy an LP by someone who's selling more records than us.
2 Some chocolate – any chocolate.
3 A packet of cigarettes.
4 I always buy magazines – I can't stop. My favourite ones are a New York magazine called *Details* and French *Vogue*
5 I never buy food (I can always eat out).

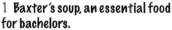

Nik Kershaw

1 Pitta bread.
2 Several cloves of garlic.
3 Assorted cheeses. I love French cheeses and blue Brie, Danish blue, a German cheese called Münster – it's horrendous stuff; you don't make any friends eating it.
4 Crunchy Nut Cornflakes – Kellogg's, of course. They cost a bloody fortune but they're lovely.
5 A bottle of Drambuie.
6 A packet of dry-roasted peanuts.
7 About a ton of potatoes. I love them any way – chips, baked, roasted. I must have an Irish ancestor or something.
8 A tin of tomatoes – you can do anything with a tin of tomatoes. We cook vegetarian at home, and if you've got a tin of tomatoes you can always get a meal out of it somehow. I'm not a vegetarian myself, but I don't eat a lot of meat.
9 Some haddock – baked or poached. I do some of the cooking but I'm home so rarely that when I'm there I tend to just collapse.
10 An enormous Black Forest Gateau from Sainsbury's. A bit of luxury.

It's terrible when you do stuff like this. You tell people what you like and the next tour you get pelted with Crunchy Nut Cornflakes or whatever. Apparently I said once, though I don't even remember saying it, that I like Marmite. And I got these jars of Marmite thrown at me! So I'll have to think of something a bit softer.

Andy Fletcher
(Depeche Mode)

1 Green Giant sweetcorn.
2 Fresh mushrooms.
3 Marks & Spencer's chunky chicken.
4 Mr Kipling's cup cakes.
5 Bourbon biscuits.
6 Mother's Pride muffins.
7 Lynne's whisky marmalade.
8 Four bottles of Grolsch beer.
9 Colgate blue minty gel (in a pump).
10 Vidal Sassoon hairspray .

Paul King

1 Very strong mature Cheddar or Stilton .
2 Toothpaste. I've just been trying one called Clearasil – no, that's the spot remover, isn't it? The minty clear one anyway, like Dentyne chewing gum. But I've discovered it's too sweet, so I'll move on.
3 Ski Yoghurt – Black Cherry.
4 Strawberry King Cones – they're like Cornettos. I'm a big fan.
5 Pizzas – they're quick 'n' easy snacks.
6 Coleslaw – from Tesco's, to go with the pizza and cheese.
7 Heinz Baked Beans – I have to have the brand-name varieties.
8 Fray Bentos Steak and Kidney Pies – because I really love the pastry. In fact, I buy them just for the pastry.
9 A bottle of Sambuca, from the off-licence. It's a liqueur.
10 KP peanuts, ready salted. I eat them by the ton.

Not a very healthy lot, is it? I do make an effort to get fresh vegetables and stuff, but it's such a bind to cook them.

Andy McCluskey
(OMD)

1 Baxter's soup, an essential food for bachelors.
2 Roses from Interflora for California.
3 White socks from M&S.
4 Aspirins – useful when listening to OMD 12 hours a day in the studio.
5 TV licence.
6 Floppy disks for Synco systems.
7 *The Times* – to do the crossword.
8 Every single British Telecom share, so I can de-privatise it.
9 Black clothes from PW Forte on the King's Road.
10 *Smash Hits* – it's still the only pop magazine worth reading. [*Your cheque is in the post. – Ed.*]

Gary Kemp

1 Bread.
2 Cheese.
3 Milk.

I'm terrible at buying things. I always end up buying bread, cheese and milk, and go home and think, "What can I make?"

Suggs (Madness)

1 A bag of King Edwards.
2 A Marks & Spencer's trifle.
3 Wholemeal bread.
4 A deep-dish Pizza Hut takeaway.
5 Peking Duck.
6 Mentadent toothpaste.
7 Italian chocolate spread.
8 Smoked almonds.
9 Mushrooms.
10 Smucker's Goober Jelly.

YOUR LETTERS

Penned by the likes of "Jungle Jezebel's Action Man" and "Bimby Boomp", our readers' missives caused belly-laughs and bafflement in equal measure. Luckily the shadowy **Black Type** was never stuck for a reply...

Dear **Black Type**,

As Britain is still recovering from the Queen Of Sleaze, Madonna, I would like to give you a few facts.

1) Madonna did not invent the beauty spot! Adam Ant did!

2) Madonna did not invent the showing off of her belly-button! Adam Ant did!

3) You've probably forgotten who Adam Ant is. Well, he's that v. famous, gorgeous singer from the early '80s who brought out v. brill records like "Stand And Deliver" and "Prince Charming" and "Puss 'N Boots". Remember them! His spirit will never die!!
Sarah, Altrincham.

Never, Sarah, never!! Why, who can ever forget that immortal refrain "a-rump-a-dump-a-rump-a-dump" from, er, whichever one it was... Or even "fa diddly qua qua" from, er, that other one... Viva Adam!

Dear **Black Type**,

Referring to the review of Erasure's concert at Hammersmith Odeon in *Smash Hits* (18-23 May): I must say that Andy Bell did not "slip on a see-through ballet skirt" as "Uncle" Reggie says he did, but in fact it was a black petticoat, which makes far more sense. (As a great man once said , "When you're feeling like life's one long bummer, slip on yer petticoat", or something like that.)
Yours faithfully, Andy Bell's "Bloomers", Belfast.

I must say, "Bloomers", that you were not the only one to experience a considerable level of distress. "Uncle" Reggie, as you call him, was so seriously sour-mouthed after the aforementioned

Look what I found in my *Judy Annual 1971*. Love the trendy haircut, Holly!
Gillian Welburn, Prestatyn, Clwyd, Wales.

"event" that he filled my prized gumboots with frog spawn and fair wiped the smirk off my jowls. Frankly, it's an outrage.

Dear **Black Type**,

What do you call a bloke who steals tarmac? Nick Rhodes.
Bimby Boomp, London N17.

Dear **Black**ingford Of All **Type**shire,

Is it true? Can it be so? Are my assumptions correct? Is the cultured era of the "ode" really diminishing? We, the great British public must keep up this centuries-old tradition. Please, Lord [**Black**]ingford, beseech your followers that life will not continue without odes.

Here, for example, is one ode which I hope will establish a firm basis for a flurry of devoted ode writers: *Ode To The Foolish*

Woman In The Heinz Baked Beans Advert Who Sighs At Her "Poor" Son Steve Davis Playing With An Assorted Array Of Kitchen Utensils.

Oh foolish woman in the Heinz Baked Beans advert who sighs at her "poor" son Steve Davis playing with an assorted array of kitchen utensils / Cheer up, you miserable old bat! / You will be rich in 20 years.

Apologies for outburst.
Mr Rick C Feeney Esq, Northants.

My useless so-called lawyer warned me not to mention this to anyone, but in fact the very same tinned cuisine manufacturers approached me some time ago to appear in one of these very same commercials. The script was appalling, however. I was supposed to be sitting at a dining table looking 15 years younger and trying not to look miserable as Cilla Black (playing my mother) screeched, "Eat up yer beans, chook, or else you'll never get a job in the nuclear power-plant down t'road!" while I fiddled with a chemistry set or something equally pathetic. And then, various unconvincing reincarnations of me growing up would appear until – there I was 20 years younger with Dame Cilla bashing me about the head with a fish slice, saying, "It didn't bloody work, did it, you snivelling little git! Call writing for that hopeless little magazine a real job!!"To which I would reply, "Oooh mum, I think it was the chronic wind on the morning of the interview that did it..." Needless to say, I forgot to set my alarm clock on the morning of the "shoot".

Dear **Black Type**,

We have just bought our *Smash Hits* at the local newsagent and, at the same time, Phil Oakey was in there buying a battery.

This is obviously much more interesting than a Morrissey interview.
Michael And Helen.

If you say so.

Found this in an unspeakable Sunday supplement. Don't they know Morisssey is always late?
A Close And Personal Friend Of Steven's, Rotherham.

Dear **Black Type**,

I have "noticed" that you have a "tendency" to put "inverted" "commas" around certain "words". What is the "meaning" of this? Is it some "secret" "code" that only "selected" "Russian" "spies" understand? Or is it a "way" of "communicating" with "aliens" from "outer" "space"? Or is it just "another" of your "tricks" to "encourage" people like me to write "dumb" "letters" to you so that the "Editor" doesn't "kick" you out of a "job"?
"Sir""William Idol's "Bondage" "Trousers", "Dagenham", Essex.

"PS" I think it is "infectious". "Help"!

Inverted commas are the best invention since exclamation marks, if you

ask me. Why, not only can you bung them round words whenever you feel like it, but you can also snip them out of magazines, gum them on your chin and – hey presto! – a foolproof Bob Geldof Disguise Kit. Here are some for you to practise with:"""""""""""""""""""" (*That's enough inverted commas, thank you – Ed.*)

Dearest **Black Type**,
Dearie me! What is the world a-coming to? I mean, is it asking too much for the Pet Shop Boys to spell one of their LP titles correctly? Last year I gritted my teeth as Messrs Tennant and Lowe ignorantly spelt pur-lease as "Please", but now this is the end! Everyone knows that "Actually" is really spelt ackcheloi. I rest my case.
Jungle Jezebel's Action Man, Nottingham.

Most odd, I must agree, especially as Mr Tennant practically invented both words. Perhaps their next LP will bear the immortal title "T-ragic", oui?

Dear **Black Type**,
Admit it. You thought Bruce Springsteen was a human being, the future of rawk'n'rawl and all that. Well, you'd be wrong. On close examination of the facts, it is fairly obvious that this "man" is a fiendishly well-disguised machine.
Take the way he plays his guitar (or should I say "gee-tar") with a decidedly mechanical movement of the arm – he doesn't even *look* at what he's doing. His latest smasheroonie record only uses six notes – is

Dear **Black Type**,
Reading through my super super super super girlie comic, I found this. I wonder where Joe is?
The Fortunate Piano Key That Wasn't Hit By Tom Bailey's Hands, Eire.

this so that Broooce doesn't overstretch his memory banks? He charges an exorbitant £15 for entrance to his concerts, then gives all the profits away. He gallivants around on stage for hours without getting tired. He sings typically "machine-like" songs about driving around in cars. He has a wistful fixation with the word "born". He wears slightly flared jeans. His music is mindnumbingly boring. He is presently getting more media attention that the C5. Hordes of people have been driven mad by hordes of other people asking them, "Have you got your Springsteen tickets yet?" when the first horde of people didn't

WRITE TO: SMASH HITS, 52-55 CARNABY STREET, LONDON W1V 1PF
THE BEST LETTER GETS A £10 RECORD TOKEN

give a Castlemaine XXXX about going to a Springsteen concert in the first place.
Bruce Springsteen the greatest man in the Universe? My bottom! I wish his batteries would hurry up and run down and give us all a bit of peace.
The Jesus And Mary Chainstore, Rugby, Warks.

Brothers! Sisters! I'm just a prisoner of rock'n'roll. Yeah! Phew! Highway! (*Shut up – Ed.*)

Dear **Black Type**,
I thought *Rambo* was a really good film, although I cried when his mother died and he was left in the forest all alone.
Porkie The Pig, London.

Me too. And what about the bit when all the elephants started laughing because he

had big ears? What a choker! Pass the Scotties Man-Size Tissues, Mum.

Dear Zwarte Typ (that's **Black Type** in Dutch, viewers),
It can't be true! Yet again the *Letters* page has been cut off in its prime! Belittled! Minimised!! What am I talking about? Why, in the last issue the *Letters* page was just one solitary page! ONE page!!! All I can say is, "Stand up for your two pages!!"
A Big BT Fan, The Netherlands.

I have, sir, I have! Hence the lovely little double-pager we are currently making our way across. And roll on that glorious day in the near future when two pages is mere so-called chicken feed and Sir Blackford has a good dozen or so to call his very own! And then it will take *Bitz*, *Get Smart!*, *Review* and all the rest of the ungrateful Sods!!! AVANTI!

Dear **Black Type**,
Ackchewelly, akchooelley is spelt like this: Atchoowelly (oh damn! My pen's slipped). Sorry, I'll start again: Akchewleh, act 2 welly is spelt like this: Actu (God! This blasted pen which I found in a pot of Pot Noodle – yum! – has run out). Sorry I WILL START AGAIN! I know I'll write acchuolly out five times to get it right. Right? Oh, well, here goes: acktchzollay, actuelley, aktoooooely, actoely, actualey.

Dear **Black Type**,
Would one not agree that Holly Johnson is suffering a jolly old identity crisis? Complete with dippy hairstyle, DIY "grow your own supadupa eyebrows" lessons from Denis Healey, and plastic surgery to correct that awful straight nose, one would be forced to say he does indeed bear a remarkable resemblance to my jolly old sonny Charlie boy, wouldn't one? Of course one would! Jolly ho and Royal regards,
E. Windsor, Buck house.

God bless you, Ma'am – one certainly would have to agree with your right royal observations. Please accept this £10 record token – a wee donation towards scraping the barnacles off the bottom of the Royal Yacht Britannia, which I know is a costly but *vital* operation. (By the by, I didn't seem to spot my name in the New Year's Honours List – some oversight here, perhaps?)

(Actually!!!) I wondered if you know how to spell it – because according to the July 3 Mega-wonderful magazine, you don't! *A Person Who Knows How To Spell Actually, Wigton Fields.*

Akkkschewellellieee is spelt like this: akkkschewellel-lieee. Actually is spelt like this: actually, actually. *Now* do you understand? (*Can't say I do, akcherleh – Ed.*)

Your constant slagging off of Bruce Springsteen in recent issues is quite pathetic and smacks of sour grapes. It's quite obvious that the reason you have

chosen to be so abusive is that you couldn't get an interview with him so you turned against him. I will not be buying your pretty little rag again.
Springsteen Fan And Proud Of It, Norwich.

Well, akchewlee, for your information, in particular point of fact, Smash Hits is the only British music publication to have run an interview with His Humble Bossiness this year – issue dated January 31 to be precise. So nyah, nyah to *you*, matey boots!

Dear **Black Type**,
    As a public service, I have scanned all your *Letters* pages for the year "1985" and have made a Top 20 chart of the characters most mentioned in your replies. They are as follows:
1) Anneka Rice
2) Bagpuss
3) Gar(r)y Lux
4) Una Stubbs (latterly known as Dame Una Nescafé)
5) Ms Vikki Watson ("the flower of English song")
6) Delia Smith ("1001 Jolly Nice Things To Eat")
7) Roland Orzabal (and a kangaroo)
8) Ronald McDonald
9) Maggie Philbin
10) Russ "prisoner of rock'n'roll" Abbot

THE NEWCOMER HAD NOTICED ONE PILOT HE HADN'T BEEN INTRODUCED TO. WHEN HE HAD TIME, HE WENT OVER TO SAY HELLO.

...THE NAME'S TAM BARTON. I HOPE WE CAN HIT IT OFF.

I DOUBT WE'LL BE FRIENDS. I PREFER TO BE KNOWN BY MY SURNAME, WHICH IS MORRISEY.

I hope you realise the pain and suffering I have gone through in order to send you this. **(V. lengthy account of the pain and suffering gone through to send me this deleted)**... but after seeing this v. revealing shot of our friendly, vegetarian whingebag... I think you'll agree it was worth it.
Stephen Adam, Whitton, Middx.

Madonna — the Dairy Blackface champion.

Before her infamous photographs in *Penthouse* and *Playboy*, Madonna did a photo session for *Scottish Farmer*. As you can see, the results are stunning.
Jennifer Sarah Duncan, Glasgow.

Here's a £10 record token to stuff into the woolly beauty's nosebag. Yum!

11) Bruce "oh what an atmosphere" Springsteen
12) Simon Le Bon (and a yachting cap full of spaghetti)
13) Rod, Jane and Freddy
14) "Winsome" Wincey Willis ("groovin' to the latest pop vids")
15) Jimmy Krankie
16) Bonnie Tyler
17) Princess Michael Of Kent
18) "Sir" Barbara Cartland
19) Michael des Barres
20) A tie between Prince, Cliff "Sir Clifford" Richard, Bilbo Baggins, David Hunter from *Crossroads* and the Queen Mother.
    What conclusions can we draw from this?
Sean Taylor (No Relation I Assure You), Winchester.

This list proves, if nothing else, that we *are* all fallible. Whatever did I see in that brazen hussie Anneka "Can't you run any faster than *that*, you pathetic excuse for a cameraman" Rice, who, last time she popped up on my telly screen, was trading loathsome and unsavoury innuendos with a slippery-tongued conjurer in a toupée, ie Paul Daniels? Grooooo! Apart from that, our chart seems pretty sound (give or take a B. Springsteen or two).

Dear **Black Type**,
    Have any other *Smash Hits* readers noticed the striking resemblance between Jimmy Sommerville of the Communards and the singing potatoes in the Smith's Crisps adverts on TV? Not only do they look alike, but they have amazing similar voices! Any chance of a duet in the future, Jimmy?
Cameo's red pouch, Burnham.

Smash Hits is still the best of all the possible music papers. Only one gripe – why are there no charts?
Richard White, Blackburn.

What sort of charts do you want, matey? Wiggly "there's-a-cold-front-approaching-from-the-satellite-picture" weather forecaster-type charts? Felicity Kendall "lookin'-the-way-you-like-'n'-likin'-the-way-you-look" diet-type calorie charts? Russell

Dear **Black Type**,
    Found in the *Chicago Sun-Times*... Obviously an Andrew Ridgeley fan.
B.C. Three Dog Night Fan, London.

KINGSTON, Tenn. (AP)—Being pinned under his wrecked sports car for six hours with a broken arm was bad enough, a teenager said, but listening to the British rock group Wham! playing continuously on his tape recorder made the situation unbearable.
    "I never want to hear it again. I swear I don't," Gordon Pickrell, 18, of Kingston, said after Roane County deputies pulled him from beneath his overturned MGB coupe Wednesday. "I thought I was going to die."

Grant "ooo-you-have-a-bit-of-Sagittarius-in-Leo-which-makes-you-very-generous-and-prone-to-nosebleeds"-type astrology charts? (*I think he's referring to record charts, actually – Ed.*)

Dear **Black Type**,
    I am 39 and read your magazine every week.
    When I take it to work the young men and women laugh. Please tell them that you can be "old" and "with it".
    Yours faithfully,
P.G. Speight, North Humberside.

Of course **you can be "old" and "with it". I am referring, of course, to that rocking elderly gent, Cliff Richard. (PS: How much LONGER must we wait for Her Majesty to unfurl the trusty sabre and whisper the joyous words "Arise, Sir Clifford!"? It is a national disgrace of climactic proportions!)**

Dire Straits are under new management.
A Girl Who's Mad About, Gravesend, Kent.

Dear **Black Type**,
    "The Adventures of an Anita Dobson Fan."
    I was camping outside my local record store waiting for the arrival of Anita Dobson's debut album. But then came the first bit of bad news. NO ALBUM!!
    So I collected my belongings and set off to the Birmingham Odeon. I pitched my tent on the pavement, to the amusement of passers-by, and sat and waited. Why, I hear you ask, am I camping outside the Birmingham Odeon? I'm waiting for confirmation of Lady Dobson's world tour!
    A whole week I camped there. Then I was finally told the bad news. NO WORLD TOUR! I felt so depressed – suicidal!!
    I slowly walked down to the nearest "news" agents and bought *Smash Hits*. I saw two fat little pigs talking on a beach. One pig said the next edition would

be "stuffed" with interesting and famous things like… ANITA DOBSON!! I then pitched my tent outside the "news" agents.

And there I waited for two weeks for the delivery of the next issue of *Smash Hits*. It finally came. I skimmed through it looking for just the slightest bit about "Dobby".

Third bit of bad news. Absolutely ZILCH!!!

I am now camping on a big piece of paper in the centre of the Atlantic Ocean.
A very-very-very-near-to-drowning person who once lived in Walsall.

That's quite enough about *EastEnders*, **thank you VERY much.**

Dear **Black Type,**
In the last issue of *Smash Hits*, I read your article "40 Incredibly Daft Questions Put To Pop Stars", but I could only find 38 daft questions. What happened to the other two, may I ask?
Caroline Who Wishes She Was Married To Francis Rossi, Manchester.

You may indeed. The missing questions were: 1) Does your mother peck cuttlefish? – to which a member of The Tweets replied: "I suppose there must be"; 2) What do you call a man with a collapsing skyscraper on his head? – to which 'Dinkie'

Dear **Black Type,**
Surely that man McCartney has made *enough* money without having to resort to supplying cleaning rags.
Mourne Observer, Co. Down.

O'Horse, lead vocalist with sadly defunct "New Romantic" outfit Gorgeous Sponge, answered: "An ambulance". On reflection, both these questions were considered far too sensible for inclusion.

Dear **Black Type,**
A few issues back you had a feature on Julian Lennon, and you said that after John Lennon had died Julian flew to New York to

find Yoko Ono and his "step-brother" Sean. But if Julian and Sean had the same father but didn't have the same mother, this would make them *half* brothers, not *step* brothers. Please tell Neil Tennant to get his facts right in future.
Ferraro Rocher, Humberstone, Leicester.

Ha! I always *thought* Neil Tennant was a slippery customer when it came to a game of "Happy Families". And *now* I know why! Miss Bun the Baker's great-aunt-by-marriage indeed!

Dear **Black Type,**
I felt the need to write this letter to you as I am most concerned about *Smash Hits'* obsession with being sick. In a recent *Smash Hits*, there was an article on George Michael and it stated that he had been sick on his girlfriend *and* on his chest. Is this true?

It was not only in this issue of *Smash Hits* that being sick in or on things was noticed. It is mentioned in practically every edition. I don't know if I have missed a joke or something with this obsession, but I am greatly concerned about such a vulgar subject. Please inform me of further details on this case.
Nicola Burnand, Berkshire.

A Publisher Writes: Take a letter, Miss Pringle. To Ms Nicola

Dear **Black Type,**
It would appear that old George has found time in between writing, singing and producing well fab records, touring China, keeping Andrew under control and rescuing all those shuttlecocks to write a book! About hunting in Africa, no less! Proof? Here I have for you the title page, plus, on page 219, a confession of his real feelings about Duran!

Must go, I've just got to an interesting bit in Nik Kershaw's book about bottle gardening…
The First Wham! Bookworm Since Sliced Bread, Worcestershire.

Whatever next? *A Life On The Ocean Wave* **by Simon Le Bon, or, yet more preposterous, a book of Nick Rhodes' Polaroids? Who can say?**

Burnand, Berkshire. Dear Ms Burnand, Thank you for your letter regarding this obsession of the Smash Hits "staff" with being sick. I too regard this as a very vulgar subject and I am doing everything within my so-called power to put a stop to the whole ruddy business. In the meantime, if you would care to take out a subscription to any of my other brilliant magazines, just make a cheque out for £3,000, made payable to The Publisher, Snoot-Mags… I say, Miss Pringle, have you ever been sick on your blouse? **(Off with you, perv-king! – B.T.)**

Dear **Black Type,**
What do you call a cat with only one life left? A careless whiskers.
J., Lowestoft.

ROY HAY'S Notebook
TAKING THINGS FOR GRANTED
OFTEN I wonder what my father, who was one of the grand old men of the gardening world, would have thought of present-day horticulture. He never saw an electrically heated greenhouse or soil-warmed frame.

(Found in a gardening magazine by Boy George's Black Nail Varnish, Walsall.)

(Found in a comic by Deborah "I think they looked a bit different in the video" Emmons, London.)

IT'S LOVELY WHEN A GIRL GETS INTO YOUR PYJAMAS
JOHN TAYLOR

(Found in "pervy publication" by Someone Who Is Definitely Still A Spring Chicken, Isleworth, Middx.)

(Found atop a carton of revolting-looking chocolate spread by an anonymous personage who comments "At LAST!")

WHAM! ★ IN CHINA

Neal Preston

Wham! were the first western pop group to be invited to play in China. The country had no pop charts, its first disco had only opened a year earlier and dancing in public was an arrestable offence. No wonder their concerts were hailed as "a cultural revolution". Peter Martin (words) and Neal Preston (photos) joined George and Andrew for the seven-day trip of a lifetime.

"**I'D LIKE TO** start by saying my partner Andrew and I are extremely flattered and honoured to be here today," says George Michael. "We just hope our performance will represent a cultural introducing between young people here and in the West and help them see what goes on in the rest of the world.

"And I think I speak for everyone when I say this may be a small step for Wham! but a great step for the youth of the world!"

"No, you go and ask for the ball back..." George Michael and Andrew Ridgeley on the Great Wall of China.

The date is April 5, 1985. The place is Peking, the capital of China. The event is a banquet held by the Chinese Youth Federation in honour of their guests, Wham!. The speakers are a certain George Michael and Andrew Ridgeley.

For the next ten days Wham! will be touring China. This afternoon they scaled The Great Wall that divides China and Mongolia. On Sunday April 7 they will perform at the Workers'

Gymnasium in Peking. On Monday they fly to Canton to perform at the Zhongshan Memorial Hall. Two days later they will fly back to Hong Kong – from where they've just got back after playing its Colosseum Theatre. And in between all that they've got a football match, about a million banquets, two press conferences and a film to make. It is, in short, an historic trip.

It's historic because China, a country with a population of one

billion, had no discos until 12 months ago, and dancing was "disallowed". There are no such things as pop charts, no singles, no LPs, just cassettes – and they're nearly all by Chinese artists. The only other music available is light Japanese pop music. Only the 'privileged' can afford any of this, anyway – most not even being able to afford a simple transistor radio.

For centuries, China has been under a self-imposed isolation

which is only now being swept away. For the first time the people of China are being allowed to have a real taste of Western culture. Already in the main cites you can find Coca-Cola, Levi's jeans, McDonald's, Sony Walkmans and now... Wham!.

Most people welcome the change. Some aren't so keen, seeing it as a form of "spiritual pollution". As a kind of compromise, Wham! were only allowed to perform after a strict vetting –

the result of which rounded off a few of their more decadent edges, such as George Michael's "sexy hip gyrations". Nevertheless the working title for their documentary film is *Wham! In China!: A Cultural Revolution!*. An appropriate title? We'll just have to wait seven days to find out.

DAY ★ 1

ALL IS NOT well; patience and energy are being spread very thin. Apart from the pressure that goes with the honour of being the first western pop group to play China, Wham! have got an awful lot more on their plate. Literally every move they make is being recorded by the film crew; they walk down the street – so do the film crew; they take a sauna – so do the film crew. For all I know, they probably get filmed going to toilet.

And then there's the Chinese themselves. Tourists are a relatively new thing for them, never mind pop stars who stroll around in tartan suits and tuxedos all day. The result is that the boys are subjected to a constant barrage of blank stares every time they set foot outdoors.

And then there's Fleet Street. Wham!'s managers have invited four newspapers – the *Daily Mirror*, *The Sun*, *Daily Star* and *Daily Express* – out here for maximum exposure back home. Each paper has forked out £10,000 each for the privilege, dead keen to have any story on Wham!. It's a fiercely competitive business. When they were in Hong Kong, for example, *The Sun*, under strict instructions to "nobble" its competitor the *Mirror*, 'leaked' a story to *Mirror* man John Blake about George Michael cracking up. Blake filed the story and it appeared on their front page. The story was completely untrue and it lost Blake the chance of an interview. Well and truly "nobbled".

After that and the previous week's stories about "Randy Andy's Bum-Grabbing Boozy Night Of Debauchery", neither George nor Andrew play ball with Fleet Street. The only occasion they co-operated was yesterday at The Great Wall, and then they only posed for photos for a couple of minutes and gave sarcy quotes – George: "It looks like one long Barratt home"; Andrew: "I can't see the point in it – who'd want to invade a country like this anyway?" The rest of the time Andrew just keeps his dark glasses on and looks moody, while George just keeps out of the way in his room.

I bumped into George at the hotel breakfast bar. He seemed very keen to give his side of the story: "All this Fleet Street business is one thing I never envisaged when we started. I mean, all those stories about me collapsing – it's just beyond me. It's absolutely horrific. It's like being bullied – bullied by Fleet Street."

At 6pm we all have to meet up again. This time it's at Peking's oldest and largest restaurant, The Peking Duck. Andrew turns up; George doesn't, choosing to eat from room service as he's a bit tired. Inside the private suite, we have the Wham! backing bands

plus Andrew on one table (there are rather a lot of them, about 40 in all), the Fleet Street reporters on another (well away from Andrew) and other tables packed with important-looking Chinese people, all stuffing themselves with mounds of stir-fried edibles.

The film's producer, Martyn Lewis, raves about his "project". He describes "Andy" as a "comic genius". Why? Because after lunch they did some location shots down on Peking's Waang Fu Jing. Andy did a bit of Jools Holland-type roving reporting. He stopped the film crew outside a shop, saying, "Hey, this looks like C&A's, let's go in!" They go in and he buys a Mao suit, a kind of Chinese 'street' uniform, for 40 Yuen (51 Yuen is an average month's pay, the equivalent of £18). Then he did a bit of a

guided tour, cracked a few funnies and was off.

The film's full of stuff like that, apparently, as well as live Chinese concert footage. Lewis reckons the film's "natural length is 60 minutes and it'll probably be shown on Channel 4 or something like that later this summer". The film is reportedly costing £1.5 million of Wham!'s money, but they're regarding it as a way of recouping some of the £700,000 their two-week Chinese tour is costing them.

Around 9pm, all the food has gone. Everyone waddles out to the waiting cars. It's here where Andrew gets – shock, horror, gasp – mobbed! Not by locals though, but by a posse of passing American tourists. They take photos, ask for autographs and make lots of noise. One American

Orange squash with a Chinese official and the British Ambassador.

Neal Preston

You've been warned about those "sexy hip gyrations", George!

woman in a flowery dress looks very pleased with herself: "That Andrew Frisbee's a true star!" she bawls at her tour coach.

The locals look on in mild disbelief. Not only do they not know what Wham! really look like, they haven't the faintest idea who they are. But that will all change tomorrow, for it's tomorrow that Wham! will show China what they're made of. Tomorrow they're playing The Workers' Gymnasium.

DAY ★ 2

"ONE OF THE many reasons the Chinese chose Wham! to play and not other groups who've asked was because of what we represent: optimism and aspiration. Also we're at the total opposite end of the scale to what China sees as the decadent rock acts of the West. You know – sex, drugs, scandal. The thing with us was that there *was* no angle. That's why I suppose Fleet Street have to make one up."

So says George Michael. Even so, despite their so-called 'whiter-than-white' image, it still took ten months of negotiations and rigorous scrutiny of Wham! videos, lyrics (translations were asked for), photos of every costume that was to be worn, and footage of a show on their recent seven-month world tour to get permission to play here. In the process, the Chinese Youth Federation considered the words to "Love Machine" "unsuitable", as was George's "sexy" hip swivelling. The Chinese don't seem to encourage displays of emotion of any kind, so it's not

surprising they want to keep check on a pair of lads who have a reputation of stuffing shuttle-cocks down their shorts. But anyway, they're here. In fact, in 15 minutes they're going to be onstage at the 10,000-seated venue. The place is a cross between a low-budget spaceship and the Royal Albert Hall. The audience, almost all kitted out in muted fawn and blue Mao suits, sit there – silent and polite – not quite sure what's about to happen. Over the PA they hear Phil Collins, Lionel Richie, Michael Jackson. It's hardly audible and all in keeping with the safe 'don't rock the boat' approach Wham! have adopted throughout.

As a warm-up we have a British dancer called Trevor, who instructs the audience on how to body pop and break-dance, whipping them into a frenzy, or rather their equivalent of a frenzy, a kind of bottled-up excitement. Then, unbeknown to us, an announcement is made (in Chinese) over the public address system. It says: "Dancing is not allowed." Those standing sit down; those sitting calm down.

The lights go down once more, the 11-strong Wham! backing band take their places. The lights go up and George and Andrew bound down their respective staircases, bursting into an ultra-fast version of "Wake Me Up Before You Go-Go". It's all very polished, almost too perfect, a very Eurovision kind of presenta-tion. After six songs (the track listing is printed in the concert programmes) there's a ten-minute break for their 'home movie' slot (minus the big kiss from the "Careless Whisper" video, which has been edited out) and six more songs, this time a bit looser – but not much – then it's over.

There is no encore. The only people dancing are American soldiers and tourists. One man at the end even got arrested and beaten for dancing by the police. Not even all the Chinese clapped. Apparently when they saw George and Andrew trying to get everyone to join in and clap, they thought they were asking for applause and were offended.

By western standards, it all seems a terrible anti-climax. But

the Chinese audience, in their own restrained way, seemed to really enjoy it. One girl, through an interpreter, told me they were "very good. Better than the Peking Opera. Next year Wham! very popular." Another said she was "so glad to be one of the people here. I was so excited, the music made me crazy."

DAY ★ 3

THE CHINESE NEWSPAPERS are full of Wham! stories and quotes from George about last night's concert. "We just couldn't bridge the cultural gap," he says. "There is a huge cultural difference which there is no way you're going to cross in one-and-a-half hours."

He told me that the concert wasn't like he'd imagined but, then again, he admitted he didn't know quite what to expect.

"I suppose I hoped that the audience might join in and dance, but I didn't realise until later that there'd been an announcement about it. I think we've been stitched up over that – if they invite us all the way over here you'd think they'd at least let us put on a show our way. Basically we were fighting a losing battle last night."

Anyway, there's always Canton, which is where we're heading right now. George, Andrew and their two managers are staying behind. The Fleet Street reporters are going home. We all say our goodbyes and head for the airport. Little do we know that tomorrow morning British newspapers will be carrying headlines like "WHAM! MAN IN HARI-KIRI TERROR".

At 3pm, Monday April 8, thousands of feet above China on CAAC flight Number 1301, something is going terribly wrong. We're only 15 minutes out of Peking on the flight to Canton when roars of pain erupt from the back of the flight cabin.

Startled, stomachs sinking fast, the passengers cautiously peer down the aisle. A man is having a fit. His screams get louder, his body wracked in pain. I'm only two seats in front – I can see a small knife in his hand,

poised in front of his stomach… and it looks as if he's about to stab himself.

There's a horrible, consuming air of panic now. The flight crew are rushing around trying to calm the passengers. Members of the Wham! party – they're all here, apart from George and Andrew and the two managers – look at one another anxiously, not quite knowing what to do.

Now the man is being restrained by two Wham! minders, Ronnie and Dave. They've got the knife and are holding him by the arms and neck. His spasms get more violent, his screams more demonic; he's like a man possessed. Shirlie and Pepsi, who are were sitting next to him, are standing on the window seat and holding on to one another nervously.

Suddenly the plane dives. Stomachs churn, heads spin. The plane begins to creak. It actually sounds like it's cracking up. It looks like we're turning back. Diving, diving, diving, we've just broken the clouds.

Land comes into vision like a zoom lens snapping into sudden focus. Meanwhile the noises from the back of the plane get more and more distressing – he sounds like the girl in *The Exorcist*.

With a loud bash we're down, the plane reeling as each side of the undercarriage hits the tarmac. One last mighty screech and we stop, dead. The aircraft then taxis to the terminal. Eventually a Chinese doctor comes on board to give him an anaesthetic. The screams subside and he's carted off in an ambulance, leaving the rest of us feeling completely shell-shocked.

But *who* is he? It turns out he's actually Raul D'Oliveria, Wham!'s 33-year-old Portuguese trumpet player. Apparently he just suddenly flipped. Talking to members of the band later, it seemed he'd been acting a bit weird for the past few days, thinking he was "the Devil", and then suddenly – without any warning – he just cracked up mid-flight. Tomorrow's newspaper reports will go completely overboard about the incident – one will say the pilot was

attacked by a mad hijacker; another that he tried to commit "hara-kiri"; another that the plane crashed and "all the passengers died". Its not *that* disastrous but it's still a pretty shaken bunch of people who settle back into their seats as the plane turns round and heads for Canton once more.

First keyboard player Mark Fisher collapsed in Hong Kong ("exhaustion" – its been a seven-month tour), now Raul's out of circulation and Wham! are reduced to a ten-piece. Coupled with this, the Wham! film director,

Lindsay Anderson, fell while walking on The Great Wall and is now confined to a wheelchair. People are starting to think the whole venture's jinxed or something.

Talking to Shirlie in the Canton hotel disco later that night, she says, "I just think what we're doing here is bad. I don't want to sound funny or anything but I just don't think it's right that we're playing here. People here are sad, they want freedom but they're not allowed to have it and, in a way, we're giving them a taste of something they can't really have. I just think it was awful the way that boy was taken out of last night's concert and beaten. That wouldn't have happened if we hadn't come here. So it was just sad. I just want to go home."

And that, I'm afraid, is the general opinion of all the 70-strong Wham! entourage at the moment. Spirits have to be raised, so we pile into the hotel

next door to see if their disco is still open. It isn't. That means it's a fridge party or nothing. This turns out to be the standard night our for the rest of the week: bit of sightseeing in the daytime, get depressed by the obvious poverty and hardship so many Chinese have to endure, go for a drink, go bowling, have more drinks, go to the disco, go to the bass player Deon's room and bring the contents of your hotel drinks fridge with you. And go to bed around 5am. Look ill the next day and start all over again. Pretty rock'n'roll, eh?

Young guns go for fit…

DAY ★ 4

TUESDAY IS A free day, so most of the party go to market. Here they see skinned dogs strung up in rows, headless cats in bins, eagles in cages all ready for eating. Rats, ant-eaters, ants, armadillos, pigeons, sparrows and even tigers are sold for the same purpose. You can even buy "boiling frogs" by the dozen. Colonials here joke that the "Chinese would eat anything with legs as long as it's not a table or a chair".

DAY ★ 5

THINGS ARE BRIGHTENING up. George Michael and Andrew Ridgeley are here and we're all off to a football match: the Wham! band versus the Wham! Chinese road crew. It's an 11-a-side to be played on the ground of the Chung Shan Memorial Hall where

Wham! will play their final Chinese concert tomorrow night.

Andrew turns up in a proper kit – Queens Park Rangers, I think. George turns up late (ten minutes into the game). The film crew are here, of course. The Fleet Street reporters have gone home, apart from the *Daily Star* and the *Daily Express* journalists, who are still in Peking but have been invited up here because "they've been the best of a bad bunch" (and, I suspect, because it would *really* annoy *The Sun* and *The Mirror*, who weren't quite so well behaved).

Anyway, the game's a bit of a shambles, most of the players just booting the ball as far away from themselves as possible. Andrew, posing like no one's business, ends up scoring two goals; Paul, the other trumpeter, scores four and that's only half-time. The team decide to "let the others try to catch up – otherwise they might not unload any more equipment!".

By the second half, the crew's team have put away two goals, and a large crowd is gathering at the surrounding wrought-iron gates. The Wham! team scores two more, making it 8-2. Ten minutes from the end, George comes off for a drink. Chatting to him by the coats they are using as goalposts, I casually point out that there's someone behind him with a ball and it looks like they're just about to score. He just turns round and wellies it down the other end, drink still in hand, saving the goal (what a hero).

The whistle's just gone and 8-2 is the final score. The winning team line up for a photo, the film crew are dragg ed back to do a shot of 'cheerleaders' Shirlie and Pepsi with a bunch of terribly cute children. And then it's back to the hotel.

6pm: there's another banquet, this time thrown by the Chinese Culture Exchange Centre, Guangdong branch. It's here where George gets dragged up to help with the after-dinner entertainment, the magician. He has to tie her hands and she has to get out of it – sophisticated stuff, eh?

According to George, "the food was awful. I hadn't eaten all day

Neal Preston

George to Mini Mao: "Excuse me, we've lost our ball – could we borrow your binos?"

and I was starving hungry after the football match, and all we got was a cold buffet!"

Back at the hotel, George heads for the sauna – the football match has done his back in again. He gets filmed in there, apparently "pouring his heart out about being a superstar and things like that", according to producer Martyn Lewis. He also gets filmed while having a massage. A massage here, incidentally, means getting walked on by a Sumo wrestler. If *that* didn't do his back in, nothing will. And, according to Lewis, in this scene there was even "a hint of buttock". We shall see!

And then it's back to the bowling alley. George can't play, of course – the bad back again. Instead we sit and watch the others. Andrew, as usual, is doing his utmost to steal the show – this time he's wearing a proper bowling glove and "throwing a few shapes". That doesn't stop him forgetting to let go of the bowl and ending up flat on his back in the next alley. Tee hee.

"Good excuse, isn't it?" smiles George. "Having a bad back can come in handy. I think I'd be useless at bowling and I don't think I want to find out – well, at least not in front of this lot."

He goes on to talk about the first concert: "Just after the concert I must admit I was a little disappointed. In a sense I thought we'd failed because only the westerners were getting into it. But that was only after I discovered there had been that "dancing is disallowed" notice. I just take that announcement as an insult to Wham!. It's like the authorities were saying you could only *observe* Wham! and not take part, which was not the premise on which we came. That just wasn't *the point*.

"In a way, I think we've been exploited by the authorities here. Okay, we've exploited it for publicity but they've taken us for a lot of money as well. The result of all this, I think, will be that they won't let anyone play here again. After Wham! I think pop music in China will come to an end."

That said, we both try to think of who else could possibly get invited. "Culture Club, purely in terms of music and presentation, I suppose," he says, adding that Boy George's old transvestite image wouldn't have gone down a storm. "Frankie are too much of a threat. Spandau are too rock and roll." Queen and Duran Duran, he reckons, wouldn't be accepted because the British papers are always trying to cook up scandalous stories about them. "They want a group who, I suppose, have a clean reputation – wholesome – and that's kind of why they chose us."

So how did the Chinese react to the Wham! concerts? What were the reviews like?

"They were so funny. We wouldn't allow any local photographers in, so they decided to kind of stitch us up. They put things like 'Wham! failed because there weren't enough solos', and that our films contained 'Wham! propaganda'. It's all so stupid."

He's not exactly in love with Canton, either. "It's very close, humid. Apart from that I haven't experienced much of it yet."

Now we're getting to the crux of the problem. The humidity, it turns out, is making George's hair go funny. His normal bouncy blo-wave is being reduced to a damp, wavy mess by the condensation.

The boys' search for a replacement trumpet player was getting desperate…

As a result he's bunged a load of wet-look gel on it to make it look properly curly. Very Kevin Keegan. But the problem is that he doesn't want to be filmed close-up when he's in this state.

So he's hit on a plan: to take the film crew back to Shepperton Studios in Surrey to do all the Canton close-up shots. The cost is undisclosed but it could run into hundreds of thousands – all that for a hair-do. That tops the one about him wanting to re-shoot the "Careless Whisper" video because he'd just had his hair cut and liked the new style better. Pop stars, eh? What can you *do* with them?

DAY ★ 6

THURSDAY IS THE day of the concert. It's also the day when the underlying reason for the trip is revealed at a press conference. George and Andrew stay in bed and leave it up to the managers to tell the story. It seems that two

A different corner: it's a long way from Bushey to Peking's Forbidden City…

strange culture: "I think its much more westernised here in Canton than in Peking. I suppose that's due to them being so close to Hong Kong. It was amazing – I met this Chinese man today who spoke perfect English. He learnt it from a dictionary and from the radio. He claimed that people here are 'for the West'. In fact he said 99.9 per cent are ready for the change, almost looking forward to it. You'd never guess by looking around."

After the photos, Cheng goes onstage to introduce Wham!. "I am their devoted fan," she tells me. "Young people here will like them very much. Their music is very loud, though. I think China will go crazy for them."

Chatting to the audience, mainly little girls, it seems they all like Spandau Ballet, Culture Club and Duran Duran, "but Wham! are the best".

This time, when the lights go down there are screams, and *lots* of them. And people actually stand up! But again they are physically forced (very politely, of course) to sit back down, which they do, for now at least. As the concert goes on, all the hits – familiar to most – are reeled off. A mass of screaming, standing girls emerges in the middle of the hall. They cannot be forced to sit down. George sees this and really turns on the pressure, pulling out all the stops.

Slowly, more and more people stand and clap and cheer, even *dance*. By the end over 50 per cent are joining in. The concert is undoubtedly a resounding success. Manager Simon Napier-Bell leaves the hall with these words: "The last 30 minutes have been the greatest of my life."

A few encores later and they're off, leaving the audience still begging for more. Later, George seems just as satisfied.

"It was only just before the end I realised it was our last concert in China, the thing we've come all this way and gone to all this trouble over. I *had* to make it work if it was the last thing I did. Thankfully it turned out a success. Now I'm just looking forward to going home.

"I can't wait for a nice cup of tea – the milk here's terrible."

Wham! tapes will be released in China. One, on April 18, will feature the best of the "Fantastic" and "Make It Big" albums.

Then, on May 1, a second cassette will be released. On Side One there will be five Wham! songs by Wham!; Side Two will feature five Wham! songs by Cheng Fang Yuan, China's most popular female artist. She will sing all songs in Chinese. The tapes are being pressed in China on an initial run of 600,000. It's

all done in association with the Chinese Culture Exchange Centre and International Yamagen (a Hong Kong company), and is expected to sell at least two million (the amount Cheng Fang Yuan sells every time she releases a tape). In China, there are 400 million people aged 14 to 35. The potential market is staggering.

7pm: we all head for the concert hall, built over 100 years ago and entirely constructed of wood without the use of nails.

Here George and Andrew meet Cheng the Chinese singer (and get filmed and photographed with her). Andrew's dad, Albert, thinks she's "lovely". He's also dead pleased to be here. "I'm very proud of our son and I'm very pleased that he's been kind enough to invite us out here to see him perform. I consider it a real privilege."

George's Dad is equally pleased to be here and appears totally fascinated by China's

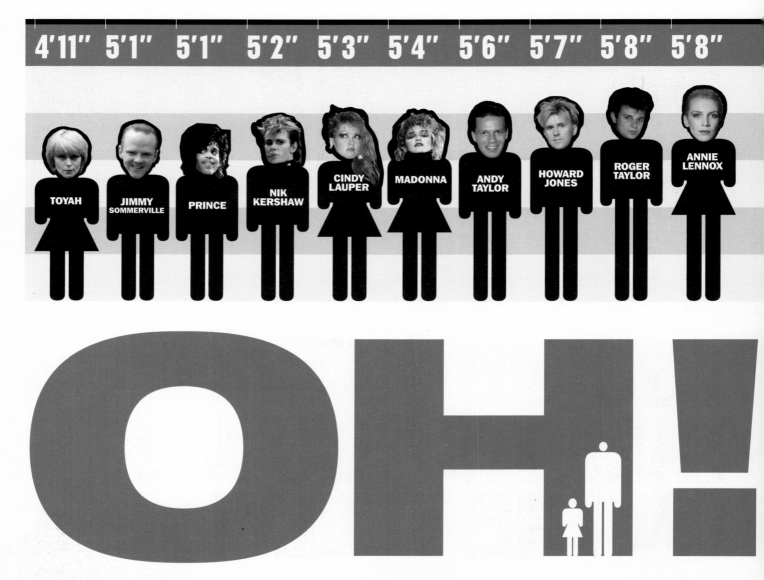

4'11"	5'1"	5'1"	5'2"	5'3"	5'4"	5'6"	5'7"	5'8"	5'8"
TOYAH	JIMMY SOMMERVILLE	PRINCE	NIK KERSHAW	CINDY LAUPER	MADONNA	ANDY TAYLOR	HOWARD JONES	ROGER TAYLOR	ANNIE LENNOX

OH!

Yes, once again, Smash Hits girlie swot productions bring you the truth about all your favourite pop stars. This time we probe into that uncharted netherworld – pop stars' heights. Discover the real length (or lack of it) of His Royal Purpledom Prince. Gasp in amazement at the enormity of Fish. Titter at the titchies. Chortle at the tallies. And see if you can work out which pop stars are fibbing…

ABOVE IS THE chart with the ever-ascending heights of 20 pop stars. But there are, not surprisingly, quite a few others clocking in at similar heights. Like there are loads of 5ft 10ins – big boy **Jim Kerr**, **Pete Burns** (6ft 1in in his stack heels), **Paul McCartney** and **Bruce Springsteen** (who'd actually be 5ft 11½in if he stood up straight and tucked in his derriere). **Shakin' Stevens** steps in at 5ft 10½in, while **Paul Rutherford** is a dashing 5ft 11in (the same as **George Michael** – must have something to do with all that bum wiggling they get up to onstage). **Paul King** is a mean 6ft in his patent leather shoes. **Mark O'Toole**

pops in at an impressive 6ft 2in. But that's nothing compared to **ABC**'s **Martin Fry**: he's one inch short of **Fish** – 6ft 3in. Phew, rock'n'roll!

On the other hand, his chum in **ABC**, **David Yarritu**, toddles in at a compact 5ft 0in. Rock chicklets **Kim Wilde** and **Alannah Currie** positively tower over him at 5ft 5in, while **Tina Turner** beats them by one inch. **Sade**, who actually does look a lot taller, is only 5ft 7in, as is **Alison Moyet**, who looks a lot smaller. Those chaps from **Tears For Fears** are like peas in a pod, both coming in at 5ft 9in, beating His Royal **David Bowieness** by one-half of an inch. Makes you think, dunnit?

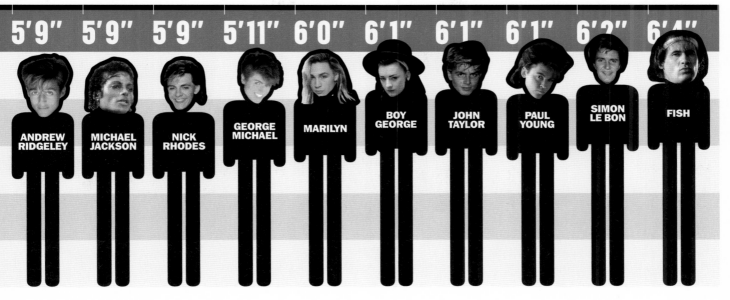

5'9"	5'9"	5'9"	5'11"	6'0"	6'1"	6'1"	6'1"	6'2"	6'4"
ANDREW RIDGELEY	MICHAEL JACKSON	NICK RHODES	GEORGE MICHAEL	MARILYN	BOY GEORGE	JOHN TAYLOR	PAUL YOUNG	SIMON LE BON	FISH

YOU'RE NOT AS TALL AS YOU ARE ON THE TELLY!

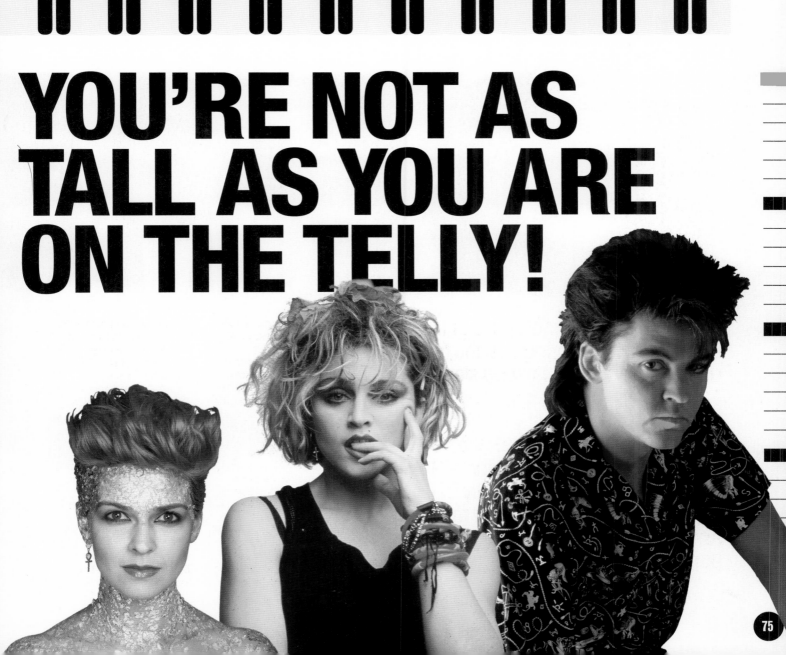

OUR FABULOUS FREE POSTERS!

Over the next 20 pages, celebrate a decade's worth of tip-top pop-rockin' '80s Smash Hits pin-ups, from Depeche Mode to – blee! – Joey Tempest and beyond. Please note, though: Blu-Tack is not provided.

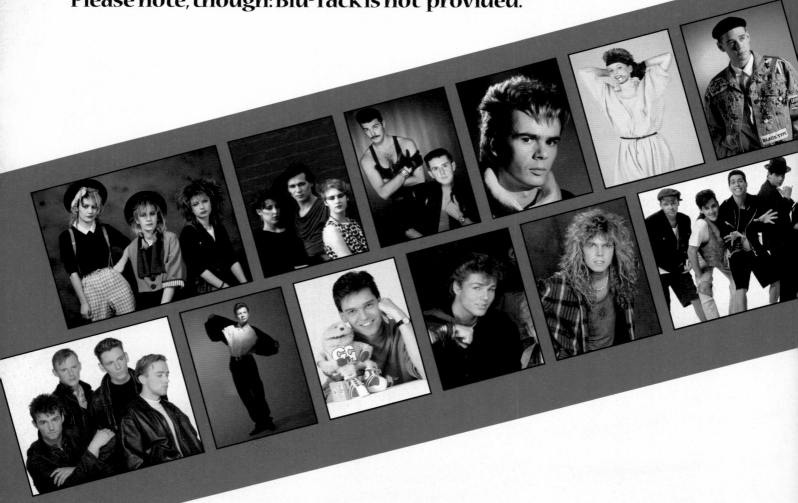

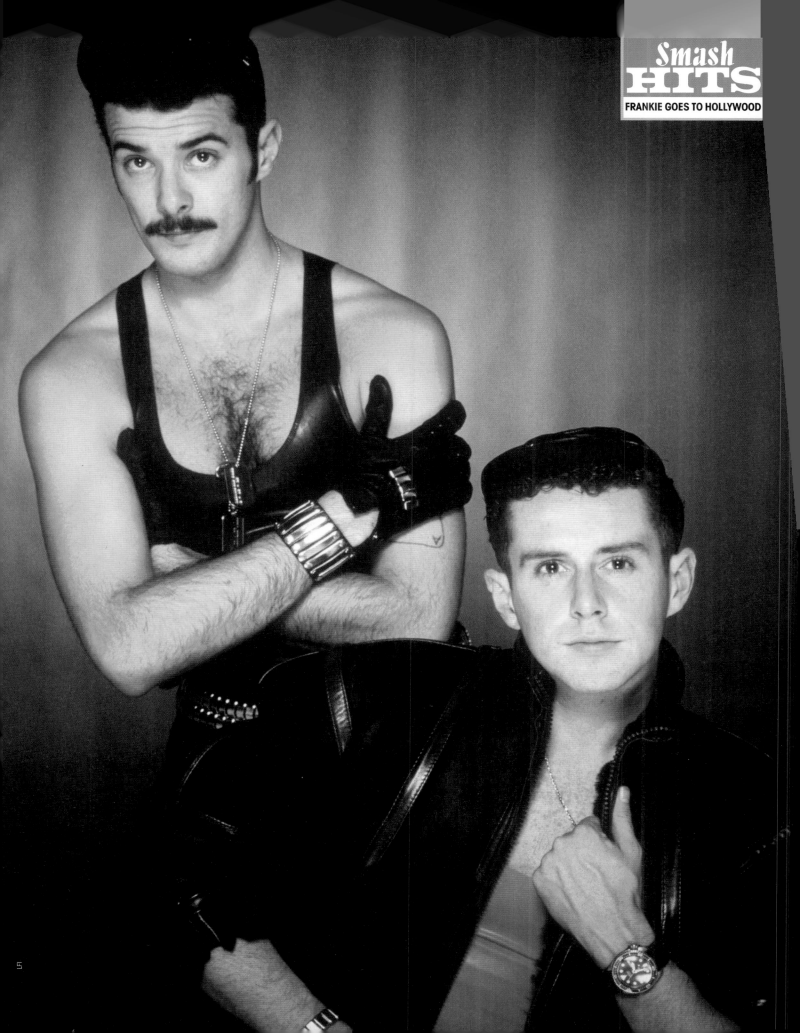

Smash HITS

JOEY TEMPEST FROM EUROPE

This Man Is perfectly

Robert Smith reckons there's *nothing* weird about The Cure taking a sheep on tour with them. He doesn't think it's odd that they once pretended to be domestic appliances either, but how about making a video with lots of socks in it? "It all just seems very normal to me," he tells Chris Heath.

Robert Smith: he had too much to dream last night.

normal

OH DEAR. IT'S nearly 2pm and Robert Smith is supposed to have been here *ages* ago. "He's always late – for *everything*," apologises the woman at his record company. Suddenly the door opens and in falls Robert, a naughty smile on his face. His hair is, as usual, all over the place and he's wearing a crumpled top, crumpled trousers and scruffy training shoes. "I don't have much time to be domestic," he explains in his slow murmur. "I just got up."

Just got up? Does he *usually* get up in the afternoon? "Depends on what time I get to bed. Last night it was half past four. I never go to bed before three. But sometimes I do get up by 12. Left to my own devices," he adds, "I wouldn't get up at all. At least not until it got dark again."

So what's the first thing he does when he emerges from under the covers at the crack of noon? "I wash my face with cold water," he mutters, "and then I go and sit down with a cup of coffee and try to remember what I was dreaming about. I used to write them all down – these days I usually discuss their more sordid aspects with Mary [*his girlfriend for the last ten years*]."

Hmmm. I don't suppose he can remember what he dreamt about last night, can he? "A sand-monster." Oh yes… of course. "He was very nice at first, he was working at the barbecue on the beach…" And then? "Then he had an axe because we were chopping wood and he was chasing people but in a sort of sandmonstery way." Bit scary, eh? "Oh I knew there was no risk."

Bit weird all this, isn't it? What about Mary? "She was an Olympic runner," explains Robert, trying to contain a snigger. "And she had pearl bracelets on, and as she was running, the pearl bracelets burst and the pearls embedded themselves behind her eyes. And then she was trying to pop them out and someone was helping her and said, 'That's it, they're all gone', but she could still feel them behind her eyes, even when she woke up. When I left her she was still convinced she had pearls embedded in the back of her eyes."

WHERE HE'S LEFT her is in his new London home – a basement flat decorated "white all over" containing nothing but basic furniture, a TV, a video and stereo, a figurehead someone made in a mental hospital and a black brass three-faced Buddha which he bought in Hong Kong. Outside, there's a communal garden "shared by about 600 people – it's like sitting on a football pitch". Which is why Robert's looking for somewhere else with his own garden – he misses the joys of cultivation he learnt to enjoy back in his original home in Crawley.

"I still try to get back there when I can – I've still got my own room and bed and toothbrush there. It's really somewhere to escape to – it's impossible for people to get hold of me if I don't answer the phone because they're not going to travel 35 miles, are they?"

And Robert is the sort of bloke who needs to get away from it all every now and again. Like last year when "I got ratty with everyone just because I was tired all the time". Mainly because he was not only keeping The Cure on the boil but also playing guitar in Siouxsie & The Banshees. He's better now, and not just because he lessened his workload by parting with the Banshees.

"I think I've come through my midlife crisis. It was the same time as anybody's – about growing up. The worst part was getting close to 25, because I'd always convinced myself I'd be dead by then, by somebody else's hand if not my own. It was a romantic idea but I had it for so long that it had become truth. I even had the date – February 1 last year. I used to have this recurring dream that I was falling through a window and I could feel all the glass going into me."

So what happened on that terrifying day?

"I don't remember. It was only when I got into bed that night when I thought, 'Bastards! It didn't come true.' I was quite disappointed in a way."

Still, he does grudgingly admit that he's had "quite a lot of fun since". As well as a few miserable moments such as his water-skiing holiday last year in the Lake District. "Was I good? No," he sulks. "It wasn't even good fun. When you hit the water at 40mph it's a pretty horrific experience. My nose was bleeding and my legs were gashed all down the side. But I thought, 'I'll do it until I can stay upright for a minute' – as soon as I could do that I stopped."

AFTER THIS HOLIDAY, Robert took The Cure on a world tour, though he has a bit of trouble recalling where ("Did we go to New Zealand? I think so.") Upon his return he did what he always does – "Got in the bath with a cup of Earl Grey tea and a piece of cheese on toast" – and then, after a bit of a rest, set about making some more music. The first result is the rather brilliant new single, "In Between Days" – "a very obvious boy/girl, go away-and-come-back song" that has got a rather strange video. "The basic video's really good," says Robert. "but now it's got socks in it. Tim Pope [*the director*] warned me he was going to put socks in it but I thought they'd be rather more… abstract-looking." He thinks for a moment, hand on chin. "There's no reference to socks in *any* song we've done ever."

"In Between Days" comes from their new LP, which has "a flamenco song, a Japanese Kyoto song and a disco song", and which is called "The Head On The Door". By now it won't be a surprise to learn that it comes from yet another dream.

"It was when I was little," he mumbles. "Before I was going to get ill with measles or chickenpox I always used to see this horrible grinning man who'd appear at the top of the bedroom door and laugh. It was like at both ends of the telescope at the same time – really near but when I tried to push it off it'd be really far away. The last time I had it was when I was 15 and ill with glandular fever. Until for some reason a couple of months ago I had a dream about it again and woke up sweating. I thought I was going to be really ill but I wasn't."

AS YOU'VE PROBABLY gathered, Robert Smith isn't a very normal run-of-the-mill pop star. He doesn't spend hours having a bevy with other pop stars ("Would I like to hang out with George Michael? I'd love to *hang* George Michael"), doesn't believe in mornings, used to take an adopted sheep on tour with him ("I left it behind in my hotel room once. When we went back they had it behind reception and were trying to feed it grass") and recently recorded an EP of Frank Sinatra songs, which he now refuses to release. But he is very friendly, nice and extremely funny. What strikes you, though, is that he doesn't really believe that other people think the things he does are weird. Like the time he told a magazine about the way he spends a lot of time at home play-acting little scenes out.

"I didn't think it was odd at all," he says, obviously a bit bemused. "Most of the people I know do things like that. Everyone's got really dark secrets. I just go a bit wayward sometimes. But," he sighs with puzzlement, "it all just seems very normal to me."

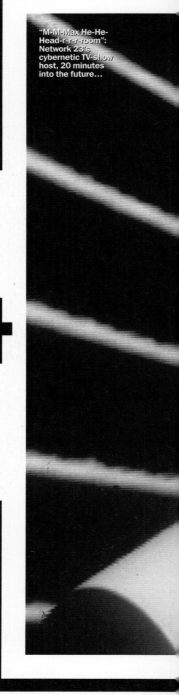

"M-M-Max He-He-Head-r-r-r-room": Network 23's cybernetic TV-show host, 20 minutes into the future…

THE WORLD ACCORDING TO MAX

He's suave! He's elusive! He's TV's most closely guarded secret! He's Max Headroom and he reveals his life philosophy (and his legs) over lunch with Maureen Rice…

MONEY

What are your feelings about money?
Money is irrelevant. You see, money is about *style*. In other words, it's not how much you have but what *you carry it around in* that's important. For example, let's take a man's leather wrist-bag. Now, that says a *lot* about a man. It says he's successful – he has enough money to afford leather. It says he cares about his appearance, and of course, it says that he's a complete nerd.

Are you rich?
Well, my producer says that some of the things I come up with on my show are pretty rich…

LOVE & ROMANCE

Everyone's curious about your love life. Are you going out with anyone at the moment?
This is a very sensitive subject for me because I've recently come to the end of a close personal relationship with a lovely girl called Anita. We never thought that being physical was an important part of our relationship – in fact, we never even met. But I loved her voice – she had a job as a speaking clock – and I knew she was always there when I needed her.

MUSIC

You play a wide selection of videos on your show, but what kind of music do you like?
Well, as you probably know I'm a great classical music fan. When I watch television I'm always most taken with those commercials that play a better class of music. Like the deodorant tune, for instance, or the advert for pure new wool. I always buy the products which have the best music in their commercials – my cupboards are full of aftershave and Hovis bread.

Is it difficult for a classical music buff like yourself hosting a pop video show?
It is a problem, it really is. But as you go through life, you'll find that we all have to do things sometimes that we don't really want to do. I'd rather listen to Mozart than any pop record. Have you seen his new video, *Amadeus*? It's gutsy, Maureen, really stunning. Of course, it's very long, so it won't get much airplay, but he's enough of an artist not to mind.

Have you ever felt any desire to make a record yourself?
Well, I think I can say in all honesty that I am a bit of a record already. In the very short time I've been in the business I have become so popular that I'm actually a record in my own right.

HEALTH & BEAUTY

Do you think the world has become too obsessed with health and beauty?
Well, I always say that if you're healthy, you usually feel beautiful. But if you're not beautiful, it doesn't mean you feel unhealthy.

What about your own health and beauty regime?
People are always saying to me, "Max – how do you do it, how do you stay in such good shape?" Well, it's simple. I'm like Jane Fonda in that I stick to one basic principle: you are what you read.

For instance, anyone who reads *Smash Hits* is unlikely to ever be overweight. Need I say more?

Do you work out?
Certainly. First thing every morning I work out exactly what I've got to do for the day.

Could you let us in on the secret of your flawless complexion?
Yoghurt, Maureen. A yoghurt face pack last thing at night works wonders. And watch what type of hamburgers you eat. A little yoghurt with that cheeseburger could make all the difference…

Rex

3 PEOPLE I'D MOST LIKE TO HAVE MY PICTURE TAKEN WITH

PAUL YOUNG, because he's tall and manly, and that's so rare these days. I hope he has lots of heirs – the pop world needs them.

NIK KERSHAW and **JON MOSS**, because it's stylish not to spell your name properly.

All of **DURAN DURAN**, because they're quite unique in that their eyes don't go red when they have their picture taken with a flash.

3 FAVOURITE HAIRCUTS

NICK FALDO
SEVE BALLESTEROS
BILLY GRAHAM (he styled himself on me, actually)

3 PEOPLE I'D LIKE TO PLAY GOLF WITH

BOY GEORGE, as I know he'd have the time.

MICHAEL HESELTINE, because he's got the same initials as me. But he'd have to get rid of that flak jacket or I might tee-off from his shoulders.

MARGARET THATCHER – we've *almost* got the same initials.

POLITICS

Are you a person with strong political views?
Yes, unlike most politicians. And I think that Wham! should run this country. They have a terrific sense of foreign policy, they're nice boys, and they already have more money than the Treasury.

SHOPPING

Do you enjoy shopping? What sort of things do you buy?
To be honest, I'm not the kind of man who likes to shop. I get asked to open so many shops that when I do get a few moments to relax I like to keep away from them. But I do need a hat at the moment and I think I'll go to *British Home Stores* or the *Army & Navy* for it. I like the styles there.

Are you interested in fashion?
Fashion is not a question of what you buy, but where you shop. Do you understand me? Now, those mail-order catalogues are the best place for keeping one step ahead. Unfortunately, I do tend to get side-tracked by the wonderful gardening sections…

Are you a keen gardener then?
Oh, certainly. I'd be even keener if I *had* a garden, but I've got my shed, and that's chock full of barbeque sets, sun shades and deck-chairs. Of course, for style that transcends mere fashion, you look to golf. I love the colours, the V-necks, the flared trousers… Golf *is* fashion to me…

TV PRESENTERS

What do you think of your rivals on television?
Well, we both know that there's a lot of jealousy in this business.

You see, in a short time – and I say this with the greatest humility – I have become mega-popular, and there are some people who don't like that one *bit*. But I'm good at what I do, and I think people are attracted by my modesty. Only the other day someone called me up to invite me to lunch at Number 10. I'd have gone too, but the fool put the phone down without telling me what road it was in!

Who are the five most wonderful people you know?
I wish I could say that I knew five people.

WHO IS POP'S MR CLEVER TROUSERS?

LFI, Redferns, Rex

YES, IT'S THAT time of year again – the time when young persons around the country sit in gloomy, silent rooms and try to remember who it was that wrote "I wandered lonely as a cloud" or to figure out just what they *mean* by Specific Gravity. Exams! Dontcha just love 'em? "Write on one side of the paper only." Huh! That's a laugh when you can't think of anything to write at all (mind you, the swot at the next desk is scribbling away like billy-o, which is just ruddy *typical*). Grrrr.

Never mind. You're in good company. Most celebrated popsters don't seem to have been much good at exams either – as this eye-opening table of O-level success and failure shows.

(But remember, readers – *adopting stern* Blue Peter-*type voice* – just because Shy Di, Gaz Numan and others have got along quite nicely despite being complete duffers in the classroom that doesn't mean you shouldn't try as hard as you possibly can. So here are some really super revision tips blah blah…)

10 O-LEVELS

GREEN
Subjects Just about everything.

HOWARD JONES
Subjects English Lang, English Lit, Maths, Applied Maths, Biology, Chemistry, French, Geography, Physics, Music. "They served me no purpose whatsoever."

9 O-LEVELS

PRINCE EDWARD
Subjects (apart from us) Maths, English Lang, English Lit, French, Additional Maths, Physics, Biology, History, Latin.

8 O-LEVELS

ADAM ANT
Subjects Art and "about" seven others.

NICK RHODES
Subjects Blurry Polaroids and seven others. "I left school when I was 16. I didn't think there was any point in doing A-levels. Sometimes it was fun and sometimes it was dreary – especially Physics."

PAUL KING
Subjects English Lang, English Lit, Art, Maths, Biology, French, German, Chemistry.

7 O-LEVELS

MARTIN FRY

Subjects Maths, English Lang, English Lit, Biology, Geography, Chemistry, Physics. "They shouldn't teach things like Religious Education. People should be taught to dye their hair."

JANICE LONG

Subjects Maths, English Lang, English Lit, French, Spanish, Art, Drama. "I hate exams – they come at a crazy time of year. I could never stand Chemistry and Physics. All I could do was write my name at the top."

ANNIE LENNOX

Subjects French, Art, Maths, History, Music, Biology, English Lang.

TOM BAILEY

Subjects Maths, English Lang, English Lit, French, Geography, Chemistry, Art, Economics.

6 O-LEVELS

PRINCE ANDREW

Subjects English Lang, English Lit, General Science, History, Maths, French.

PRINCESS ANNE

Subjects English Lang, English Lit, French, History, Geography, Biology.

5 O-LEVELS

GEORGE MICHAEL

Subjects French, English Lang, Music, English Lit, Art.

ANDREW RIDGELEY

Subjects English Lang, Art, Biology, Physics, Maths. "The academic side of things wasn't any use to me by the time I was 14, so I sort of gave up. I only went to college to escape going to work."

4 O-LEVELS

CURT SMITH

(Tears For Fears)
Subjects Maths, History, English Lang, Physics.

3 O-LEVELS

MERTON MICK

(The Style Council)
Subjects Geography, Art, English Lang.

GARY DAVIES

Subjects English Lang, Geography, French. "I hated them – I was lazy when it came to revising. I can work my guts out for something I believe in but I didn't see the point of exams."

2 O-LEVELS

SIR CLIFFORD RICHARD

Subjects English Lang, Religious Education (!)

1 O-LEVEL

ST. BOB GELDOF

(Irish O-level)
Subject English.

TOYAH

Subject Music.

DAVID SYLVIAN

Subject Art.

NICK HEYWARD

Subject Art.

BILLY OCEAN

Subject "I can't remember."

NO O-LEVELS

PRINCESS DIANA

BLACK LACE

(Nought between them.)

GARY NUMAN

PAUL WELLER

(But he *did* get 3 CSEs.)

HOLLY JOHNSON

ANDY TAYLOR

"Having no exam qualifications hasn't done me any harm."

101

SATURDAY 13 J

THE GRE
SHOW ON

ULY 1985

Live Aid at Wembley Stadium: 72,000 people watching 25 acts-over 10 hours as 1.5 billion viewers worldwide raise £150 million for famine relief.

ATEST EARTH

LIVE AID

LAST DECEMBER WHEN Bob Geldof and Midge Ure assembled a choir of extremely famous pop stars to record a song in aid of starving Ethiopians, no one quite realised what a big deal it would turn out to be. Band Aid's "Do They Know It's Christmas?" quickly became the biggest-selling British single of all time and generated a staggering £8 million towards relief of the famine. But that wasn't the end of it. A torrent of similar projects from other countries followed, and food and supplies bought with the profits started to get through to Ethiopia.

Through pop music, concern for the plight of the Ethiopians had been aroused worldwide, and with funds still urgently needed, Bob Geldof began to work on plans for a massive benefit concert on both sides of the Atlantic. With a mega-star cast and a global link-up, the project seemed like an impossible dream. But thanks to the efforts of all concerned, it came off – the biggest pop concert ever staged and the largest fund-raising event in history.

Condemning the apathy of politicians towards the human crisis of Ethiopia, Geldof remarked: "For six months I've been dialling 999 but the ambulance still hasn't arrived." With Live Aid, pop stars had done more than any government to alleviate the tragedy of the famine.

LIVE AID

12.00 Wembley erupts as their Royal Highnesses Chuck and Di shuffle into the royal box accompanied by Bob Geldof and triumphal trumpets. Within seconds, **Status Quo** will be kicking off the show.

FRANCIS ROSSI "I spoke to Bob Geldof three months ago and he was a very depressed – he couldn't get Wembley or the police to do it for free. Then it all snowballed, so we said, 'Let's go for it.' We had some hesitation at first about playing live again after we said we'd given up forever, but it's only two or three numbers. I said to Bob, 'I don't know about this,' but he said, 'It doesn't *matter* how good or bad you are.' I never used to like him at all – I thought he was a bit of a loudmouth – but now he seems really nice."

12.01 A raucous shout of "'Allo! Y'alright?" booms from the stage. 'Tis Francis Rossi. As Quo bounce into boogie favourite "Rockin' All Over The World", the atmosphere is, as they say, "electric"…

12.17 It's the turn of **The Style Council** next.

PAUL WELLER "I've got certain criticisms of Live Aid, but you can't criticise the fact that it will raise millions of pounds and save lives. *That* far outweighs any criticisms. There's no one backstage I particularly want to meet, but what I would like to do is set up a sort of musician's union where we could get a list of people involved in some of the political things we're interested in, and maybe meet once a month or something…"

12.18 Weller, in new sensible haircut, and "Merton" Mick in routine stripy blazer, take the stage and soften the mood with their snoozy jazz flutings – "You're The Best Thing", "Walls Come Tumbling Down", etc.

12.43 The Wembley masses welcome hero of the hour Bob Geldof as **The Boomtown Rats** launch into their enormous hit of yesteryear, "I Don't Like Mondays". "I've just realised today is the best day of my life," Bob announces and thousands of fists punch the air in salutation. A moment charged with emotion.

12.59 Adam Ant is about to make his first live British appearance in three years…

ADAM ANT "I saw the documentary at Christmas and I've never been moved that way before. It's a very human thing – it doesn't involve politics, logic, business or anything, it just involves seeing people in distress and raising money to invest in people's future in Ethiopia. It's a great gesture and it's nice that it's come from a business which is usually known as very spoilt. Am I scared about the huge audience? Well, it'll be the audience in the stadium that'll be the problem. Just being in the stadium when it was empty was bad enough!"

13.00 Adam steps out into the sunlight in biker's gear. "The world is watching. Let's feed it!" he exclaims… and straight into the blurry guitar sounds of "Vive Le Rock", his only number. Possibly the shortest set in rock history.

13.05 Prince Charles leaves for v. important official engagement (ie, a game of polo with ver lads).

13.06 Telly coverage whips across the globe to Australia for **INXS**'s rockin' contribution to Oz For Africa. Australia's TV compere Molly Meldrum is wearing a v. silly "jolly swagman"-style hat.

13.17 Inside Wembley Stadium, it's getting very hot indeed as that other Band Aid initiator, "Magnificent" Midge Ure, comes on with mirrored shades, a greatcoat and **Ultravox** to perform live for the first time in ten months.

13.33 A very sweaty Ultravox leave the stage.

MIDGE URE "I was really nervous at the beginning, but we got through it! I didn't have much to do with organising Live Aid because Bob's much better at doing it than me. He's taller, for one thing. He deserves all the credit for this. Bob's proved that complete tossers from Ireland and Scotland can put this together, so surely other tossers can do the same."

13.34 TV coverage goes live to Tokyo for some "scorching" heavy metal "licks" from **Loudness** and contributions from other top Japanese acts. Until the satellite conks out… Temporarily…

13.45 Gary Kemp is *bursting* to get out there…

GARY KEMP "It's not just the bands that should be thanked for their efforts, it's all the people who've donated their services for free and all the fans who have bought records, tickets and supported the cause."

13.46 "Ladies and gentlemen, will you welcome on stage **Spandau Ballet**…" This simple announcement draws the first excited screams of the day. With a jaunty "'Ello world!" from T Hadley, it's straight into a breezy rendition of "Only When You Leave". Steve Norman's wonky leg holds up nicely and – yes siree! – the Spands are in fine fettle. (And Gary Kemp's orange shirt is *completely unbuttoned!* Crikey!!) "You're looking

Status Quo kick off proceedings with their dependable brand of Brit boogie.

Sade brings a slice of cocktail cool to Wembley's sweltering masses.

presenters introduce *not* some Dutch pop phenomenon but footage of American blues guitar "legend" **BB King** at the North Sea Jazz Festival.

14.52 It is announced that 1.5 billion people around the world are watching Live Aid. (But how many of them have ever heard of Dennis Waterman or Rula Lenska, who are being interviewed on TV?)

14.54 Perfect music for a warm summer afternoon is provided by the day's first female entertainer, **Sade**. The "mellow" cocktail meanderings of "Why Can't We Live Together" help to cool down those who are simmering at the front – until a huge close-up shot of Sade's face, and enormous earrings, appears on the giant TV screens, at which the crowd goes bonkers. Stewards rush to the rescue of a young man who has passed out, overcome, apparently, by Sade's breathtaking beauty…

15.08 Live by satellite to Yugoslavia for *their* band aid song, "For A Million Years" by **Yu Rock Mission** (lots of popsters holding tots in their arms, etc).

15.17 Noel Edmonds bounds on stage to "rap" to the audience and to introduce… "Ladies and gentlemen… Mr Phil Collins… and… first of all… Sting!" Enter **Sting** in clean white shirt and baggy trousers. "Phil'll be joining us in a minute," he says. Then he performs a "laid-back" version of the old Police hit "Roxanne".

15.26 "*Now* Phil Collins," says Sting. And there he is – **Sir Philip Collins**, at the pianoforte playing "Against All Odds".

15.30 Sting does a solo version of "Message In A Bottle"…

15.35 Phil performs v. touching pop ballad "In The Air Tonight"…

15.40 Phil and **Sting** team up to do "Long Way To Go" and "Every Breath You Take"…

15.47 Phil Collins leaves to catch a plane. (Apparently, he has a pressing engagement in Philadelphia…)

15.48 Sporting a highly "sensible" sports jacket, **Howard Jones** awaits his turn to face an *enormous* public…

HOWARD JONES "The most exciting thing is that there will be so many people watching, all involved in a completely unselfish pursuit. If that many people can get together and direct their thoughts towards people who are starving and much less fortunate than themselves, then I think that's bound to be a good thing."

15.49 "Ladies and gentlemen, the beat goes on. Will you welcome **Howard Jones**…" "Hello," says Howard, "I'm just going to do a little song at the piano." And he does…

15.54 Live by satellite to Moscow – an historic moment – where a presenter with an impeccable US accent welcomes us to the Soviet

---

beautiful," Tony tells the crowd. "Every one of you." Swoon…

14.05 Spandau Ballet retire to the backstage area for a few glasses of rock'n'roll mouthwash.

GARY KEMP "It went very quickly. The greatest moment of my life and it just flashed by! I can't believe they're just wheeling the bands on and off. Normally you come off stage and loads of people are giving you towels and drinks and things. I fell off the stage and nobody gave a toss!"

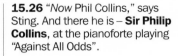

14.07 A bearded **Elvis Costello** arrives on stage. Accompanied only by his electric guitar, the "committed" troubadour treats the masses to a surprise solo treatment of The Beatles' "All You Need Is Love". The masses sing along with gusto.

14.11 TV goes live by satellite to Vienna for **Austria For Afrika**'s band aid effort "Why", quite a rousing workout from Austria's

top pop attractions (**Opus** and, erm, a lot of other singing folk…)

14.21 Backstage, **Nik Kershaw** is sweating quite a lot. Is it the heat? Is it blind panic? Well, a bit of both actually, but it's worth it for such a good cause.

NIK KERSHAW "The music business is too often associated with things trivial, negative and destructive, so I feel pleased to be able to play even a small part in an event which proves otherwise."

14.22 Now Nik's up there doing "Wide Boy" in cool and confident fashion. At the back of the stadium, many spectators are taking a siesta in the sun.

NIK KERSHAW "I didn't enjoy it really. It was a bit fraught – a lot more than supporting Elton John last year. Is there anyone I'd like to meet backstage? Yeah, Sheri, my wife…"

14.40 Live by satellite to Holland, where three exotically clad TV

Sir Philip: in the air tonight…

A big hand for serial collaborator Mr Sting.

Rex

LIVE AID

Union and introduces "Top of the pops... **Autograph**!" Autograph perform a jaunty Eurovision-type number followed by a "progressive" rock "workout". No threat to Wham! (or anyone else) seems to be the general reaction of the Wembley spectators.

16.07 Bryan Ferry trots on to the boards, looking as spruce and dapper as ever, and proceeds to wake up a dozing Wembley with his newly formed backing band (which appears to consist of about seven million musicians). A welcome breeze has arrived to take the edge off the mid-afternoon heat and people are actually *dancing* again...

16.26 Live to Cologne for the German band aid song, "Naked In The Wind". Before the singing starts, however, German rock person **Udo Lindberg** delivers a long and "heavy" speech – condemning the "sick powers" in Washington and the Kremlin – which is treated with hoots and cheers in equal numbers...

16.35 A live report from Ethiopia reminds the millions just what all the pop festivities are about...

16.39 Things get "swinging" back at Wembley once again as **Paul Young** scampers into view. After an a cappella verse of "Do They Know It's Christmas?" comes a lusty "Come Back And Stay" featuring much jigging about from Young and his musicians.

16.48 Paul Young bids welcome to a "very special lady... **Alison Moyet**". Alf and Paul duet on the old soul classic "That's The Way Love Is"; the audience warms to this corking and unlikely-looking vocal team.

16.57 During "Every Time You Go Away", stewards rush to the assistance of a young woman who has passed out, overcome, it seems, by P Young's breath-taking beauty...

17.00 "Wembley! Will you please welcome America to Live Aid!" – Geldof is at the Wembley mike while over in Philadelphia **Bryan Adams** prepares to get the US leg under way...

BRYAN ADAMS "I guess this just about says it all: 'We can bridge the distance / Only we can make the difference / Don't you know that / Tears are not enough?'" [*From the Canadian Band Aid record, "Tears Are Not Enough"*].

17.01 "Everywhere I go the kids just wanna rock..." squawks Bryan Adams above squealing guitars. Sweating it out in the JFK Stadium, thousands of "kids" prove him right by going slightly bananas...

17.08 Bryan takes a breather from "rockin' out" to sing "Tears Are Not Enough", the Canadian band aid song (which he helped to write...) and to declare, "I think Bob Geldof is a saint!"

17.19 V. famous actor Jack Nicholson comes onstage in Philadelphia to introduce **U2** in London. Backstage at JFK, Bryan Adams is shaking his head and gasping, "God, what a great day!" as if he can't quite believe it all...

17.21 "Sunday Bloody Sunday" shouts Bono at the Wembley

Mark Knopfler: he's with the 'band.

terraces, and hundreds of waving flags and banners come out to greet U2. "We're an Irish band," says Bono (as if anyone still didn't know by now) and draws the biggest roar of approval of the day so far. The "shimmering shards, sepulchral majesty and gentler pockets of sound" of U2 help to revive any flagging spirits.

17.33 Bono leaps off the stage, and takes a girl at the front of the pack in a tender embrace. He *would* wander further but yellow-shirted security men dissuade him...

17.38 U2 take their leave after the most "uplifting" performance of the day.

17.40 Rapidly ageing pop veterans **The Beach Boys** are dishing out some more of their perennial summery harmonies. "I wish they all could be California

girls" they warble and 90,000 people inside JFK join in (well, *some* do...)

17.56 The Beach Boys depart from the stage. Singer Mike Love, in a sweat-soaked, gaily-patterned shirt, hoots: "Goooooooood vibray-shuns whoo!" at nobody in particular...

18.00 At Wembley, **Dire Straits** come out waving and are immediately joined by... **Sting**! Yes, *he's* back again, singing "I want my MTV". Was he invited, one wonders? Evidently so, because he's soon "boogieing down" in no uncertain fashion with Straits' Mark Knopfler (who is sporting the day's very first headband). Despite Sting's distracting presence, ver Straits "deliver" their usual "tight set" and prompt fresh outbreaks of inter-audience frugging.

18.25 In JFK Stadium, it *should* be **Tears For Fears**. But they've

Really up for it: barricade-storm[...] performance fr[...] U2's Bono.

Rex

MUTTERINGS

pulled out for some reason or another (see *Mutterings*, right), and **George Thorogood And The Destroyers**, dodgy "cult" rhythm and blues combo, are given a chance to trade some meaty riffs with the entire world…

18.39 Back at Wembley it's time for a bit of "zany" humour from "funnymen" Griff Rhys Jones and Mel Smith, who come out dressed as British bobbies. After a couple of not v. popular "gags", they announce "Her Majesty… **Queen**" – and on to stage centre prances Freddie Mercury in skimpy white vest and tight jeans. The roar from the crowd is *huge*, reaching an alarming crescendo as Freddie starts to tickle the ivories and sing the opening lines to that hoary old chestnut "Bohemian Rhapsody"… The "epic" song never gets finished, though, for after a few bars, Freddie leaps up from the piano stool and – while Rog, Bri and John steam into "Radio GaGa" – the moustachioed, strutting popinjay of rock stalks the forestage enticing the masses to sing "Day-Oh", to clap their hands, to play invisible guitar along with Bri's squiggly solos, etc. Just about *everybody* seems to be wigging out to Queen. Who'd have thought it?

19.02 It's absolutely *sweltering* inside JFK where rather a lot of people wearing not very much are staring up at the giant TVs. Why? Because any moment now they're going to be shown an "historic" sight – **M Jagger** and **D Bowie** a-groovin' together on the hilarious and totally brilliant "vid" they've made specially for the occasion. "Dancing In The Street" – it's a classic!

19.07 The old fogeys' sizzling video finishes. And then… **Simple Minds**. Jim Kerr's voice rings out loud and clear through the Philly air and, long before the group get to the familiar US favourite "Don't You (Forget About Me)", he has the people in the palm of his hand.

19.20 You've just seen the video – and you're about to see the real

Chuck and **Di** impressed everyone no end. First Chuck met **Bob Geldof** and promised that his charity trust will, in the future, give the Band Aid trust "every help in its endeavours", by helping with the supply of trucks, loading equipment and labour, etc. Then the pair passed on a note to **Mark** "very stupid headband" **Knopfler** saying how much they enjoyed the **Dire Straits** concert thing earlier that week. Di, humorously, of course, wrote that she was v. annoyed at them for being so good that she had to "make a fool of herself by getting up and dancing". How sweet.

Well, there it is. All 16 hours of it. But apart from the comings and goings onstage and on telly, there was a load of stuff that went on relatively unnoticed. And guess who got the job of sorting it all out? Yep, Mutterings. So here goes… **Tears For Fears**: where were they? Seems they were billed as appearing before they agreed to do it. "Emotional blackmail" was how they saw it, apparently. So they didn't do it. **Bono** referred to this before the big day: "Bob Geldof used moral blackmail to get a lot of groups to appear but I approve of that. The end justifies the means. But TFF came through with this compromise: they've pledged all profits from their future concerts. Well done. ● **Julian Lennon**… what happened to *him*? He was billed to appear with **Sting** and **Phil Collins**, but it just didn't happen. Rumours hint at the reason being his deep fear of a possible Beatles get-together with him on guitar. ● **Prince**? Well, he said from the start that he wouldn't turn up, promising instead a video contribution. This gem turned out to be a stupid little black and white film of him saying "Feed The World" while lying on a bed stark naked! By an act of supremely wise judgement the clip was not used. Just think, one billion people feeling not very well all at the same time. Yukky. ● **Culture Club** – whatever happened to them (Part 3). It seems they were asked to appear but their management forgot to give the OK by the agreed date, so they weren't allocated their 20 minutes. Instead, they promised to fly in to do the last bit. And did they? No, they ruddy well did not. ● Did you see **Michael** "pardon the voice" **Des Barres**? *Honestly!* Can we use the expression "bit of a state"? ● Man Of The Match award goes to the mighty **Bono**. Not only did he fall off the stage, drag the cameramen all over the place and have a tongue sarnie with a member of the audience, he managed to get the loudest cheer during the big finale. Worra man. ● **Duran Duran**. Pur*lease*! Andy Taylor – get that hair cut! And **Simon Le Bon** – he got a bit carried away, didn't he? We know it was a v. big deal and all that, but did he really need to go all waily and pained-looking like that? ● Poor Unfortunate Person award goes equally to **Paul** "Fab **Macca**" McCartney and **Bob Geldof**. Both their mikes went off for an embarrassingly long period. ● Big Div award goes to Mr Sincere himself, **Noel Edmonds**. He made a real meal of doing his onstage introduction bit. ● Fifty thousand v. brill Live Aid programmes went like hot cakes, selling out in minutes. ● All the way through the Wembley concert the huge video screens flanking the stage kept showing ruddy awful adverts. Lots of money was probably raised from them, but it still looked a bit daft having horrible Marlboro cig ads in between an event geared towards saving people's lives. ● The concert cost £3.3m to put on, but they still managed to raise around £40m clear profit through tickets, merchandise and telethons, etc. ABC TV in America gave £5m just for the exclusive TV rights backstage at Wembley.

Initially announced as **Elton John** and **Wham!**, it turned out that the pair simply joined Elt for a moving rendition of "Don't Let The Sun Go Down On Me". It was also planned that George and Elt would "air" their new "fab waxing", but they didn't have time. It was also planned that Andrew would go onstage to announce His Royal Holiness D Bowie, but that didn't happen either. But then life's a bit like that, really.

LIVE AID

thing. **Bowie** is about to grace Wembley with his presence...

DAVID BOWIE "I wish I could say that this year's money-raising efforts have brought to an end the starvation and death inflicted upon the African continent, but many more millions of pounds over many more years are needed to get anywhere near alleviating their misery."

19.22 "David Bowie!" and there he is, gyrating in his nattily cut blue suit and singing with aplomb – just him, a piping-hot, unswanky backing crew and a selection of popular "gems" from the archives – "TVC 15", "Rebel Rebel", "Heroes". It's getting cooler but after *this* those crushed at the front could well do with another hosing down...

19.40 Bowie leaves the stage in triumph, then returns to say *"You're* the real heroes at this concert!" Hurrah! Then follows a specially made video which shows harrowing film footage from the famine area (accompanied by music from **The Cars**).

19.45 In Philadelphia, Jim Kerr has been replaced on stage by his wife, **Chrissie Hynde**, and **The Pretenders**, whose perky power pop is accompanied by some welcome puffs of wind at last. Assorted frisbees wing across the auditorium as Chrissie jigs about in calf-length boots – *très* chic.

19.59 Jack Nicholson announces that, as soon as they can find some hoses, the roasting Philadelphians will be treated to cooling showers...

20.00 In Britain, the re-formed **Who** have presented themselves on stage. They look a bit, erm, doddery as they crunch into the age-old anthem "My Generation". After a couple of bars, the TV satellite conks out again – as if in sympathy – but the old-timers soldier on regardless: singer Roger Daltrey unbuttons his shirt and Pete Townshend does the splits in the air.

20.22 Over in Philadelphia there are further archive sounds from ancient Latino-rock "outfit" **Santana**. Many members of the US audience have decided that this is as good a time as any to take *their* siesta... (Backstage, Mr and Mrs Kerr are having a bit of a kiss...)

20.33 Pat Metheny joins **Santana** for some sleepy-headed guitar jamming...

20.40 Live by satellite to see the video of Norway's band aid song, "All Of Us" (featuring a man standing in the sea playing a guitar and squillions of children).

20.50 "Jokester" **Billy Connolly** is talking to Wembley: "I'd like to introduce a friend of mine from planet Windsor... **Elton John**..." Wearing a silly hat with a feather in it, and a gaudy smoking jacket, Elton takes his place at the piano for "I'm Still Standing", "Bennie And The Jets" and others from his bottomless repertoire. By now vast sections of the audience are flagging – but *still* they manage to give Elt and his hardy old backing stalwarts a friendly reception...

21.05 Chanteuse **Kiki Dee** steps out to join Elton in a re-enactment of their 1976 duet "Don't Go Breaking My Heart".

21.09 And *now* joining Sir Eltonford on stage is a man with a beard, a leather jacket and faded jeans. *Most* unsavoury! But wait! Is it? Can it be? It *is*. It's **George**

Who's next? It's only Roger Daltrey...

Michael (with friend **Andy** in tow) and, taking the microphone, he performs a "soulful" and really quite moving reading of Elton's ballad "Don't Let The Sun Go Down On Me". Flashbulbs pop in the darkness as George proves, once more, that he's a wizard little singer (Andy and Kiki's backing vocals are rather more wobbly...)

GEORGE MICHAEL "When we did the Band Aid record last year I don't think any of us quite realised what a big deal it was. But now, with this concert... I mean, one billion people will be watching it – that's like every single person in the world with a television. It's the first thing for ages I've been nervous about, but I just hope we can help raise lots more money."

21.29 The Philadelphian throng shrieks, squeals and gets rather excited as – gasp! – **Madonna** appears on stage, doing some "delightful" disco twirling and skipping with a couple of dancing playmates. "Are you ready to get in the groove" she enquires. "Oh, alright, then!" roars Philadelphia. "I thought so!" says the saucy entertainer and rattles her tambourine. She does some quite frisky singing, too...

21.42 Mr Bailey and his **Thompson Twins** join Madonna for a performance of "Love Makes The World Go Round"

21.48 Oh no! Crowd-teaser **Freddie Mercury** is back on stage. Accompanied by **Brian May** on a Spanish guitar, the "preposterous" Freddie croons a lilting ballad (which, thanks to malfunctioning microphones, goes horribly wrong...)

21.51 Piano notes chime from a darkened Wembley stage. The lights come up on His Most Royal Wonderfulness **Paul McCartney**, who is singing the old Beatles ballad "Let It Be" – or trying to. The microphones are *still* playing up – and so the crowd spring to the rescue, taking over the singing en masse...

21.54 Fab Macca's still playing "Let It Be" when a tremendous roar erupts to greet a quartet of

Heroes: Bowie et al onstage the grand finale at Wembley.

Rex

backing vocalists that's just wandered into the spotlight – **Bob Geldof**, **David Bowie**, **Alison Moyet** and **Pete Townshend** of The Who…

21.56 The entire British Live Aid cast is on stage for the finale – "It might be a bit of a cock-up. But if you're going to cock-up it's best to do it with two billion people watching!" says Geldof. "Do They Know It's Christmas?" has Wembley swaying and singing in rapture… There's not a dry eye in the house as the "best day" of Geldof's life comes to a joyous, triumphal conclusion… Back-stage, a few minutes later, he's still gushing about how "terrific" it's all been. So what's he going to do now? "I'm going to bed." Meanwhile in Philadelphia…

 22.14 A memorable day at Wembley is over – but not in Philadelphia. **Tom Petty** and **The Cars** pump out orthodox rock tunes; legendary folk-rock supremo **Neil Young** wins the hippie vote by whining a lot and puffing down a broken mouth organ…

23.42 The Power Station bash on to stage. New singer Michael Des Barres sports fetching white bootees. Andy Taylor's locks are more straggly than ever. John T's pouting is formidable. There's horrid "axe" solos, feverish onstage struttings and boundless determination. But, by and large, the Philadelphia thousands remain unimpressed…

00.20 They're back! They're proud! They're fizzing! **The Thompson Twins**! And who's that on squeaky backing vocals? Step forward **Madonna**! And who's that on squawling lead guitar? Step forward **Stevie Stevens** (*Who? – Ed.*) (Oh sorry, he's the "axeman" for no less a personage than Sir William Idol!).

 01.01 Backstage at Philly, **REO Speed-wagon**'s drummer appears to be engaged in "friendly" conversation with *Madonna*! What can it all mean?

01.02 Does this man *never* tire? **Phil Collins** is on stage *again*! He's tinkling the ivories. He's singing "Against All Odds" and "In The Air Tonight". He's recalling memories of Wembley, 13 July, 1985 (about eight-and-a-half hours ago, to be precise…)

01.11 P Collins dons yet *another* Live Aid hat and acts as compere, introducing **Jimmy Page**, **Robert Plant** and **Paul Martinez** – ie, the (sort of) re-formed Led Zeppelin (boring old band). And guess who's playing drums in this hard-lovin' combo. Is it Sir Philipford Collins? It certainly is! It's turning out to be a strange night on rock's missing highway…

01.23 The Page/Plant band thingy perform the Led Zeppelin (or "Led Zep" to give them their full title) "anthem", "Stairway To Heaven", which is one of the most "symbolic" and "classic"

rock songs of *all time*. Well, according to spectators Ray and Signe (who've travelled all the way from Chicago to see their fave singer and guitarist) it is…

01.44 And here come… **Duran Duran**. Bursting into "A View To A Kill", Simon slides around the stage as if practising for his forthcoming tempest-tossed yachting adventure, while Andy flicks his shaggy mane about as though auditioning for The Power Station. John T's pouting is *formidable*. Somehow, Nick and Kevin – oops – Roger manage to hold it all together – but still it's a pretty reluctant and unconvincing showing. Philly stagehands rush to the assistance of a young lady who has passed out, overcome, no doubt, by the staggering beauty of N Rhodes.

 02.08 Back in London, a young acoustic-guitar-strumming singer makes an impromptu appear-ance on the BBC's broadcast and upstages Duran Duran (and just about everyone else for that matter). His name, of course, is **Sir Clifford "Cliff" Richard**…

02.48 The incredibly famous **Daryl Hall** and **John Oates** are rockin' Philly – Hall's hairstyle, cunningly modelled on that of *Dynasty*'s Krystle, proves particularly popular. After 15 hours of non-stop music, rock no longer holds any mysteries for your team of *Smash Hits* reporters and the secret of Hall and Oates' success becomes crystal clear: they are quite good.

 03.06 Clodagh Rodgers wins the Eurovision Song Contest at the second attempt with "Jack In The Box". Oh… no. Sorry. Forget that bit.

03.12 A wildly gyrating **Mick Jagger** has appeared to entrance anyone who's still paying attention (the viewing figures still run into the hundreds of millions, actually). **Hall**, **Oates** and

the Hall & Oates band provide the backing as Sir Michaelford preens, struts and postures through "Just Another Night" in vintage fashion. Yes, like many of the celebrated codgers who have take part in this marathon, Jagger seems remarkably chipper…

03.28 Mick whips a towel over his left shoulder and bawls: "Awright! Where's Tina?" Why, *there* she is: **Tina Turner**, tucked into a slinky and not very sizeable leather dress. Mick and Tina duet with energy and much "suggestiveness"… Mick reveals his torso *in its entirety*… And – gosh! – what long legs Tina has! (particularly when the bottom part of her dress "accidentally" falls off)… Phewee!…

03.40 Jack Nicholson intro-duces "one of America's greatest voices of freedom". And there, for the world to see, is **Bob Dylan**, flanked by Rolling Stones persons **Keith Richard** and **Ron Wood**, both of whom have acoustic guitars and cigarettes drooping from their mouths. Average age of this untoward trio: rather a lot. But who cares? They may be making a terrible jumbly racket but these unkempt banjoliers are also making a history as the penultimate act at the biggest pop concert ever staged…

03.55 Lionel Richie is singing the opening lines to "We Are The World" and he's joined on the grand finale by a huge cast – just about everybody who's already performed along with extra guests like Sheena Easton, Harry Belafonte and Cher. There are children on stage; there's rejoicing in the audience; there are thousands of lumps in throats. But, far, far more important than any of this, people around the world have responded to Live Aid by donating money – at least £40 million has been raised, probably a lot more – to alleviate at least *some* of Ethiopia's misery…

The Smash Hits Live Aid Special was put together by: David Bostock, Steve Bush, Chalkie Davies, Chris Heath, Tom Hibbert, Vici MacDonald, Peter Martin, Steve Rapport and William Shaw.

Messrs Townshend and McCartney chariot a tired but triumphant Bob.

A FRIENDSHIP MADE IN HEAVEN

Lion-maned dance-goth Scouser Pete Burns and bequiffed Mancunian pop-poet Morrissey make the oddest of best buddies, as Ian Cranna discovers.

"IT'S A BIG step for us, doing this piece together," says a bouncy, good-humoured Pete Burns. "We *could* have done it for *The Sun*. Can you imagine what *they* would have made of it?" Indeed – this seemingly unlikely friendship between two of pop's most "awkward" and "news-worthy" stars is a scoop the tabloids would undoubtedly go *bonkers* for. Morrissey and Pete Burns – bosom chums!? Who'd have thought it?

We're in Pete and Lynne Burns' new flat. Unlike their previous home, with its ferns, mirror tiles and clutter of kitsch *objets d'art*, this is v. smart and modern (almost hi-tech) with lots of gold discs and framed magazine

covers on the walls. The only animal skins *here* belong to the two (live) cats snoozing on the cushions.

Pete and Lynne are fussing around Morrissey like a pair of mother hens. "Toasted sand-wiches?" enquires Lynne solicitously. "What would you like to eat?"

"Cheese?" suggests Pete, arching an eyebrow. "Cat food?"

Eventually the odd couple are seated side by side on the slim red sofa, Morrissey with his Marks & Spencer Apricot and Guava Thick & Creamy Yoghurt – yum! – and Pete Burns knee-deep in packets of biscuits.

"I know people who think, 'My God! What can Pete see in

Morrissey?" says Pete. "Yes," says Morrissey, "and *I* know people who think, 'What can Pete see in Morrissey?'" The pair dissolve in laughter. Quite clearly they adore each other – but why?

Morrissey Before I met Peter I had a very strange impression of him – I just went by stray gossip and mythology, and so I thought he was a half-crazed oddball. But deep down inside, as time began to pass, I began to really concentrate on this specimen and I thought, "Oh no, it can't be true. I refuse to believe in all the curious things I've heard." And I really wanted to meet him because I saw a video which was wonderful.

Paul Cox

Pete Which one?

Morrissey Um, the weird one with the women bodybuilders…

Pete That was *crap*…

Morrissey …and then we met and it was really odd because all these preconceptions I'd had about Pete were completely untrue. I approached him at *Top Of The Pops*…

Pete In the toilet…

Morrissey And I thought it would either be a black eye or it would be heavenly harmony…

Pete He came up and spoke to me, which was a brave thing to do, so I decided to be polite to him and from then on we struck up a friendship that's been enduring. Before I met him, I thought he was a malicious little prat sometimes the things he

says about other musicians are *so* strong. Morrissey has no mercy, you see, and that is where we differ… I'm a lot more charitable than other people would expect but he's not, you see. I'd be very careful what I said about other people's records because I don't think it's fair…

Morrissey Oh, *I* do. It's only because I really care about popular music that I feel this Samaritanesque duty to go out and nail those that need to be nailed.

Pete I heard him on *Roundtable* and wrote him a letter saying he should hire three bodyguards and a tank – he's *really* the one with the nasty tongue.

Morrissey I think it's sad that Pete does so *few* interviews; as

a symbolist he is quite a critical figure, and he's *certainly* one of the most threatening, and I think people need to hear his spoken voice as well as is singing voice. I think it's a shame that now he's come to massive prominence, he's locked himself away in a broom cupboard.

Pete But I have no wish to be acknowledged for anything I *say*. Before we started to become successful nobody paid me any attention – I could have shot the *Pope* and I still wouldn't have got on the cover of a magazine. But then *everybody* wanted to talk to me and it went mental – "the return of the gender bender" and all that crap. People set me up as something that I'm not. It's like with Morrissey – he can inspire

hatred. He makes the most outrageous statements and everyone prints them and he *stands by them*. Everybody wants him to say he's a clapped-out old drag queen, but he isn't and so he won't say it.

Morrissey Pete is seen as a sour character and a bit of a trouble-maker, but that just isn't the case. He has an endless array of humour that has been gagged by the press.

Pete Yeah, I'm really *not* such a bitter old sourpuss. But when I'm under pressure and working, my sense of humour isn't always there. When people try to pour custard on me… We did a TV show where they wanted to walk on halfway through the song and give me jam sandwiches, and I

Moz and Pete: reeling around the fountain and spinning like a record, baby…

won't *have* things like that. Morrissey can cut himself off a lot better than I can; he doesn't have second thoughts about knocking the phone off the hook and not going out through the door for five days. I'm too nosey – I want to know what everyone's saying. Old Mozza here is dead good at doing runners and dismissing the business for a week or so, don't you think?

Morrissey Yes. Yes. It's just a safety net, really; I have to seal up the door and roll down the windows and hide.

Pete But despite these differences, I feel a very strong affinity with him – almost a brotherly thing. We've got a lot in common. We're both outsiders of the music business: we don't blend in on

the showbiz party circuit; we don't stage huge publicity stunts; we don't throw Page 3 girls over our backs and get photographed at the Hippodrome…

Morrissey Peter is so detached from the pantomime element of the whole industry and the whole party ethic, and so are The Smiths. The only people we know in the industry are Dead Or Alive…

Pete And I'm a Smiths fan, embarrassingly enough – I'm not supposed to admit that but it's always exciting when they're on *Top Of The Pops*…

Morrissey It's only exciting because we're the group that shouldn't *be* there…

Pete I followed them on a whole tour. I was like a crazed groupie. Morrissey would be in some clapped-out hotel somewhere and I'd show up – because I could *always* find him. Do you want anything to eat or drink?

Morrissey No, I'll have something quite soon.

Pete Why's that? Are you feeling queasy?

Morrissey No… can I open these Coffee Creams?

Pete Of *course* you can… I'm still getting to know Morrissey, really, but it's great having a friend like that, because in this business you sometimes think you're going insane because you're not at the Wag Club with the famous starlets. Meeting him was great because we're both public figures and yet we're both at home eating toast at 10.30 on a Saturday night. We both know that we can phone each other up at any time of the day or night and we'll be at home.

We keep in touch all the time, but I doubt if you'll see us braving nightclubs together or anything. Whereas most pop stars who strike up a friendship, the first thing they'll do is whizz out to every public place together. But we went for a three-hour walk in the park the other day, didn't we, and froze to death and we walked through teams of rugby players… It does seem at the moment to be a friendship made in heaven, doesn't it?

We had a screaming row the other night – it was an absolute screamer. I blew my top.

Morrissey It was horrible. It was terrible.

Pete It's great to find a friend you can row with. I phone him up from Italy and everywhere, don't I? Even my own mother doesn't hear from me…

Morrissey I think he *means* to phone his mother but he gets confused and dials my number instead. And he doesn't realise until we're halfway through the conversation that I'm not actually his mother…

Pete He's *not* my mother…

Morrissey As long as I don't have to breast feed…

Pete Oh, that was a sharp one, Joan Rivers.

Morrissey He sends me flowers lots of times…

Pete If I hear that he's down or depressed, I'll send him a bunch of flowers. Send him a bunch of daisies and he's anybody's. It's true, we have these little Interflora men running between our flats, don't we, eh? He's *anybody's* for a lupin.

When we were in Italy we had to have all these armed military police to guard us, which was so stupid and it was freaking me out, so I phoned him up and he was making a piece of toast in Manchester. It really brought me back down to earth – you know, "What are you doing?", "Oh, I've got a piece of toast on the stove and I'm watching *Brookside*." It makes you realise it's still the same world. That's why our friendship is really important. I know it's more important to me than it is to him because he'd gladly go off and be a recluse.

Morrissey No, that's not true. He sent me 26 roses when it was my birthday and I sent him 48 naked sailors.

Pete See. I've met my match, tongue-wise. I always cheer you up, don't I?

Morrissey Always. Always. Most of the people I have ever met have somebody who they can fall back into their arms – Peter's relationship with Lynne is enviable. When I fall back, I hit concrete.

Pete But I phone him up and cheer him up. If *I* was alone in this business – alone in my bed at night – I'd have flipped out. I certainly wouldn't meet anyone

now – there's no way I'd get involved with somebody *now* due to the fact that I'm successful. It's very easy when you're famous to get into somebody's underpants. Or knickers. It's served up on a plate with relish – but you would not glean any relationship from it.

If Morrissey was to get a relationship now, a lot of people would treat him with kid gloves and think, "Oh Morrissey! Morrissey!" and relate to him in awe. You'd have trouble finding a steady relationship now…

Morrissey As opposed to before when it was really easy…

Pete He's best without all that aggro because he'd immediately feel used by whoever he was with…

Morrissey I *want* to be used. I *want* to be used.

Pete See. That's how Morrissey sells records – by making himself sound available and cheap. I don't think you'll find a relationship for a while – until you've had four flop records. And I think his creativity would go down the toilet – Morrissey's appeal is in his public face of loneliness. What else could he write about? "Everything's wonderful. I'm so happy today."? There'd be no sense of drama in it.

Morrissey *Peter's* appeal is that he's relentlessly exciting in every single way.

Pete Isn't he lovely?

Morrissey 'Specially the first time "You Spin Me Round" was on *Top Of The Pops*. That was just barbaric; it was demonic. "You Spin Me Round" is a hallmark in British music and it will never ever date.

Pete You provocative little minx, you.

Morrissey But to be perfectly serious about this whole thing, Pete has been a wonderful friend to me. He really *does* care and when I get depressed he'll pester and he'll persecute in a wonderful way. Other people will just leave me alone but he won't do that. He'll stay there and take me out of the whole thing. And that is really priceless to me.

Pete That's a lovely thing to say. I'm touched.

THE GREAT SMASH HITS NUCLEAR DEBATE

We ask: "Do you believe in nuclear disarmament?"

NIK KERSHAW

"I believe in unilateral disarmament. Nobody is ever going to say, 'Let's all put down our nuclear arms all at once!' Multilateral disarmament is impossible, but one country has got to be brave enough to say, 'We don't want them in our country.' I'd like it to be the UK. The chances at the moment? Nil."

ROBERT SMITH
THE CURE

"My views are pretty much the same as my childhood hero, Spike Milligan. I still think that the idealism involved in nuclear disarmament is laudable, but the knowledge to create the bomb is there and there's nothing we can do to take that away – nuclear disarmament is a very naive dream. Nevertheless, The Cure are playing Glastonbury [*the festival that supports CND*] because there always has to be a level of public and private awareness, otherwise people in power get too complacent. With the threat of civil unrest lying near the surface, I hope that keeps certain political leaders from being too extreme."

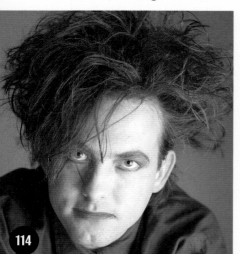

THE DOCTOR
DOCTOR & THE MEDICS

"Whoooooooer! I don't know, I don't know… this is a toughie actually. My mind's in two halves, as is everyone's, ha ha. I mean, say they got rid of all the weapons and there was a war – that could mean us all being sent the call-up papers and being told to take a gun and go off and shoot people… I think it's very naive to think they're just going to chuck all the bombs away. And let's not forget about germ warfare. They've got as many scientists working on that as bombs. To me it's far more frightening that someone can come over here with something in his suitcase and put it in the water and the next day the nation's dead and no one can drink water for a hundred years or whatever. Germ warfare is far more sinister. Apparently, the Russians have got a gas that they can drop on a country and the whole nation wakes up as Reg Varney. Now that's frightening…"

GARY GLITTER

"Before the bomb, European countries used to bash the hell out of each other, and when there were a large amount of kids on the dole, which there has always been, they used to create a war to get rid of some of them. Maybe in some ways the bomb is necessary – I mean, I hate the idea of having a bomb hanging over us but I also hate the idea of a kid being sent to war and blown away that way."

PATSY KENSIT
EIGHTH WONDER

"I'm disgusted with the world at the moment. All we've talked about for the last week in our house is the nuclear cloud. It's disgusting, so unfair. How can people decide what happens to us? They're idiots. Margaret Thatcher – I hate her. Ronald Reagan – eurrrgh…"

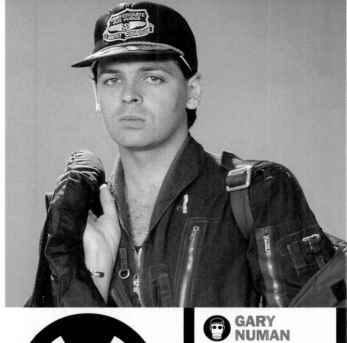

GARY NUMAN

"I'm not in favour of it. I did some shows at American airbases last year and we were warned to take special care of our aeroplanes because peace women were damaging them. If peace women are damaging our planes then I can't understand it."

DR ROBERT
BLOW MONKEYS

"I'm all for it and I hope that if Kinnock gets in – though I do think he's a bit soft – he's hard enough to kick them out. Nuclear power they shouldn't stop; nuclear weapons, yes."

BILLY OCEAN

"I think nuclear weapons should never have started in the first place – it's dealing with sciences that are nothing to do with the spirit of the Lord. Maybe it's too late to do anything now. Just as an individual, don't buy a gun, don't join the army, don't kill. As individuals, we can all do something. But so many people would rather fight to make a decision rather than sit down and talk."

MICK HUCKNALL
SIMPLY RED

"I don't see how anybody in their right minds could consider not supporting disarmament, bearing in mind Chernobyl. Do I think something will happen to get rid of weapons? No. Sad, isn't it?"

SADE

"Disarmament would be a way to preserve a future but it won't happen. It's as simple as that. There are too many people who don't understand the danger of it. It's idiotic."

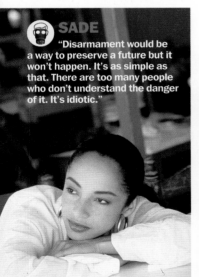

MARK KING
LEVEL 42

"I'm really scared. It suddenly occurred to me that my kids trusted me implicitly, but that I didn't know what was going on and I certainly didn't have it under control. Politicians are frightening, and it's not just the Reagans and Gaddafis. With Reagan you're talking about all the mad advice he's being given by all these Weinbergers and Weingums and Beefbergers… It's frightening."

BILLY
BRAGG

"Actually, I think the events of the last few months have proved the case for nuclear disarmament. Chernobyl was only a fraction of what would happen if a nuclear bomb went off. Imagine what would happen if 30 of them went off in France. I'm not convinced that all the governments are going to turn around at once and give up their bombs. In the States, their whole economy is based on making and selling weapons, and likewise in the Soviet Union – they need that fear of war to keep their punters in order. But I do feel strongly that the pressure from people like CND results in governments realising it is possible to change direction."

ASK A SILLY QUESTION...

"What colour is January?""Do you know anyone called Tarquin?""Why did you get so fat?"These were just some of the bizarre, probing and downright rude enquiries pop stars had to handle during an interview with Smash Hits. How did we get away with it?

Do you empty your own hoover bag?
"No, I must admit I don't. I found it very difficult to live on my own without a mum. I have someone who comes round to do the cleaning. I'm sure she finds some disgusting things in the bag." *Gary Kemp, Spandau Ballet*

How do you like to travel?
"By carpet." *Steve Strange, Visage*

Did you ever pass your Cycling Proficiency test as a child?
"No, I didn't, and I should have done because I was brilliant! It was a real bone of contention at the time. I could do fantastic wheelies but they didn't seem to think that counted for much." *John Taylor, Duran Duran*

How would you say you got on with Jerry Hall's ponies?
"They think I'm terribly handsome, poor things… I do like a nice cup of tea, don't you?" *Mick Jagger*

What colour is happiness?
"I'd have to say blue and yellow. Because yellow is just happy. It's just *there*, it's vibrant and it's happy. Yellow doesn't spell anything bad. And blue is the sky and

Are you gay?

"No, not in the conventional sense, but I *can* appreciate men of my own sex as well." *Paul Weller*

"I go with both. Well, at the moment I go with one of each." *Pete Burns, Dead Or Alive*

the sea and neither of those are bad. What we're putting into them is bad, but to me they're happy. Um… that's it!" *Stefan Dennis*

What colour is January?
"I think it's going to be a red one this year because we're going to be on tour in Germany. If we were recording it would probably be grey-green; if we were on holiday it would be yellow." *Wayne Hussey, The Mission*

Is it true you applied to be the new drummer of The Housemartins?
"No! Where do you hear all these *silly* rumours from?" *Samantha Fox*

Are you any good at potato sculptures?
"I used to do sculptures in butter, but not potato. I used to do little people and things. My mother wasn't very pleased." *Nick Kamen*

What's the secret of the universe?
"I think the world is a dead carcass, and I think the purpose of human beings is as maggots. We're stripping the dead flesh off the carcass." *Alison Moyet*

What's your favourite item of clothing?
"Brogue shoes. And I have a leather jockstrap that's quite nice." *Holly Johnson, Frankie Goes To Hollywood*

Do you like sardines?
"I love sardines in their can with mustard. But I take their spines out and their tails off." *Madonna*

Have you ever considered posing in the nude?
"If anyone's interested, I charge around £39.50 for a session." *Nick Heyward, Haircut 100*

If you were married to Freddie Mercury, would you let him keep the moustache?
"I'm not into that. I really like clean-shaven guys. I always have and always will." *Susanna Hoffs, The Bangles*

Have you ever been beaten up for no reason?
"Only for being pansylike. I used to encounter a certain amount of hostility at school, basically for being a bit of a snobby poof." *Lloyd Cole*

Has getting married changed your relationship?
"Yes. It's really good fun saying 'my wife' – don't you find that?" *Simon Le Bon*

What was the stupidest thing you did as a kid?
"The *silliest* thing I ever did was to nick a lightbulb and a container of crab paste. I got a conditional discharge. I didn't need the light-bulb or the crab paste." *Ali Campbell, UB40*

What's the worst song that you've ever written?
"'Bad Boys'. I *hate* it. It's like an albatross around my neck." *George Michael*

Rex

Did you have a nickname at school?
"Yes, the Norwegian for woodpecker, 'Hakkbspetta', because of the resemblance to my name, 'Harket'."
Morten Harket, A-Ha

Do you believe human beings can spontaneously combust?
"I think it's probably caused by people's pacemakers and things exploding. I'd love to see it!" *Roland Gift, Fine Young Cannibals*

Have you ever heard voices in your head?
"Yes. I used to pretend that Tchaikovsky could compose through me, and it worked."
Chris Lowe, Pet Shop Boys

How come you share your life with two fawns, a sheep, a llama, a boa-constrictor and an aviary?
"I just love all animals. I think they're sweet. I like to pry into their world and watch the way they move about. I just stare at them. They're gorgeous." *Michael Jackson*

Did you have any strange habits as a youngster?
"I would arch my back and, placing my hands by my feet, I would scuttle like some demented crab about the house. I did this for about a year." *Bob Geldof*

Did you ever have a rocking horse when you were a child?
"I never had a rocking horse. But I had Action Men, about six of them. And my sister had a Sindy doll. Sindy had a horse and I had a jeep and a tank. I learnt a lot about girls, chat-up lines like, 'Heeey. I'll come pick you up later in my tank.'" *Dave Gahan, Depeche Mode*

Why did you get so fat?
"It's due to pizza in New York. Ever had a pizza from New York? You'd be fat as well."
Jim Kerr, Simple Minds

What's the most horrid thing you've ever done?
"I once threw a cream pie in this girl's face. She was alright, but she was very tall and for some reason she had a crush on me."
Midge Ure

What's your favourite word to use on *Call My Bluff*?
"'Whange' – a Chinese walking stick, or 'poltroon' – a spiritless coward."
Roland Orzabal, Tears For Fears

Does your mother play golf?

"She does, actually. Until recently she was Ladies Captain of the City Of Newcastle Golf Club."
Neil Tennant, Pet Shop Boys

"She does not. She's got a really bad back, my mum." *Andy McCluskey, OMD*

"She attempts golf annually, but usually retires to the nearest pub."
Kim Wilde

If you were a car, what kind would you be?
"An Aston Martin DB5. Although it's sporting, it looks real mean… all big and formidable. It commands respect." *Paul Young*

Do you think that *Antiques Roadshow* is boring?
"No! I think it's one of the *best* programmes I've ever seen! All these people with little vases that they've had in the attic for 19,000 years and they think they're worth £40,000. The look on their faces when they're told the vase is worth £6.20 – ha ha!"
Owen Paul

Can you think of a good poem about Wet Wet Wet?
"Yes. 'I know a little singer / I wish he was my pet / If we jumped in bed together / It would be wet wet wet.' I think he's gorgeous." *Boy George*

Do you put up your own shelves?
"I don't, but I've just built a chicken shed."
Alison Moyet

Have you ever milked a cow?
"No, but I'm working on it." *John Taylor*

How successful was the hair transplant?
"It was perfect. It hurt a bit but it was worth it. I had 96 plants and only one of them turned out a little bit dodgy. It should have had 10-15 strands and only has about six. But I'd strongly recommend it for anyone, although it does hurt a bit." *Gary Numan*

What's your favourite item of clothing?
"Tight jeans. People seem to find something sexy about tight jeans. I do."
Mike Nolan, Bucks Fizz

Did you know that the world's biggest spider had a leg span of ten inches?
"I think I did, yeah. Do you know, I go mad if I see anyone killing an insect." *Kim Appleby, Mel & Kim*

Have you ever thought you were a bus stop?
"Sort of. I went to four or five different bus stops one day and never got a bus at any of them. And when I tried to sit down at one of them, I fell over. I suppose at some stage during that day I might have thought I actually *was* a bus stop."
Shane MacGowan

Are you any good at marbles?
"No. But I'm not bad at basketball. Oh, and I play table tennis as well."
Fish, Marillion

What was the best excuse you used to get off PE?
"I never wanted to get off PE – it was the only intellectual subject in school." *Morrissey*

Have you ever owned an Austrian shepherd-boy puppet?
"I had a teddy bear that had a musical box in it. One of my uncles, in a fit of spitefulness, took the box out and killed him. I was devastated." *Kirk Brandon, Spear Of Destiny*

If you were a kangaroo, what would you keep in your pouch?
"Marbles… so I could have a game with the other creatures." *Andy Bell, Erasure*

What do you wear in bed?
"Not a sausage."
Carl, Madness

Have you got any nice crockery?
"I've got a nice hand-painted tea set. It's lovely – it's got cornflowers and poppies on it. I use it all the time." *Holly Johnson*

Have you ever placed a lonely hearts ad?
"Yes. It said: 'I'm dying of loneliness and need to be rescued or else I'll sink into obscurity', which I did. I also put that I was mad, ugly, spotty and totally odorous. No reply." *Morrissey*

Did you ever phone a number at random and annoy the person at the other end?
"Yes, I did. It was very fashionable in Germany when I was about nine." *Tanita Tikaram*

Have you ever been so violently sick that your earrings fell off?
"No, my earrings are very sturdy. But I've been pretty sick in my time. Usually in the bathtub. I don't even bother aiming for the toilet, because I need a big space. I clean it out, of course – lots of Dettol and TCP." *Melissa, Voice Of The Beehive*

Where do all the missing pens in the world go?
"I think there's probably some creature that eats them. Have you ever read that book called *The Borrowers*? All these tiny people come and steal everything like that. It's got to be true." *Patsy Kensit*

Have you ever thought that the world was just a little crouton floating in God's minestrone Cup-a-Soup?
"Uh, that's a neat way to think about it. I'm *actually* very religious. I go to church each week I can, and I pray to God every night to help me do my best." *Glenn Medeiros*

Have you ever accidentally swallowed a fly?
"Yeah, on my motorcycle, and I accidentally ate a worm the other night. I was eating spaghetti sauce and I could definitely taste a worm." *Belinda Carlisle*

What was your biggest thrill as a child?
"Nothing whatsoever. I hated every minute. My biggest excitement was when my parents went on holiday and I ran off for two weeks." *Toyah*

Do you think flowers scream when you pick them?
"Very possibly. There's an old legend about the mandrake that if you pick one and it screams it means you're going to die soon." *Dave Vanian, The Damned*

What would you do if you were Prime Minister?

"I'd halve the price of cigarettes, double the tax on health food, then I'd declare war on France." *Mark E Smith, The Fall*

"I'd have the Union Jack pulled down and have a new flag with a big banana to be hoisted in its place." *Malcolm McLaren*

"I'd open up the banks and let lots and lots of money flood up north." *Garry Christian, The Christians*

"I would make every Saturday a public holiday. And I'd also declare a two-party political system: the Party Party and the All-Night Party." *David Grant, Lynx*

"I'd stop cruise missiles, ban fox hunting and make Glenn Hoddle stay at Tottenham." *Steve Severin, Siouxsie & The Banshees*

"I'd make everyone grow beards and all those who couldn't grow a beard I'd make join the army." *Nick Heyward, Haircut 100*

What's your least favourite expression?
"'Where's the beef?'" I'm just sick of it – pur*lease*!" *Madonna*

What did you have for breakfast this morning?
"The usual health diet. A handful of Vitamin B, a handful of Vitamin C, some jalapeno peppers and a shot of Jack Daniel's." *David Lee Roth*

What keeps you awake at night?
"Sneezing. I think I'm allergic to beds." *Shirlie, Pepsi And Shirlie*

If you had 15 minutes to live, what would you do?
"I'd make sure I was at home for a start. And I wouldn't start any long books. Oh, and I'd cancel the milk." *Nik Kershaw*

Did you ever pull the legs off a Daddy long-legs?
"I never did that but I did bite the top off a rabbit's ear once. I was very tiny and the rabbit bit me, so I just bit it back and I took the very top of its ear off. My mother hit me all the way home. My feet didn't touch the ground – I was constantly in the air because she leathered me all the way." *Phillip Schofield*

What are your ambitions?
"I want to be an astronaut or a member of the SAS, because you're always on the move." *Toyah*

Have you ever hit your sister with a wet fish?
"No, but [*my sister and Voice Of The Beehive singer*] Melissa used to have a dried sting-ray and she used to chase me round the house with it! She used to put it in my bed when I was sleeping." *Tracey, Voice Of The Beehive*

How would you describe yourself?
"A sleazy, funky, lowdown woman!" *Alannah Currie, Thompson Twins*

What were you in a previous life?
"A black prince. I must have been, because of my eccentricities and regal manner." *Leee John, Imagination*

Why did you wear men's suits?
"I wanted to look like a white Grace Jones." *Annie Lennox*

Redferns, Rex

Do you know anyone called Tarquin?
"No, but if I did I'd admit it to you. I *think* there's someone called Tarquin that works at our record company." *Phil Collins*

Did you take sandwiches to school or have school dinners?
"At primary school my mum used to make me digestives and cheese, but then later on I had school dinners. I thought they were disgusting." *Edwyn Collins, Orange Juice*

Who was your first crush?

"A girl called Patricia Hookway. I took her to a film, but I didn't concentrate as I was plucking up the courage to kiss her. I gave up the next day when she turned up in checked socks." *Mike Nolan, Bucks Fizz*

"Her name was Lesley Duffy. I kissed her in the library and I was ten." *Chris Lowe, Pet Shop Boys*

"Probably Valerie Singleton from *Blue Peter*." *Joe Elliott, Def Leppard*

Who would you most like to be stuck in a lift with?
"Sylvester Stallone." *Marilyn*

Do you think "Meat Is Murder"?
"I do feel guilty, but one has to eat something solid once in a while." *Julian Lennon*

How much would you have to be paid to pose in the nude?
"Let me think… a year's supply of Mars bars." *Paul Young*

How often do you cut your toenails and where do you put the clippings?
"I cut them when they start sticking out of my socks and put the clippings in the rubbish bin – like all good boys do." *Nick Rhodes, Duran Duran*

What TV programme do you always have to turn off?
"*Coronation Street*. I can't stand it. *Emmerdale Farm* and *Little House On The Prairie*. I watch just about everything else." *Rick Parfitt, Status Quo*

Do you pick the white, stringy bits off oranges before you eat them?
"No. They add a definite flavour to the orange." *Roger Taylor, Duran Duran*

Did you ever play an angel in the school nativity?
"No. I played Bilbo Baggins in *The Hobbit*. I remember I had to faint. I don't think I was very good. I was pretty much like David Bowie as an actor – tragically on the edge." *Boy George*

Do you snore?
"I used to. When I was on aeroplanes, they had to wake me up because I was disturbing the other passengers. But I lost about 100 pounds and it's not so bad now." *Divine*

Why do so many girls fancy you?
"I don't know. I think they just want to clean me up a bit – give me a shave and a good wash." *Jimmy Nail*

What is your goal in life?
"To breed dogs and open an exotic pet store." *Dee Snider, Twisted Sister*

Has anyone ever told you that you look a bit like Beethoven?
"Funnily enough, someone in Germany *did* tell me that once. But I think I look more like a young Paul Newman." *Feargal Sharkey*

Do you ever cut yourself shaving?

"Lots of times. I've been shaving since I was 13. I've been plucking my eyebrows too since I was 13." *Paul King*

Do you mow your own lawn?
"No, my girlfriend's brother does it. Oh… actually she's not my girlfriend any more, she's my *wife*." *Paul Hardcastle*

What's your favourite hat?
"A sailor's cap. But I had to stop wearing it as it was giving me a headache." *Madonna*

Have you ever written a fan letter?
"Yes, I wrote loads to Michael Jackson, but he never replied. Then I wrote loads to Donny Osmond, but he didn't reply either." *Dee C. Lee*

Did you know that the world's longest parsnip was nearly 12ft long?
"No, I did *not*. And to be quite honest I'm not that *bothered*! What kind of a question is that?" *Hazell Dean*

Would you say you had any eccentricities?
"I used to have a fetish about clean hands but now I only wash them about every five minutes." *Andrew Ridgeley, Wham!*

If you could contact one dead person in a seance and have a chat with them, whom would you choose?
"Jean Cocteau." *Nick Rhodes*

What's your most disgusting habit?
"Picking my toenails. But I always tidy the bits up." *Mick Hucknall, Simply Red*

Which member of Duran Duran would you most like to play golf with?
"Andy Taylor. If we could both get out of the club house standing up." *Nasher, Frankie Goes To Hollywood*

What does Boy George remind you of?
"An aubergine… all shiny and plump." *Paul Young*

Have you got one of those flush things that you hang down inside the loo?
"No. I don't like blue water. I don't *trust* blue water. I like to see what colour my piss is." *Richard Butler, Psychedelic Furs*

Have you ever done a jigsaw puzzle in hospital?
"No. But when I was six I went into hospital to have my tonsils out, and I used to play with this tea set that had little dollies with it." *Wayne Hussey*

When you were young did your mother ever lock you in your room with a plate of cold cabbage?

"What's that? Cabbage? What's that? Oh, a vegetable. I don't know what that is! My mother probably did lock me in my bedroom when I was young, but she would have brought me a blanket or something. My mother is very nice – she never even hit me." *Joey Tempest, Europe*

Do you have a big mirror in your bathroom?

"No, I've just got a picture of a chimpanzee in there. It just looks at me while I'm having a bath." *Shane MacGowan*

If you were a domestic appliance, what would it be?

"I suppose I'd be a video. Show some films and that. Or a TV." *Kim Wilde*

Do you know anybody called Igor?

"No, but I do know someone called Wilf." *Dave Vanian*

Do you still sleep in a coffin?

"No, I stopped doing that about seven years ago." *Toyah*

What would you do if you were invisible for a day?

"I'd go to Buckingham Palace and see if the Queen really does go to the toilet and I'd follow her into the bog." *Jimmy Somerville*

Is there anything more infuriating than putting on a duvet cover?

"*The* most infuriating thing is when you can't find a bottle-opener. Of course, *I* just pull it off with my teeth. I tell you, though, there's some girls in Thailand…" *Michael Hutchence, INXS*

Has Pete Burns got nice legs?

"Yes. They're very smooth. I think he uses wax." *Wayne Hussey*

Have you ever been sick into a cowboy boot?

"Yes, it was this guy's brand-new cowboy boots. I thought I'd never see him again, but we ended up getting engaged for a while." *Carol Decker, T'Pau*

Do you like Rupert the Bear?

"Yes. He's so innocent and charming. He always reminds me of Winnie The Pooh." *Michael Jackson*

Have you ever grown parsnips in your gumboot?

"No, I haven't. But I used to collect fluff bunnies under the bed. You know – little balls of dust. I used to cultivate them, grow them into different shapes, and I even used to give them names." *Terence Trent D'Arby*

"No, but as a child I used to grow cress in a hippopotamus." *Stan Cullimore, The Housemartins*

"It depends whose gumboot. If it was Madonna's gumboot… but then I doubt she's got any gumboots. Anyway, I don't like parsnips – maybe swedes?" *Wayne Hussey, The Mission*

Do you own a stuffed Alaskan timber wolf?

"Yes. He has a really scary look in his eye, so for a while I kept him locked away in a room. I thought I'd build him his own tundra setting in my lounge, but I never got around to it." *Gary Numan*

Do you believe in God?

"Well, no one has ever taken a picture of him, have they? There's always a picture of Jesus with that thing on his head but no one's ever seen a picture of God." *Samantha Fox*

Aren't Big Audio Dynamite just a bunch of boring old punks?

"That's a bit bloody cheeky, isn't it? I'm not a dinosaur." *Mick Jones, Big Audio Dynamite*

"What's your favourite Spandau Ballet record?

"I wouldn't know one if it came up and rapped me across the back of the thighs with a hairbrush." *Chrissie Hynde, Pretenders*

Have you ever worn a dress?

"Yes, when I was 13 in the school play, *HMS Pinafore*. I was a soprano, so I played the woman." *Neil Tennant*

Have you ever found any silverfish in your mattress?

"No! It would scare me to death." *Mags, A-Ha*

Do you own a stuffed panda?

"Yes. I bought it in Singapore in 1981 – he's got a really lovely face." *Gary Numan*

What's your favourite Indian meal?

"A quarter tandoori chicken with samosas and a naan and Bull's Blood and yoghurt." *Ali Campbell*

Why do you look like Jimmy Osmond?

"I don't know! I can't remember what he looks like… did he have dark hair? I know that a lot of girls liked the Osmond brothers, so… ha ha ha!" *Joey Tempest*

What colour is your bedroom wall?

"White. But I'm going to redecorate." *Midge Ure*

Don't you think The Jam's Rick Buckler looks just like Dennis Waterman?

"Does a bit, doesn't he. Lots of people say that. Going a bit bald too [*sniggers*]. He's over the hill." *Paul Weller*

What words do you find interesting these days?

"'Interesting'. And 'boomerang'." *Kate Bush*

Have you ever eaten a hamster?

"Not a *live* one, no." *Belouis Some*

What order do you take your clothes off in?

"First socks, then I move to the top. I always leave the middle to the last minute." *Paul King*

Why are you so ugly?

"I think it was the porridge." *Rose, Strawberry Switchblade*

What do you think about Mrs Thatcher?

"She's alright. I don't talk about politics. I was going to live next door to her, but the garden was too small." *Samantha Fox*

Redferns, Rex

Are you a vegetarian?
"No – I couldn't dream of it. I mean, you are what you eat, and who wants to be a lettuce?" *Pete Burns, Dead Or Alive*

Does it bother you that Howard Jones is better than you at water-skiing?
"Not really. He can't do anything else, can he?" *Robert Smith, The Cure*

Can you mend a puncture on a bicycle tyre?
"Certainly can. You have to make sure there's no air left in the inner tube, get a tyre lever, lever the tyre off, then take the inner tube..." [*continues in this fashion for several years...*] *Simon Le Bon*

Have you got a Ronald McDonald toothbrush?
"No, but I *have* got a plastic Hamburglar. It's for my daughter." *Suggs, Madness*

Should we scrap the Royal Family?

"People who want to get rid of the Royal Family should be shot, traitorous scum." *Gary Numan*

"I'm afraid I'm all for them. I'm interested in history and they are part of history." *Mick Jones, Big Audio Dynamite*

"The Royal Family are *laughable*. Andrew and Fergie are a really *gruesome* couple. He's really obnoxious and she's really ugly." *Robert Smith, The Cure*

Have you ever been sick in a kangaroo's pouch?
"No, I haven't, and to be totally honest with you I hope I never will! It would be a very weird situation to be in! I mean, the last time I threw up was years ago when I drank too much at school and came home feeling a bit wheezy and puked a little bit. What a weird question!" *Jason Donovan*

Were you ever a cheerleader?
"Give me a break! I never even went to one high-school dance. I used to hang around with the ugly people in the art room." *Chrissie Hynde*

Do you ever go "a bit weird"?
"Yes. If anyone calls me 'dear', I throw things at them." *Annie Nightingale*

What's your favourite thing from childhood that you've still got?
"My penis." *Roland Orzabal*

Did you have a wildly exciting job before the band started?
"I carried sacks of potatoes for two days, then I gave up. And I was a wine waiter." *Lloyd Cole*

Is it true that David Bowie once gave you a lovebite?
"Oh that's so boring, it's not even worth mentioning." *Marilyn*

What's your favourite breakfast cereal?
"Sugar Frosties. I love cornflakes but I hate the hassle of having to put sugar on." *Annie, Amazulu*

Are you a cricketing genius?
"Well, I played cricket with David Gower once. We got thrashed." *Stephen "Tintin" Duffy*

Have you ever worn a kilt?
"No, but our keyboard player Mick wears one in bed!" *Jim Kerr*

What do you wear in bed?
"Nothing. My daughter is too young to be upset." *Falco*

Do you often get recognised when you're shopping in Tesco's?
"Yes, but I don't really have anything normal I can wear – unless I go out in my dressing gown." *Siouxsie Sioux*

Did you really once go to a fancy dress party as a car-crash victim?
"No, I went as a motorbike victim." *Paul Young*

What's the worst job you ever had?

"I was a secretary, but my hair would always go messy or my false eyelashes would curl up. I got fired, and was told I was the worst secretary they'd ever had." *Cyndi Lauper*

"Working in a weedkiller factory over the summer holidays." *Paul Young*

"Making window frames. I lasted three days." *David Coverdale, Whitesnake*

"On a building site in Wapping." *Holly Johnson, Frankie Goes To Hollywood*

Do you think you're good-looking?
"Not really, but I think I can fake it." *Pål, A-Ha*

Who do you not like?
"Hippies. I'm into chasing hippies out of town. I wouldn't want no hippies tromping all over my cows." *Mick Jones*

Do you own a teddy bear?
"Yes. It was given to me on the day I was born. It's soaked with tears." *Robert Smith*

Does Prince know any good jokes?
"Stop asking stupid questions!" *Sheena Easton*

A tabloid newspaper makes up a story about Princess Margaret calling you "a poor excuse for a dog's dinner" at a film premiere (at which you were not even present). Go forward ten spaces.

27

HOSPITAL: Throw 6 or pay forfeit set by opponents to escape.

25

Your pet llama eats the master tapes of your debut LP. Go to VET.

24

During recording of the charity record you're asked to sing harmonies with Simon Le Bon and Willie Nelson. The ordeal causes you to collapse with nervous exhaustion. Go to HOSPITAL.

LAWYER: Throw 6 or forfeit set by opponents to escape.

28

59

Nose job. Go to HOSPITAL.

58

57

56

A waxwork of you goes on display at Madame Tussauds. Throw again.

54

53

"Jig-A-Jelly" is used as the theme music to *Rocky XIV*. Go forward 6 spaces.

Barry Manilow sues you for stealing the tune of "Dib-A-Dum Dib-A-Dee" from "Bermuda Triangle". Consult LAWYER.

82

Britain's Brightest Pop Mag prints an ancient photo of you in horrible platform boots and sequinned hot pants. The shame! Lose two turns.

80

You become the first ever pop singer to play a concert in Albania. Millions of journalists fly out for the occasion leaving no room in the venue for Albanians. Albania sues you. Consult LAWYER.

30

60

83

David Attenborough announces that he is making a film of your pet llama's life starring Morrissey, Tina Turner, Anneka Rice and Sting as The Vet. Go forward two spaces.

96

95

Richard Attenborough announces that he is making a film of you starring Rupert Everett, Toyah, Lionel Blair and David Bowie as Barry Manilow. Go forward two spaces.

31

61

84

98

100

At a music awards ceremony, Elton John describes you as "possibly the greatest musical genius of all time". You break down and blub uncontrollably as your pet llama delivers a deeply moving speech about having sex on the phone with Holly Johnson. Congratulations! You have made it to THE

Torvill and Dean, Motörhead and a member of the Labour Party all appear in the v. expensive video for your new single, "Jig-A-Jelly". But you decide to scrap the "vid" as your hair looks too "fluffy" in it. Visit HAIRSTYLIST.

Your waxwork is melted down and replaced by one of Keith Chegwin. Go back 12 spaces.

Chas and Dave record a version of "Trumpiti-Tra-Banjola (Meat is Not Very Nice)" (changing the words to "…Let's 'ave a right-old fry-up") for a sausage TV ad. Outraged, your llama tramples your TV set, injuring his trotters. Go to VET.

99

32

63

85

86

The Fates are catching up on you!! Throw again: if dice shows even number, go to HAIRSTYLIST; if odd number, take DETOUR to DOOM.

87

88

You buy a useless football team. During first match under your directorship, pet llama runs amok and eats the referee. Go to PRISON

VET: Throw 6 or pay forfeit set by opponents to escape.

64

You're picked to represent the UK in the Eurovision Song Contest with "Po-La Po-Lum (The Chemical Warfare Song)" but are disqualified when your pet llama destroys the electronic scoreboard. Go to VET.

65

You land a role as an alien in dodgy sci-fi film and nearly suffocate in a spiky blue rubber costume. Gary Numan takes over your role. Go to HOSPITAL.

67

68

34

Your book of blurry photos taken off the telly, *Images Within A Tangent, Man*, is published. Not even your mum buys it. Miss two turns while you "reassess" your artistic direction.

35

During an appearance on breakfast TV you fall asleep on the sofa. Miss a turn while Wincey Willis chortles on about the weather.

37

38

As a publicity ruse, you take part in a transatlantic yacht race. Yacht is attacked by giant jellyfish off Isle of Wight. Go to HOSPITAL.

39

1

2

Your group is seen in a pub by a mad record company boss. He signs you and your first single (which none of you play on and consists mainly of electronic whistling noises) is released. Go forward five spaces.

3

4

5

Your mad boss writes sleevenotes for the 12in remix: "The hammer of illusion? Rungs of the ladder + next is indecision = sideways into the future…" Miss a turn while you try to work out what it means.

6

POP SWIZZ!

The Smash Hits V. Bored Game

21 A tabloid newspaper makes up a story about your "Sizzling Nights Of Saucy Sin" with someone you've never heard of. Go forward eight spaces.

20

19

18

17

You're asked to appear on a charity record along with lots of v. famous people. Go forward six spaces.

You decide to become a radical vegetarian and record "Trumpiti-Tra-Banjola (Meat Is Not Very Nice)", a soaraway dancefloor hit. Pet llama chokes on one of your nut cutlets. Go to VET.

51

50

49

78

77

You make guest appearance as someone or other's long-lost millionaire cousin on *Dynasty*. Joan Collins flounces off set muttering about "bloody amateurs". Go forward seven spaces.

76

75

You sue yourself for stealing "Jig-A-Jelly" from "Dib-A-Dum Dib-A-Dee", Channel 4 make a documentary about the unprecedented court case. Go forward eight spaces.

Your solo single is banned by a wholesome BBC DJ who reckons that "Dib-A-Dum Dib-A-Dee" might mean something rather rude in Morse code. Throw again.

16

94

93

92

74

48

15

DETOUR TO DOOM: Your private plane is hijacked by terrorists disguised as heavy metal singers. You are never heard of again. Bad luck!

In a speech to the nation, Ronald Reagan muddles you up with Bruce Springsteen and calls you "A great patriot... a true American". Your new LP, "It's Swinging, Pops!", goes platinum in US overnight. Go forward two spaces.

Appearing on *Pop Quiz*, you correctly identify all the members of Dire Straits. Return to START.

73

The Krankies invite you to appear on their TV show. Go back two spaces.

47

14

46

During an interview on *Wogan*, you remark: "y'know, Terry, success to me is, like, a very double-edged thing." One-and-a-half million viewers die of boredom. Go back four spaces.

90

72

Barry Manilow sues you for stealing "Jig-A-Jelly" from "I Made It Through The Rain". Consult LAWYER.

You release your first solo single, "Dib-A-Dum Dib-A-Dee". Little And Large invite you to appear on their TV show. Go forward one space.

45

You meet Brian "Nasher" Nash in a pub, and subsequently go bonkers in Madame Tussauds, attacking the waxwork of Keith Chegwin with a blowtorch. Go to PRISON.

70

"Dib-A-Dum Dib-A-Dee" is used as the theme music to *Porky's VII*. Go back four spaces.

71

44

12

40

To try to get "Jig-A-Jelly" played, your manager films a "vid" in his garden featuring an out-of-focus wheelbarrow. It is hailed a "masterpiece" and "Jig-A-Jelly" zooms up the chart. Go forward ten spaces.

HAIRSTYLIST: Throw 6 or pay forfeit set by opponents to escape.

Hairstylist

42

During your debut *Top Of The Pops* your hair is ruffled by a balloon. Visit HAIRSTYLIST.

43

Prison

PRISON: Throw 6 or pay forfeit set by opponents to escape.

7

8

CONTRACT

You tell a journalist that the sleevenotes on your 12in remix are "a load of toffee-nosed rubbish". Mad record co. boss sacks you from group. Go back to START.

9

10

You win a heated trolley and a bedside lamp on *The Price Is Right* and swap them for a super Boots cassette recorder. Miss two turns while you make a demo tape and secure a record contract.

Excuse me, my mate fancies you...

What do people most want to know about their favourite pop stars? Their top five production hints? Their "seminal musical influences"? Not ruddy likely! What people really want to know is who they fancy. Bev Hillier asked lots of v. famous people how they'd rate each other in the pin-up stakes – the blokes on this page and the amazin' rock'n'roll ladies on the next...

Toyah

Samantha Fox

Curt Smith on...

"When she's got all her make-up on she looks good. Not a very good actress though."

"Horrible. I don't know her personality but I think she has put sexual equality back 20 years."

Nick Heyward on...

"I wouldn't go out with her. She looks quite headstrong and she's ambitious, which is good. She's good-looking but I've never seen her without any make-up on."

"She's got a lot of puppy fat, which she should have got rid of by now, but I like it because she looks very cuddly. Her breasts are too big for me; I prefer smaller ones. If she was taller she'd be more attractive – and if she had a little more talent."

Paul King on...

"I think she has a charming personality, lovely complexion and would totally win you over with her charm and beauty. The fact that she is quite tiny wouldn't bother me."

"She looks a bit too young for me. I've never really been a big bosom man either. I met her once and just said 'hello'; she seemed very pleasant but very young."

Paul Weller on...

"Stick to acting."

"Blueegh!"

Martin Fry on...

"Tiny, too short for me. Looks like she has a heart of gold but she's no Aretha Franklin."

"Not my type. I'm familiar with her and so are thousands of others. I went off her when I saw her on *Wogan*. She doesn't have the attributes I look for in a woman. She's not my type but there again I'm probably not hers."

 **Kim Wilde**	 **Dee C Lee**	 **Alannah Currie**	**Cheryl Baker**	**Strawberry Switchblade**
▶ "I don't know what to say about her. She looks great in her short tight black leather mini-skirt. A bit too tough for me – a hard woman I think."	▶ "Gorgeous, really nice and very good-looking! A great singer as well. I wish there were more singers around like her."	▶ "Don't talk to me about Alannah Currie! We toured with the Thompson Twins a long time ago. I think she takes feminism to ludicrous extremes. Definitely not for me."	▶ "I think Jay Aston was a lot nicer. On the surface I'm not attracted to her but she's maybe quite interesting. I've never spoken to her."	▶ "Nice Scottish girls. I said 'hello' to one of them once and she seemed very nice and down-to-earth."
▶ "I like Kim Wilde. I find her voice sexy and she's quite attractive. I've met her before and we got on alright. She's quite friendly and jovial. She's also got a little puppy fat but, as I said, I don't mind chubby girls."	▶ "I don't really know what she looks like. When she sings those political lyrics it looks like she doesn't have a clue about what she is singing. I'd like to take her to the Houses of Parliament for a cheese roll and a cup of tea – that way I'd find out what she looks like."	▶ "She's a very 'up for a laugh', forward girl, which I think is great. I don't find her attractive but that go-for-it attitude is good. I met her at a Thompson Twins party."	▶ "Bit of a mother figure really. She's chirpy and looks like a bubbly, mature woman. I like mature women occasionally. I despise most of the stuff Bucks Fizz do but she looks alright – I've met her a few times. She looks like she should be in *EastEnders*."	▶ "Jill reminds me of a young Elizabeth Taylor. I like Scottish girls. I'm also into all the stuff they wear – it would probably take me about 16 hours to get through that lot, which would be fun! Jill's got a nice character."
▶ "Mmmm. She's got a very nice mouth. Mmmm."	▶ "Let me think. Oh no – I was just going to say something outrageous then but I won't. Very raunchy, definitely turns me on – she has the sort of face that you could imagine you could have a very good laugh with."	▶ "Interesting. She looks to me like the sort of lady you could have lots of conversations with, but intense conversations aren't really my idea of fun. What I'd do is take along a few bottles of wine, and I'm sure she'd be a really good laugh."	▶ "She looks very laid back and appears to me the sort of lady who, rather than go out to a disco, would invite you around to her flat for a nice meal. And a good laugh."	▶ "A bitter-sweet experience when sugar-sweet pop meets a visual shock."
▶ "Who?"	▶ "A nice chick who can hold her drink."	▶ "Doesn't drink real ale."	▶ "Nice TV personality for a cockney."	▶ "Nice girls who support CND, so I like them."
▶ "She went through a strange period of wearing rubber clothes – I wasn't impressed. She has a mouth like Brigitte Bardot and reminds me of her a little. Is she a born blonde or bottle blonde? I think she should loosen up and be herself."	▶ "I like her more with her hair down. She's very pretty. If I was given the opportunity I'd take her out."	▶ "Not me type at all. She looks like Cruella Deville. She should loosen up a little as well. I don't like that tattoo on her head. Anyway, she goes out with Tom Bailey."	▶ "Bubbles and blondes are not my style. She seems like a south London girl who'll be too pushy for me. I prefer the silent type. She's very chatty and would probably think I was very miserable."	▶ "Sharp dressers. I don't think they should wear so much make-up. I like them because (a) there's two of them and (b) there's an element of punk rock in what they do, which is refreshing in this day and age. Original with individuality."

Toyah on…

Samantha Fox on…

Kim Wilde on…

Dee C Lee on…

Curt Smith

"I kind of like Tears For Fears. He's good-looking in a boyish way; he's sort of got a roundish face. My first visual impact is that he is very attractive."

"Lovely eyes and a good voice. Quite sexy-looking."

"Which one is he? They're both quite cute (as in teddy bears as opposed to Ryan O'Neal). They look like brothers. Their 'Mad World' single was great – so was 'Shout'. He's obviously very talented and it's great to see them slaying them in America."

"He seems quite an intense sort of person. I've never met the bloke but I get the impression he likes staying in and watching the telly."

Nick Heyward

"He's very good-looking in a different way. He looks totally English and always looks well scrubbed behind the ears. Very attractive, Nice dimply smile."

"Cute and always smiling. I think he looks so young. He's lovable."

"When 'Favourite Shirts' came out I went straight out and bought it; it had a really fresh sound. I really like the LP 'Pelican West' – and Nick's cool charm, of course. I'm just waiting for the next song now."

"Looks quite a sweet boy but just a bit too sweet for my personal taste. I can see why girls go mad for him. He seems like a nice boy!"

Paul King

"Very handsome. He makes me think of a Roman gladiators. I don't think I could go out with him as I'd hate to go out with a rock star. He hasn't got a pretty face, it's unique… he has a very strong profile. An acquired taste but very handsome."

"Good bone structure and lovely silky hair. I've seen him in real life and he's much better looking. Overall I think he's dark, hairy and macho – very appealing."

"Well, I'm waiting to hear something that I like. Paul reminds me of this person I know, which is rather unfortunate 'cos he's a real pain. Paul, however, has never caused me any real grief – yet!"

"I can't handle his hairdo but I'm sure he's a nice chappie.

Paul Weller

"Not my type at all. A great songwriter but too thin for me. I like big muscley hunks."

"I think he moves well when he's singing – he has a funny way of moving actually. Also I love the way he's always chewing gum when he sings. I used to like him in The Jam when I was a little mod. I've never met him before and always wanted to at the age of 12."

"I had a dream about him once and I really liked him for a day after that, but I'm afraid it ended all too soon. I wouldn't be seen dead wearing some of the clothes Paul Weller wears. I haven't bought any Style Council records, but I used to buy a lot of Jam records."

"He's the most miserable person I've ever met and he's not very hairy and can't hold his beer. But having said that, he's a lovely old bastard."

Martin Fry

"I quite like him. I like his height; he's also very attractive. I prefer the way he used to look rather than his new outfit."

"Tall, hunky and dresses really nice."

"I met him at a pop quiz thing once and he knew everything, which was quite good as I was on his team."

"Again, I've never met him but just from watching him on TV he seems a bit too flash for me."

Alannah Currie on…

▼

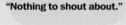
"Nothing to shout about."

▼

"He's quite sweet but he gets too excited about chord progressions."

▼

"I'd like stilettos!"

▼

"Old misery guts. You've got to be joking?!"

▼

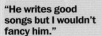
"He writes good songs but I wouldn't fancy him."

Cheryl Baker on…

▼

"I like him. I think he looked a bit odd at first with his slicked-back hair but I've got used to it now. When he sings he always looks like he's enjoying it, whereas with the other one it looks like he's singing through a sneer. Curt's quite handsome."

▼

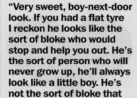
"Very sweet, boy-next-door look. If you had a flat tyre I reckon he looks like the sort of bloke who would stop and help you out. He's the sort of person who will never grow up, he'll always look like a little boy. He's not the sort of bloke that I'd fancy."

▼

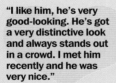
"I like him, he's very good-looking. He's got a very distinctive look and always stands out in a crowd. I met him recently and he was very nice."

▼

"I prefer him now in the Style Council, I like his music better. I think he's good-looking. He reminds me of the sort of blokes I used to go around with in my skinhead days."

▼

"Very, very manly face. He reminds me a little of Tony Hadley as he's got a very masculine face as well. I can see him in a film like *Superman* going up, up and away. He's very handsome but not my cup of tea."

Jill, Strawberry Switchblade on…

▼

"He's quite nice. He's got four cats and I like people who've got cats. Quite attractive, I'd say."

▼

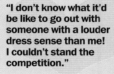
"Pretty good-looking. He looks like a schoolboy. I like him 'cos he's quite charming in a cheeky way."

▼

"I don't know what it'd be like to go out with someone with a louder dress sense than me! I couldn't stand the competition."

▼

"I like him, I think he's attractive. I don't think men have to be big and butch to be attractive. He's a socialist, which enhances his appeal. I agree with his politics. I also like his new haircut; it looks good sticking up."

▼

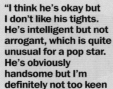
"I think he's okay but I don't like his tights. He's intelligent but not arrogant, which is quite unusual for a pop star. He's obviously handsome but I'm definitely not too keen on those tights of his."

Our Stars' Choices

Curt ♥ Jamie Lee Curtis

"I think she's very attractive. She is very striking and has got the most amazing body – Not that I've looked."

Nick ♥ Cybill Shepherd

"Cybill Shepherd was great in *Heartbreak* and *Taxi Driver*. I just like everything about her."

Paul King ♥ Jessica Lange

"She's definitely on my mind quite a lot. Unfortunately she's married and has got a baby."

Paul Weller ♥ "Nobody"

Martin ♥ Katharine Hepburn

"She has great cheekbones and a sense of authority. I like power."

Toyah ♥ Paul Young

"I just love tall men, and he's got wonderful legs. I like men to look like men – I go for natural sex appeal. Paul Young looks very rugged. But only to look at."

Samantha ♥ Owen Paul

"He's just signed to CBS Records. He's got a cracking little figure. He looks to me like a young Bruce Springsteen."

Kim ♥ Christophe Lambert

"For obvious reasons."

DC Lee ♥ Paul Weller

"I like a man who likes a good drink, so it's got to be Paul Weller."

Alannah ♥ Sam Shepard

"But Nile Rodgers has offered me a lot of cash to say he's best!"

Cheryl ♥ Harrison Ford

"He's got such a lovely mouth and teeth. A great face and a very cheeky grin. His sense of humour always comes across in the parts he plays. He's definitely my ideal man."

Jill ♥ Morrissey

"He's not too good-looking, not too ugly and not likely to ask me out – that's my ideal man."

"We Barbeque Our Neighbours' Bodies!"

Goodness gracious! Can that really be what Five Star told Chris Heath? And we always thought they were such nice people…

IT'S JUST A normal day for Five Star: up at seven in the morning, make-up on, Lorraine helps their mum make a packed lunch, the five of them pile into a car with their father Buster and head off to a south London video studio, a-munching Jaffa Cakes and cheese sandwiches on the way (groo!). Then they spend the rest of the day – until two o'clock the next morning in fact – making a video for their latest single "The Slightest Touch". Nothing too strange about *that*, is there?

So! If Delroy and Lorraine are having a dressing-room chat, it's a fair bet they'll be talking about "normal" Five Star conversation topics – music, useless TV programmes, carp fishing, etc. Let's just have a listen…

"We used to have a string across the garden with a big knife at the end, and if you touched the string the knife would go straight through your head."

Yeauucchhh! *Surely* this can't be that nice Delroy Pearson talking????

"You know what we used to do? We used to play out in the street and we used to put cotton across the road, and whoever ran into it got their eyes and their head cut off."

Bleugggghhh! And surely *that* can't be the nice Lorraine Pearson? Except – it is!

"We had a minefield."

"If you ran through it you got blown up."

What, pray, happens when you get blown up? Delroy looks at me as if I'm stark raving bonkers and have never *seen* a Sunday-afternoon film with a minefield in it.

"You're dead!" he explains impatiently. "You're in the air and in pieces all over the garden."

Urrrghhh! Can't be very nice for the neighbours to have bits of bodies flying over from next door, can it?

"We have a brick wall up," explains Lorraine practically, "so it just splats against the wall. We clean it up afterwards."

Oh. That's alright then.

"Anyway," continues Delroy, "we invite the neighbours over for a barbeque and say, 'Lets have a race down the garden.' They all run and then they get blown up."

"And we barbeque the bodies," adds Lorraine tastefully.

Taste nice, do they?

"Yeah."

"They're not *bad*," says Delroy, clearly a man with a more discerning palate than his sister.

"The one up the road, Isabel, didn't taste very nice, did she?" says Lorraine, reconsidering. "She was a bit stringy."

"And George," she adds, "he was a nice person. It was quite sad when I ate him."

"Agatha," says Delroy, "was just a big mistake. She came running over one day because she was so happy with Five Star and ran straight through the mines. We didn't have time to warn her."

Poor Agatha. So did they feel bad about it?

"We pickled her eyes ha ha ha ha!" laughs Delroy (presumably this means 'no'). They're in a jar in the cellar."

Next to?

"Just a few fingernails," chuckles Lorraine nonchalantly. "We pull them out of people while they're still alive. We paint them and put them on a wall."

DEAR ME. THIS is going to be an interesting day. Already a few things are becoming obvious: a) that Five Star have got a stronger sense of humour than most people might suspect, b) that eating Jaffa Cakes and cheese sandwiches in the morning makes you go a bit squiffy in the head, c) it's probably not a very good idea to accept invitations chez Five Star. It's also quickly obvious that Delroy and Lorraine certainly don't think they should be talking about decapitation, neighbour mutilation, bottled eyes, etc – for the rest of the day they seem quite embarrassed by how carried away they got and instead concentrate on the video.

The story – such as it is – revolves around Deniece. She, along with the rest of Five Star, just happen to be in a fruit 'n' veg market (hence the £55 worth of fruit 'n' veg that one of the video workers had to buy at four o'clock that morning). Deniece prances round, looking very fond of herself, then picks up an old man's leaflet about how science can help improve you and goes to him for treatment from a spook machine (actually an 'mazing spark-generating globe) while the others laugh at her. And then… well, er, that's about it really. As Lorraine succinctly puts it, "it's just basically a lot of fun and dancing".

Five Star are one of the few groups in the universe who claim actually to *like* making videos and they therefore stay in good spirits for most of the 14 hours they're on location today. When they can, however, they retreat to the dressing room and Mrs Pearson's packed lunch; when they can't, they clown about on the set. Deniece runs around feeling people's hands (she wants to know who has the hottest) and throttling Stedman. Stedman practises his tapdancing, cracks his knuckles (*not* v. nice) and wonders whether she should take one of the large white pillars home. Lorraine demands a chocolate chip ice cream (she doesn't get one). Doris blows a raspberry at the *Smash Hits* "reporter" (the cheek of it!) and Delroy stands around loooking much older and thinner than he did a few months ago, as Lorraine is only too happy to point out.

"I just turned round one day," she laughs, "and said, 'Delroy!

Lorraine

Deniece

Stedman

Tim Bauer

You've got skinny!' He started looking good in his clothes."

Hmmmm. So how, pray, did he look *before*?

"He was fat!" she exclaims. "Don't you remember him being fat? He was *so* big."

Charming. The conversation inevitably moves on to food, clearly a pet topic of Lorraine's.

"I've been on a diet and lost nine pounds," she boasts proudly, before ruining things by explaining her rather suspect diet. "Every day when I wake up I have a cup of tea and biscuits and in the afternoon I'll have a cake or sandwich. In the evening while my mum's cooking dinner I just eat sweets and biscuits until dinner's ready. And then I always have a bowl of Ready Brek before I go to bed at night." Apparently it "keeps your bed warm".

This may all sound a bit odd but Five Star are, it turns out, *horrified* by other people's eating habits, especially their breakfast ones.

"Lots of English people have cereal in the morning, don't they?" says Delroy, looking a mite disgusted at the thought. Though he has "nothing", Doris joins in with "biscuits" and Deniece in particular goes straight for the sweets. "Sometimes," giggles Lorraine, "we open a jar of chocolate eclairs and then go and play a game like tennis." Or, like this morning, pig themselves on Jaffa Cakes.

But weren't they on the cover of *Fitness* magazine only a few months back, giving some sensible advice about keeping fit 'n' fresh the Five Star way? What happened? "Oh yes," says Lorraine with pride, "those were healthy hints."

Er, yes, but Jaffa Cakes for breakfast?

"Well," says Lorraine, clearly foxed, " I *do* drink a lot of water and I have an apple every day." Which might have got her off the "hook" if she didn't admit seconds later that she actually places sweet supplies in strategic places "all round the house" so that whenever the urge takes her she "can just quickly take one".

Apparently, these bad habits have only really taken hold since they moved into their posh new home. ("A palace?" says Delory. "Well, it looks like one.") It's here that they record demos, rehearse, watch the swimming pool being built, peer through the windows at the two gardeners tending the flowerbeds, and feel glad they never have to go to discos or anything.

"We have our own disco in the house," explains Delroy.

"We play Sam Cooke music," laughs Lorraine, "and sit round eating chocolate eclairs."

It's here they sit looking at their posh cars and feeling glad they'll never have to go on a bus ever again...

"I don't miss public transport," says Delroy incredulously. "I prefer to take the Mercedes (*his*

car, which he'll start driving if he passes his test in a few weeks*). It's easier. I don't think it's very big to tell you the truth. There *are* bigger, and the bigger the better I'd have thought."

It's here also that Delroy can go and stare in the fishpond while he moans about having missed the fishing season. "It's not something I do a lot," he says, "just once in a while. When did I last catch a carp? Ha ha ha. Last year, in the summer." The pond is well stocked with carpish things – "all different types of carp, a few goldfish, a few tench" – all transferred from their old house in dustbins. "We just put them in the removal truck."

AND SO THE day ticks on as they whirl and they twirl again and again (the "Slightest Touch" dance routine took them, you will be disgusted to know, just one-and-a-half hours to learn).

They chat to an 11-year-old fan called Gary whom the fan club have invited along as an extra ("I fancy Doris," he says breezily to anyone who'll listen. "Too old? She's only 20!"). Delroy even starts cracking "jokes". When he spots the *Smash Hits* journalist taking notes he shouts, "Show us your short hand!" Apparently, waving a pad in his direction isn't the right response.

"Your supposed to go like *this*," he explains, holding one of his hands very close to his body (*short* hand, geddit, har har har). Oh well. At least they aren't talking about grisly murders any more.

"Why don't we saw his head off..."

Uh-oh, spoke too soon.

"...and burn his eyeballs out." Lorraine looks chuffed by the nastiness of her suggestion.

"He'll have to wait till tomorrow," says Delroy sinisterly, "if he wants my bazooka. I'll aim for the heart..."

For the heart???? I think it may be time to slip out quietly.

Five Star: going back to their fruits for the video.

Doris

Delroy

pet shop boys

West Coast Boys:
it's all glowing well
for Chris and Neil
on Sunset Boulevard.

SMASH HITS

Weird Tales From
AMERICA

Snooting around in big black cars with TVs in, being accosted by religious loonies yelling, "Video stars are evil!", getting presented with glass dumb-bells called "Infinity"… As Simon Mills reports from LA, it's all happening to the Pet Shop Boys now they're famous in the USA.

"LOOK! LOOK!… OVER there! Behind that bush!… it's Robert Palmer having a pee!" An English record company person is getting very excited indeed. You see, not only has he been "invited" (ie forked out $150 for a ticket) to the MTV Video Awards and the ensuing after-bash party here in LA (man), he's also managed to spot somebody very famous doing something very, um, "natural". Just wait till the guys in the office back home hear about this.

While poor old Robert fumbles with his trousers, the assembled party turn and search for another pop star to gape at.

"Look! There's one of the Pet Shop Boys," squawks a teenage girl, and dashes off towards Neil Tennant clutching her MTV programme and a pen. She's beaten to it by a middle-aged woman who explains to Neil, "I don't know who you are but could you please sign here otherwise my kids'll kill me."

This rather ignorant lady is the exception rather than the rule – for almost everyone else in America *has* heard of the Pet Shop Boys, and they seem to be especially popular here in California. While she's waiting patiently for her turn, the eager young autograph hunter informs me that, along with "Day-pesh-ay" Mode, "the Pet Shop Boys are the hottest thing in America right now". This is true. Their LP,

"Please", has sold over a million copies and "West End Girls" was a Number 1 hit. They've been asked to write a couple of songs for Steven Spielberg's new film, *InnerSpace*. They might be doing the music for a very famous American soft drink commercial. They've been nominated as Best New Band Of The Year by MTV. And they've been asked to perform live at the prestigious awards ceremony.

"No, you tell him he looks like JR…" The PSBs and that EMI America bigshot.

THE MTV VIDEO Awards is the US equivalent of the BPI Awards, but being America it all operates on a much larger scale. The programme is broadcast live from both The Universal Amphitheatre in Los Angeles and the cavernous Palladium disco in New York. Guests performing live are Robert

Palmer, Whitney Houston, The Monkees, The Hooters (?) and Mr Mister (among others), presenting awards are Huey Lewis and Janet Jackson (who confirms many "Is Jacko Wacko?"-type rumours by announcing the winner of one particular category from the safety of her dressing room instead of on stage). Receiving awards are Dire Straits, Madonna (who walked on to the Palladium stage and said, "Hi, is

this New York? I'm so tired I don't know where I am!") and Robert Palmer, whose video for "Addicted To Love" enjoyed "heavy rotation" on MTV; ie it was on quite a lot.

Unfortunately, the Pet Shop Boys lose the Best New Band Award to A-Ha. Boo! Nevertheless, Chris and Neil do manage to get the all-seated auditorium audience (most of whom are clad in "rock'n'roll attire" as requested on the invite) "whoopin'" and "a-hollerin'" when they perform funky rearranged live versions of "West End Girls" and "Love Comes Quickly". Actually, only Neil sings "live"; Chris just stands there looking extra fab in his bright yellow rubber windcheater and round chrome glasses miming along to the tunes.

Neil's voice is helped along by soulful backing singer Ava Cherry, and ver lads "deliver a tight set",

"Wot, no Bee Gees! It's, um, a *tragedy*." Choosing tunes at radio station KROQ.

as they say, despite the fact that their stage monitors have broken and they can't hear a thing they're doing. Rock'n'roll, eh?

After much autograph signing and socialising at the "exclusive" après-bash party (about a zillion people, none of whom seemed to know each other but all of whom were hoping that Prince or someone would turn up).

The Pet Shop Boys climb into their waiting limousine and begin to make their way to their own little "do" at a private club, where they are to be presented with Platinum albums for one million sales of "Please". But they don't get very far – the journey is soon interrupted by a mob of religious nuts grasping banners that read "Video Stars Are Evil" and "It Is Immoral To Worship These False Gods". Neil takes particular exception to this.

"I felt like getting out of the car and saying, 'Oi! I'm not evil,'" he snaps. But, wisely, he does not get out of the car…

WE FINALLY DO make it to the Pet Shop Boys party, which turns out to be a rather embarrassing, back-slapping music-biz affair, the climax of the evening being a profound but painful speech by the head of EMI America. Dressed in dark tie, dark shirt and dark suit, he takes the stage looking like a baddie from *Dallas*.

"In a very short space of time, Chris and Neil have reached the paramount of achievement in the rock industry," he drones. There follows a well rehearsed, dramatic pause. "It's called Platinum."

Tennant and Lowe then leap on the stage with their roly-poly manager Tom, and both get a shiny record mounted in a

With one million album sales in the USA, it's time for reflection.

"tasteful" frame. They make their respective speeches and leave the stage. Everybody breathes a sigh of relief – that's quite enough yukkiness for one night, thank you. But no – there's more. The EMI bigwig is back, BACK!

"In addition to this," he says even more "sincerely" than before, "on behalf of everyone at EMI I'd like to present Chris and Neil with a special token of our appreciation. Hopefully this object will symbolise the Pet Shop Boys' relationship with EMI… Infinity!" And what does "Infinity" look like? You really want to know? Infinity is a glass dumb-bell! This is all too much, so the boys and their entourage decide to "hit" the dancefloor – well, the edge of it anyway, where the DJ is playing a remixed version of "Opportunities". Chris and Neil are mesmerised. They've never heard their record played in a club before and they stand watching the local groovers sweating away to the complicated metallic rhythms and atmospheric synth noises.

Judging by their delighted reaction, this sort of thing means a lot more to them than their glass dumb-bells. They decide not to venture out on to the floor themselves, though.

"It's a bit naff dancing to your own records," says Neil.

"And anyway," says Chris, "there's no need – I dance to Pet Shop Boys records all the time… in my bedroom."

NEXT DAY WE'RE back at the Mondrian Hotel, Sunset Boulevard, West Hollywood, a beautifully designed "theme" hotel based on a grid and colour block painting by an artist called – you guessed it – Mondrian.

Chris and Neil are spending a half day wandering around the hotel's "lee-shur" (leisure) complex; taking the occasional dip in the pool, relaxing in the jacuzzi or just sitting in the sun. Neil is wearing a pair of tinted John Lennon specs and a pair of cream and red tracksuit trousers designed by Giorgio Armani for the Italian soccer team, and Chris is sitting on top of the poolside cocktail bar dangling his legs over the side like a cheeky school boy.

Dressed in Nike trainers, Nike T-shirt and Nike shorts (all donated by Nike), he could be aged anything from 12-32. If they want to order a drink, a waitresses will bring them a drink, and if they want to call home, someone will bring them a telephone so that they can talk trans-Atlantic by the pool, *à la* JR Ewing. Isn't this all a bit, erm, "flash"?

"In LA, riding around in a limousine is no big deal," says Neil. "For a start it's not very expensive – it costs about the same amount to hire a limousine as it does to hire a couple of taxis, and if there's a lot of people with you, like there often is with us, it makes lot of sense. It's also very nice to ride around in a great big car with a TV in it. The secret is not to call it a 'limo' though, because that shows that you're really into it! We'd also never have a limousine in London, any smelly old mini will do us."

And the bloke from EMI making the speech? "Well, it's very easy to snigger, isn't it? Because you're English the words they use sound funny and all that, but really they're dead sincere. Our record company is dead pleased that we've done so well. They take their jobs really seriously, and if you laugh at what they're saying you're laughing at *them*, really, and we don't want you to do that because we're rather proud of how well we've done in America. It is quite an achievement to sell a million records, don't you think?"

But does he think the Pet Shop Boys could get used to all this and become a boring "rock band"? Neil doesn't think so.

"You see what has happened with all these groups from the New Romantic period? That moody façade just seems to have been a means to an end. Like the Eurythmics and Tears For Fears, for example – they used to be moody synth bands but now they're becoming authentic rock groups. I don't think you'll ever see us going that way. I could never lead that sort of lifestyle," he decides. "I could never live in LA – I see myself spending my later years going mad in an old castle in Italy." (He's got his eye on one at a bargain price of £60,000.)

CRIKEY! HE'S A POP STAR

In '85, the Hits' Assistant Editor Neil Tennant ran off to become a Pet Shop Boy. How odd it was for us to be writing about *him* just a few months later.

AUF WIEDERSEHEN, PET!

At one minute past six on the evening of April 5 1985, the lights went down in Carnaby Street. The flag flying proudly atop the Smash Hits Tower was lowered to half-mast. People in the street wailed and blubbed openly. For why? What was the cause of all this commotion? Choking down a gallon of tears, *Bitz* brings you the awful news that **Neil Tennant**, he of the flowing quill, sabre-toothed wit and 'really happening' shirts, has left *Smash Hits* for pastures new. Yes, it's as bad as that.

We are absolutely *convinced* that you will wish to join us in wishing him well in his new career as one of the most exceedingly talented persons ever to grace the bright firmament of popular music. But put away the hankies girls, for *Bitz* predicts that in a matter of weeks Neil's pop duo The **Pet Shop Boys** will be down the dumper and he'll come crawling back on bended knees hahaha.

In the meantime, we bid a sad 'Adieu!' with this poem especially written for the occasion by the Poet Laureate (or someone like that).

Lines On The Retirement Of Neil Tennant

So!
Farewell then Neil Tennant
You of the ready pen and knowing wink
You of the extended lunch break

No longer shall our hallowed portals
Ring
With cries of
"Sir William Idol
Is the Greatest Living Englishman"
Or
"Tell them I'm in a meeting pur*lease*"

No longer shall our happy office
Purr
With sounds of
Mid-afternoon zuzzing at the desk

Thank goodness for that

PET SHOP BOYS – Chris Lowe and (right) Neil Tennant: they came to rock and roll!

Photo: Eric Watson

Smash HITS
52-55 Carnaby Street
London W1V 1PF
Telephone 01 437 8050

Editorial
Editor: Mark Ellen
Assistant Editor: Neil Tennant
Design Editor: David Bostock
Design: Kimberley Leston, Vici MacDonald
Staff Writer: Tom Hibbert
Staff Writer (Bitz): Peter Martin
Staff Writer (Reviews): Chris Heath
Research Get Smart: Linda Duff
Lyrics: Lisa Anthony
Reception: Samantha Archer

Special thanks this issue:
Ian Cranna, Michael Conway

Opportunities: (from left) the send-off, April 1985; the 1985 Smash Hits masthead a fortnight before Neil's departure; reviews from November 1985 (West End Girls), February 1986 (Love Comes Quickly) and March 1986 (Please).

**PET SHOP BOYS:
West End Girls (Parlophone)**
A tumble through Soho in the seedy wee, wee hours accompanied by the kind of jaundiced horns that are more often found on soundtracks of films about Hollywood actresses hitting the bottle and cracking up with mascara running down their faces (*Valley Of The Dolls* springs to mind). Set against this, the electronic bleats and the demi-rap (Grandmaster Flash And The Furious Five's "The Message" without the baseball bat) create an atmosphere of danceteria sleaze that's almost *sinister*. Brrr.

THE PET SHOP BOYS: Love Comes Quickly (Parlophone)
This has a good chorus and it's *very* catchy – a good follow-up to "West End Girls". I hope they have a crappy looking video again because I liked that – Jonathan King slagged it off as cheap and horrible, the most appalling video ever made, but *I* thought it was simple, straight to the point, and I really liked the moody guy in it. It's funny reviewing a single sung by someone who used to interview us – I *should* be getting my own back. The runner-up single of the fortnight, I suppose.

PET SHOP BOYS: Please (Parlophone) If there's anyone who still needs convincing that "West End Girls" wasn't a one-off fluke then this should do the job. Here the Pet Shop Boys romp through ten thoroughly catchy songs (including the last three singles) all about dark mysterious love affairs and whispered crimes, all crammed with millions of wonderfully tacky atmospheric sound effects. Most of it's the usual rather moody hi-energy but there's also – gasp! – a piano ballad and even *that's* good. Oh dear – it doesn't look as if they'll be able to retire for *ages* yet. **(9 out of 10)**

Chris Heath

"You see," he says, summing up his thoughts, "I see the Pet Shop Boys as one of the last surviving synth duos like Soft Cell."

LATER IN THE day, when the Pet Shop Boys are down at a local radio station, KROQ, Chris chooses Soft Cell's "Say Hello Wave Goodbye" as one of his "classic rock tracks". Others include "Eyes Without A Face" by Sir William Idol, "The Look Of Love" by ABC and "Invisible Sun" by The Police. The DJ, an Englishman called Richard Blade, doesn't have any Bee Gees, much to Chris's disappointment. Then it's time for the "boys" to take some calls from the listeners.

"Hi! This is Stella from San Diego. Can you tell me why you cancelled your tour?" This is a big question with KROQ listeners.

Many of them seem to have bought tickets for the now postponed shows, which were to have taken place later on in the year at a small theatre for five nights in a row. All 10,000 tickets sold out within two hours despite the fact that the group had not given the venue the final go-ahead. Chris explains patiently (for about the millionth time this week) that the dates were cancelled owing to some financial problems which meant that they might end up losing a lot of money but adds not to worry because they would definitely be playing next year.

Stella is thrilled to be talking to the group; she likes Depeche Mode a lot too, but the Pet Shop Boys are her favourite. She thinks it's really great that they have taken the time to come down to

KROQ as a sort of thank you to the station for their early support. "It's nice to talk to some down-to-earth rock stars," she says.

Stella is right. Success hasn't really spoilt the Pet Shop Boys yet. Neil still says things like "tragic" and gets excited when he hears that Sir William "Billy" Idol is staying in a nearby hotel. They both still like pop stars who are "down the dumper", their latest fave being Andrew Ridgeley: Neil recently told a "VJ" (video jockey) that he thought Andrew was much more talented than George Michael. "You know, Neil," said the sincere video person, "you're the first person I've heard say that." And Chris, meanwhile, remains unimpressed with the US sales of "Please".

"When you consider how big America is, a million isn't very

much. I think it's a bit disappointing, really." Well! Best of all, though, the Pet Shop Boys have retained that invaluable British quality, the ability to laugh at themselves.

"Have you seen our fantastic neon sign on Sunset Boulevard?" asks Neil proudly, referring to the very striking fluorescent pink neon words reading "Pet Shop Boys" and "Please" which glimmer brightly high above Sunset Boulevard.

"Well, the other day I was having this meal," he continues, "and the waitress came up and asked, 'Are you the Pet Shop Boys?' So we replied 'yes', expecting her to say something like, 'I think your record's great,' or 'Can I have your autographs?', but instead she turned round and said, 'I just *lurve* your neon sign'!"

Andy Catlin

Oh no! The Editor had flounced off to some so-called "conference", with half an issue still to edit. *Who* could fill his shoes? In desperation, we phoned "Dial-An-Editor". No reply. And then we remembered Neil Tennant – ex-Deputy Editor of *Smash Hits* and now pop "singer" with the Pet Shop Boys. As Chris Heath reports, he was happy to help. For a while…

NEIL TENNANT
Smash Hits Editor for a day!?

10.40: THE EDITOR ARRIVES "FASHIONABLY" LATE…

"I'm *sorry* I'm late," trills Neil Tennant a touch unconvincingly as he breezes through the door. "Though I've always thought it was fashionable to arrive at least ten minutes later than expected." Er, yes, but isn't Neil rather more than just the ten minutes late?

"Howdy!" The Boy is back in town…

"Forty minutes," he says definitely. And incorrectly, as he's *supposed* to have been here at 9.30. "Nine-thirty???" he exclaims, clearly horrified. "I always thought it was ten." Quite. In any case, he continues in defence of his lateness, "They never complain when you stay an hour late, do they?" Indeed they don't.

His "excuse", it turns out, is something to do with the pop music lark that he always used to go on about when he last worked here.

"I was in the studio last night," he says, "until about a quarter to two in the morning finishing off the very wonderful record that the Pet Shop Boys have just made with Dusty Springfield [*rather brilliant ancient '60s singer*]. It's called 'What Have I Done To Deserve This?' I was quite nervous about meeting her because I've liked her since I was young and…" And on he goes, though of course everybody else is *far* too busy to listen, so in the end he shrugs and sets his mind to some hard work…

Neil receives a Fuzzbox picture disc – but is he going to use it?

10.50: OPENING THE MAIL

"*What* is this?" he exclaims, tackling a large brown envelope.

"It" turns out to be a heart-shaped Fuzzbox picture disc. "Lucky" Neil! "I met them at the BPI awards!" he exclaims. "I was talking to that one," he says, pointing to Jo. "I was giving them some fatherly advice about the music industry. I was probably boring them to death. Actually, they were really, really nice…

"Oooh, I *must* stop saying everyone is really nice. They were really *horrible*." That's more like it… "Except," he whispers apologetically, "they were dead nice." Oh.

"*This* looks very boring." Neil has just moved on to a dull brown envelope. "Oh. A Peter Gabriel press release – 'so Peter Gabriel sledgehammers his way into the big time'. What a *good* press release. I think this is for *Bitz*. Or maybe 'Happenings'?" He looks unsure – this editing lark is clearly a tricky business.

Next, Neil discovers the new copy of *Star Hits* – the American

Paul Rider

Only another 25 minutes staring at the "flatplan", Neil, and it will be perfect!

version of *Smash Hits*, with Glass Tiger on the cover (?????). He leafs through the poll results and finds a Sigue "Sigue" Sputnik feature. "We were there when the Sputniks were in Manhattan," he says. "We like the Sputniks. We're going to start an organisation called Save The Sputniks. I think they should get an Arts Council grant. It's *unfair* the way everybody's gone off them."

Finally, Neil gets to an odd-looking package he's been saving. "It's always exciting when you get a bumper pack – it's

always some silly promotional thing," he coos in thrilled anticipation. And he is right – it's a box of truffles that have some tenuous connection with singer Helena Springs. It's also a very spooky coincidence. "Uncannily enough," says Neil, "she is the woman who sings on 'West End Girls'! Actually, we've co-written a song with her for her solo career – it's called 'New Love'."

Meanwhile, the rest of the staff wonder: how much longer can Neil Tennant stay here without doing any *proper* work…?

11.15: COFFEE

A while longer, it seems. An underling is sent out for a coffee from across the road – "large, milk, no sugar" (*45p – a snip (?)*) – and rushes back in with a charming polystyrene cup in his hand. Neil looks aghast. "It *should* be on a tray…"

11.25: TINKERING WITH THE FLATPLAN

The "flatplan" is a very big sheet of paper with all the pages for the

next issue laid out in order. Throughout history when editors have wanted to pretend to be busy they "tinker with the flatplan". Neil Tennant duly does this.

11.55: WRITING CAPTIONS FOR THE BPI AWARDS FEATURE

As the photos are placed on the Editor's desk by an eager designer, a horrified look comes over Neil's face. He has just realised a very significant fact – that his day back in the office isn't a joke at all. He genuinely *is* going to have to do lots of work. "This is for *real*, isn't it?" he gulps. "You all thought, 'What can we do to get someone in to help?'!" Rumbled too late, haw haw!

12.10: A POP STAR PHONES UP

Yes, that's right. Internationally famous megastars from the pop world keep the *Smash Hits* telephone line "a-buzzin'" all day long, as we shall now discover... *Bring! Bring!*

"Hello," chirps Neil. "You want to speak to Ian 'Jocky' Cranna? Yes, I'll put you through. Who's calling? Oh. It's one of the Virgin Prunes! (*Opens door*) Ian! It's a Prune for you!" (???????)

12.50: LUNCHTIME

Smash Hits staff are allowed one hour for lunch but, says Neil, "You can be flexible." And with that he tidies his desk (not a v. complicated operation as he's hardly done any work) and off he shoots!

3.20: ARRIVES BACK FROM LUNCH

"I met a very important video director – let's just call him Zbig – with Chris Lowe at a restaurant in Marylebone Road," Neil announces to the staff (who of course have only been able to pop out for a meagre sandwich as a) they're too busy and b) they only get 50p luncheon vouchers a day – swizz!). "I had mussel soup, scallops with spinach and cheese – en Florentine or something – it was very nice. And two hours and 20 minutes was no longer than I used to have." Quite. And with that Neil starts reminiscing...

"We used to go to this café that we christened the Bomba. I went off it though in the end because I got food poisoning and after that I refused to go back. Do I miss luncheon vouchers? No, not fundamentally, though I *do* miss lunch. It was always a good laugh. I must say, though, that before *Smash Hits*, when I worked for a book publisher, I used to have these very healthy lunches – brown rice from the Indian vegetarian round the corner – and when I came to

Choosing pictures: it's blimmin' hard work, you know.

Smash Hits it was sausage, beans and chips with rum baba afterwards, which was the start of my downfall. After I left I got healthier but I've got unhealthy again. I'm trying to start jogging regularly again."

3.20: WRITES *CONTENTS* PAGES

"Oh no," says Neil, when he realises the dreadful task in front of him. Every single fortnight someone has to think of something witty and amusing to put after *Star Teaser*, *RSVP* and *Crossword*. "It's not much fun." Soon, though, he gets down to business, stopping only to ask some perfectly reasonable questions: "*Who* is Greedy

Smith? It's not Frankie Goes To Hollywood to hell and *back*, is it? Shall we put 'To hell and staying there!' ha ha ha? Do I *have* to put 'killed the cat' after Curiosity? *Who* are The Jets? How do you spell 'genuinely'?"... Then he's interrupted by "journalist" William Shaw, who asks timidly "Can I have The Jets article?"

"I *suppose* so," says Neil *very* snootily and hands it over. From then on his concentration begins to wander. First he notices a Sex Pistols book on the bookshelf. "That's *mine*!" he exclaims. Next he starts criticising the office equipment – "I thought you might have got some new typewriters in the last two years," he moans. Then he decides the staff need

"Jocky? There's a Prune on the line for you..."

some "encouraging" words from the "editor"...

"I'm coming out in a moment," he shouts from his office, "to see what you're up to. It seems to me that you're all wasting lots of time wandering around the office chatting." The ruddy cheek of it! As a "subtle" distraction someone persuades him to reminisce again, this time about his personal contribution to *Smash Hits*...

"The main thing I invented," he laughs, "the last one in fact, was 'They're back, Back! *BACK*!' in July '85. 'Tragic' is another one, and '*pur*-lease', though they're not used so much any more. Having sexy things in was also something I started, being an essentially erotic personality (????) It never used to have *any* sex in it."

And with that he types the last few words of *Contents* and whips his "masterpiece" out of the typewriter. "Well, that's *that* polished off. I don't know what you all make such a fuss about."

4.10: SENDS UNDERLING OUT TO CRANKS (SWANKY HEALTHFOOD PLACE) FOR BANANA CAKE, AS HE'S FEELING PECKISH

"It's nearly an hour since lunch," explains Neil, "so I'm feeling peckish." And so he sends out an underling, just like in the old days, to get him a healthy after-lunch "snack".

Unfortunately when he unwraps it...

"*This* isn't banana cake!" he screams.

Er, yes it *is*, insists the poor "underling".

"*Why* then," says Neil, in his familiar 'I'm right, matey' voice, "has it got *dates* in it?" He does seem to have a point. Luckily he says, "As it happens I like dates anyway." Phew! To make up for such a clottish mistake, the underling scampers off to make a mug of tea. A bad idea, as it turns out...

"Are *all* the mugs round her of Sarah and Andrew?" screams Neil. "You *know* I don't like the Royal Family. Don't you think she looks like Miss Piggy? *Devastatingly* like her?" Suddenly Neil remembers that his mother – a keen royalist – reads *Smash Hits*. "Oh, no. She'll be very upset."

Paul Rider

Neil struggles to reacquaint himself with a typewriter.

hand, the party in the room afterwards, going in the swimming pool, signing the autographs, wrecking the mini-bar… The only thing I don't like the idea of is being on the stage and having to sing for rather a long time. I think one of the biggest mistakes we ever made was performing live at the MTV Awards. It would have been much better if they'd never seen us and thought we were an amazingly enigmatic creative band from England instead of two total wallies who can't 'cut it' live…"

5.50: A PHONE CALL REMINDS NEIL HE'S ACTUALLY A FAMOUS POP STAR

Suddenly Neil's reflections are interrupted by the phone ringing. Apparently it's EMI Records. "Oh my – silly me," says Neil down the phone, already packing his things away. "I forgot I was a pop star… We've got some tracks to lay down? OK. But I'll just have to finish sorting things out first, because, frankly, everything's a bit of a mess here since I've left. I came here just as a bit of a joke but as it turns out I'm having to do some pretty hard work just so they have a half-decent issue." The cheek! Still, Neil very kindly stays and helps finish off the issue. At the end he sighs wearily.

"It's been hard work – I'd forgotten what hard work it is," he puffs. "Especially the really difficult things like trying to write something funny in *Contents* for *RSVP* or *Star Teaser*. I've enjoyed it but, yes, it *is* more fun being a pop star. You get paid more – at *Smash Hits* you get paid absolutely *nothing* – and you can get up later. Pop stars don't really get a long lunch hour," he says, trying to think of a drawback, "but then that's because all day is lunch for them." Huruummmphhh…

"But then again, as a journalist you don't have to work until two in the morning as often, and I do miss working in an office. Some people hate offices but I like all the gossip, the trying to get paid more money and the jokes. So I've really quite enjoyed today. Particularly the banana cake. Even though it *was* date slice…"

4.20: LISTENS TO HALF MAN HALF BISCUIT LP

Neil wanders over to the not v. swanky office record player to do his album review. Unfortunately once he gets there he spots – among the disgusting mound of sleeveless records, mostly by **Black Type**'s favourite, Red Box – a couple of things he'd rather hear. First he "spins" "Shades" by Iggy Pop – "practically the best record ever made," he claims – and then plays Boy George's new single, the first time he's heard it. After the first minute he declares, "Not very good, is it?" but after he's played it a couple more times he's changed his mind and decides "it is rather good after all". What, though, about "Ver Biscuits"? After a while he decides he'll have to "take it home over the weekend for more serious consideration".

What a toff.

Another coffee break – and that disappointingly banana-free cake.

5.25: DECIDES HE'S BEEN WORKING TOO HARD AND STARTS REMINISCING SOME MORE ABOUT THE "GOOD OLD DAYS"

"The thing I most regret writing," he says in the tone of an older and wiser man, "is my Bardo review". This was when he announced that Bardo – useless British entrants for the 1983

Eurovision Song Contest – were absolutely *guaranteed* a great musical future. They have never been heard of since. He also starts chatting about how scared he used to be: "It was much more nerve-wracking interviewing someone like Annie Lennox, who you've heard is difficult, than appearing on some massive television show in front of 20 million people." This, he explains, is something that his pop combo – called the Pet Shop Boys, he says – do rather frequently. At the moment, though, they're finishing off their second album and thinking about doing their long-promised world tour, though just at the moment "we all seem to have gone off the idea".

"I can't see the point really," he explains. His attitude is the exact opposite of most pop stars. "I quite like the idea of being on the coach, having the meal before-

Sylvia Patterson takes notes as the Beastie Boys go to Brighton, don't blow up a single deckchair and decide…

"HEY! YO! THIS IS MY GOD DAMN KINDA PLACE, MAN!!"

Mike D (left) and MCA pose as Ad-Rock tries to get the sound of a disgruntled taxi driver out of his head.

THE TAXI "TIFFS"!

"YO! LOOK AT *that*, man! Quick! You gotta get a picture of that – that's the *coolest*! Hey! Quick! Ho!!" Mike D and Ad-Rock of the Beastie Boys are in the back of a taxi trundling along the Brighton "seafront" and they are mightily impressed. Mike pokes at Ad-Rock to take a photo of everything in sight while Ad-Rock seems more content to hang out of the window whistling the loudest whistle ever peeped. But the taxi driver is not so impressed and pulls his taxi into the kerb.

"I can't drive properly with you carrying on like that," he grimbles.

"Uh… you *can't*?" pipes a bemused Mike.

"No, I can't. I suggest you put the window up."

"Aw, but he just wants to take some pictures of the sights, y'know? We're just laughin', y'know?" pleads Mike.

"I suggest," the taxi driver repeats even more grimly, "you put… the… window… UP."

"Hey!" snips a well-miffed Ad-Rock. "You don't have to tell me twice – I understood the first time. Don't worry about it, I won't scream, I promise."

"What you do on *stage*," snorts the driver, "is your business. What you do in my taxi, is *mine*."

"Jeez," whispers a subdued Ad-Rock, "we're gonna come back and hang out in this town…"

"Pthpthttpth!" splutters Mike, much amused by this, and thus commences several minutes of not-very-stifled sniggerings.

"Hey!" shrieks Mike all of a sudden, ignoring the stony glare of the driver, "there's a rock shop! Is that all the Brighton candy rock? That's so *coooool*. Hey, y'know this is *my* kinda town. You ever been to Coney Island in Brooklyn? Well, it's just like this – a wild, crazy place! Y'know… when I get old and retire from life I'm gonna be a bartender on Coney Island. And I'll get myself a little apartment facing the sea even though it's cold all year round. Well, I suppose it gets hot in summer. Uh…" (??)

Ad-Rock, on the other hand, has other things on his "mind".

"Did you see any girls back at the venue with big tits?"

Aherm, can't say I noticed, actually (*blush*).

"I haven't seen *one* girl with *big big* tits in Brighton. Or big *big* fat asses… or… uh, oh sorry, I'll shut up now…"

"Hey! *Ya*!! Bus stop comin' up," booms Mike. "Bus stop with girls hanging on them, and you know what they say about *them*!" (?)

"Hey baby!" gurgles Ad-Rock, hanging not-very-appealingly out of the windows to address two bewildered foxtresses. "Wanna hang out with some *real* men? Y'know I'm gonna be 21 soon, so I really *will* be a *real* man!" he continues more realistically, "and my birthday's on Halloween, which means I'm a wizard with a big funny pointy hat."

"I got my beard comin' in!" announces Mike proudly. "I *really* think I'm gonna start shaving soon!"

"Michael!" gasps Ad-Rock, putting his arm around him, "you are a 21-year-old *man*! You're *of age*, bitch! You're an *of-age* bitch, Mike! And you're the most handsome one in the band. I, of course, am the most… hunky, though. Macho."

"Hmmm," ponders Mike, "you're the most loveable and I'm the most *debonair*."

"I'm *manly*," decides Ad-Rock. "I think you know what I'm saying here, right? I've got a rocket between my legs."

"Golf!" shrieks Mike, thankfully, spotting a distant golf course.

"SHSHSHSHSHSH!" hisses Ad-Rock even more loudly, pointing at the smouldering driver and giggling like a lunatic.

"But it's *golf*, man!" continues Mike – not for one second having this "great" discovery dampened. "Aw, man! I could really play a

Words: Sylvia Patterson. Photos: Paul Rider, Rex Features

"C'MON, THIS IS *cooool*!" flaps MCA leaping into the seat of one of the rides.

"I am *not* goin' on that ride, man!" protests Ad-Rock. "No *way*. I'll throw up, man, I will *throw up*!"

"Aw, you're soft, man, soft!" jeers MCA, as the others join in a general attack on Ad-Rock's "manly" character.

"OK! I'm soft! Soft, soft, *soft*! I still ain't ridin' on that thing!"

The Super Twister begins to twist and the various faces on "board" begin to look as if Ad-Rock had the right idea all the along.

"I'll tell you," he sighs, weedily watching the others, "I went on a roller-coaster when I was nine and I was *real* sick. I mean *sick*. I ate 16 Zepilese [*pieces of fried dough – bleee*] and then threw up all over the ride and everybody on it. It went right round three times like this [*swirls hands all over the place*] and that was *it*.

"And in my neighbourhood there's this thing every year called The San Anthony Feast and you get sausages and sugar stuff and there's all balloon races and a ferris wheel and rides like this and it's right outside the school for three blocks and... well, I threw up all *over* those three blocks. I once went on Space Mountain in Disneyland and I threw up on that too. I tell you, you don't *want* me on those things, man! In fact, I'll go on the ladybug ride... I'm getting sick watching that thing..."

"Maaaaaan, that was the *best* ride!" gasps Mike while fumbling off the Twister, dropping his money all over the place and looking mightily green around the 'gills'. "We gotta do that one more time!"

"Do you *mind*?" sniffs a women's voice from a pay-booth, none-too-chuffed that MCA has now seated himself, rather happily, on a ladybird. "That's for children – not *you*. You're *too* big!"

"OK!" he grins, whisking himself off the ladybird seat, "sorry, maaaaan!"

game of golf *right now*! I only ever played it twice before but I *love* it. Aw, yo man! Hey! This is my god-damn kinda place!"

Does your mother play golf?

"Uh... naaah, she doesn't do any of that fool stuff."

"She plays stick-ball!" retorts Ad-Rock, who's obviously "in the know" on such topics.

"Stick-ball?" quizzles Mike. "Y'know, you're absolutely *right*. She does play stick-ball and she's in a league! Hey! Aw yo! Yeah! Look at that cliff, man! It's like the time we went to Niagra Falls!"

"Y'know , Molly can't say the word Niagra," mumbles Ad-Rock of his girlfriend Molly (*as in Molly Ringwald, the actress, fact fans*). "She says 'Nagra'. That's cute, though."

Aw! And on and on they burble about how "the sea is a great dividing force" and on about their "crazy, delinquent but *very* intelligent" pals back home... and on about how we're really in Holland because they've spotted a windmill and on about how we are, in fact, completely lost.

"Aw, I knew it..." sighs Mike. "It was when *he* [*huffed taxi driver*] stopped to reprimand us – we didn't follow the others. We've messed up..."

But! With a quick swirl and a screech in the opposite direction "the others" are spotted hovering by a mini funfair halfway along the "front".

"Hey!" bellows Mike for the billionth time, "they got a choo-choo train!"

"That's the stupidest thing I ever seen!" replies Ad-Rock, obviously more disgusted at Mike's goofiness. "Imagine goin' on a beach an' ridin' on a bunch of *those*. That *sucks*. Aw, I don't think I wanna lay down on those god-damn rocks, man!" he continues, obviously unimpressed with Brighton's pebble beach.

Out of the car we jaunt, to be met by the scruffified MCA, the "tour photographer" Ricky and The Other Beefy Minder.

MCA gets the bug at Brighton's beachfront fair.

"Hey!" shrills Ad-Rock as he begins "dancing" to a not-very-good heavy metal "tune" thrusking in the background. "AC/DC! Do you like AC/DC? You gotta! Yeah!" and off he grooves to go and have a look at the children's ladybird train thingie...

Car trouble of a
different kind as
Ad-Rock grapples
with the steering…

6 THE SCOFFING OF THE "GOODIES"!

VER BEASTS PURCHASE ice-creams and escape to the beach. "Aw! What's with these rocks, man?" grimbles Ad-Rock The Weed. "Everything's too god-damn hard in this place!"

MCA, however, fearlessly sits on the pebbles to finish his ice-cream. Hmmm. Tell us, Adam, why *do* you all clutch your groins so much on stage?

"Well, it's just something to do… I don't think it symbolises any particular desirableness – it's just sort of… it's to display one's male prowess, as it were."

And why do you think you've become The New Sensation?

"Y'know, I don't think I really know! I guess it's because we don't have the same attitude like most rock'n'roll bands have these days – y'know, a *serious* attitude. We just wanna have a laugh and… well it seems that no one wants to *let* us have that laugh. But we're gonna go right ahead and have that laugh anyway!"

3 THE WEEDINESS OF AD-ROCK!

"THUMPER CARS!" BEAMS Mike, heading to the dodgems. "Hey! I heard that in England you really try to avoid the other cars – is that *true*? In America, you try to *hit* each other. You people are all insane…"

And off they all spring into the cars and try to hit each other – except for Ad-Rock The Weed, of course, who seems to be finding steering something of a strain.

Over the road in a shop two faces are peering out at the antics before them – obviously waiting for some great misdemeanour to take place involving the Beastie Boys. One of the faces is that of the miffed taxi driver, the other a perplexed shopkeeper. "Oooooooooh! They're naughty boys, aren't they?" she wimples. "Well, so the papers say anyway! *You're* not with them, are you?" she gasps at him.

'Me?" he booms, horrified at the thought. "You *must* be joking! I'm only driving 'em…."

Jings!

4 THE GRAPPLING IN THE, AHERM, BALLS!

BACK OVER THE road, a netted playpen thingie filled with balls has been gleefully discovered as one by one ver "Beasts" leap in for a frolic.

"Ahoooooooo!" wimpers Ad-Rock The Weed, leaping straight back out again. "They're hard, man! *Hard!* Jeez, that sucks, man – I thought you said they were soft balls? No way! You can't even bounce on the god-damn stuff!" And he limps off in the distance – much to the glee of the others – muttering, "This whole park sucks, man…" and generally being in a huff.

"Hands up who likes me!" smirms MCA, all of a sudden pretending to be Rik from *The Young Ones*. He is thoroughly ignored. "Hands up who likes MEEEE!" he bawls, finally inciting the "hands on the ground" reaction, which everyone finds hugely hysterical. How extraordinary…

5 THE BIKE PINCHING!

"HEY! YOYOYOYOYOYO!" bellows MCA, spotting an innocent couple on a motorbike. "Hey! Gimme a go! YOOOO!" He sprints off. Seconds later he comes semi-screeching round the corner going the wrong way up a one-way street. "Get outta the god-damn waaaay!" he screams, eventually piffling to a halt in disgust. "It's crap, man!" he concludes. "You call that speed?"

"Hey! Gimme a go!" MCA "borrows" a local's motorbike, then polishes off a "99" (above).

Paul Rider

Rhymin' and skimmin': Ad-Rock gives up as Mike D gets ten "bounces".

THE QUITE-GOOD "GIG'!

GLIMMERING ORANGE lights beam on to the "Gill Pringle Sucks!" banner being displayed proudly by a fan (Gill Pringle being the *Mirror* "reporter" responsible for the "stories" about crippled young persons), while MCA stalks to the front and bawls, "We just been on the dodgems, maaan!"

The excruciating sexist "dancers" do their "thing" in their cage (ie take their clothes off), are joined by Ricky, who does his "famous" "Oh dear, all my clothes have just fallen off!" routine, the gigantic 21ft willy hovers skywards from its box, the seething crowds are doused in Budweiser – which seems much preferable to The Boys than actually drinking it – and most of

all they leap, bound, shriek, holler, bend over double and screeeeam the words of their pop songs like "men" demented. Never before has anything quite so simple, idiotic, definitely embarrassing and certainly different been so *utterly* brilliant.

What an *extraordinary* group…

Is photographer Ricky trying to release the, er, "caged birds"?

THE BEACH JINKS!

AND WITH THAT, MCA's up and stompling down the beach.

"Y'know, my grandfather was Scottish!" he peeples on the way back to the stony-faced taxi driver. "His name was George and he married my grandmother after my real grandfather died. He was the *best*, y'know. He used to stand on the tables with a glass of Scotch in his hand and, even though no one knew what the *hell* he was saying, he'd go, 'It's a braw bricht moonlicht nicht the nicht!' and then he'd take me aside and explain what it all meant and all about the 'bonnie lasses' and all that…"

…and so on for several thousand decades…

"…And I'll tell you the *best* thing about George, and that was that he laughed a lot, y'know? He was a laugher and every time there was a family party or somethin' we'd always be in the corner together laughing. Hey, maybe I'll follow in his footsteps and when I'm old I'll be getting up on the tables and rappin', 'When I was young I was no good!' Ha haaah! Aw, he just died a year back too, which was too bad – real sad for me. Oh George, you were the best…"

Oh dearie me (blub!).

THE WHISTLING OF THE FANS!

OUTSIDE THE BRIGHTON Conference Centre, one hundred million be-capped, be-T-shirted, be-Budweiser-in-handed, be-whistle-in-gobbed (?) Beastie Boys fans are blooooowing those whistles! Brandishing those cans! Shrieking obscenities as their "heroes" zwing back into the venue. There, ver "Beasts" transform themselves into the most monumentally sexist, beer-flinging, foul-mouthed hoodlums in the history of popular legend.

The referees convention gets into full swing…

Onstage, Mike D spots the angry owner of a badge-less VW enter the hall…

THE MARGARET THATCHER INTERVIEW!!!?

Come with Tom Hibbert, why don't you, inside the hallowed portals of Number 10 Downing Street, where the so-called "Iron Lady" awaits your "pleasure"…

AS I WALK into the drawing room of Number 10 Downing Street, the figure in the matronly maroon outfit and pearly necklace shoots up from a golden armchair, proffers a hand and enquires in a treacly tone "How *do* you do?"

"Sit down," she urges, a 'radiant' smile playing across her famous features and, hitching up the trouser leggings of my Mr Byrite suit (£19.99 – a snip!), I do as I am told. "Now, dear, would you like something innocuous to drink? Orange juice? Tea? Mineral water?" I plump for the water and she scuttles to the drinks cabinet crying, "It's Malvern Water. British. We only serve *British*." Quite.

Here I am being poured a glass of refreshing mineral water by the steady hand of Margaret Hilda Thatcher, Prime Minister of the universe. It's all *very* peculiar…

So what, might you ask, is Mrs Thatcher doing talking to *Smash Hits*? Simple, really: you see, pop goats, she wants *you*, the youth of the nation, batting on *her* team. Fancy that. So here we are, me, Mrs T and a couple

of "helpers" – a young press officer to lend support on taxing youth-oriented questions, and a bloke with an impressive tape-recording machine to record the conversation for posterity.

I present the PM with a token of your affection – a Black Type tea towel, which she appears to mistake for a Fairy Liquid advert. "Have you seen that Nanette Newman Fairy Liquid advertisement on television?" she asks. "Lovely. *Lovely!*" she proclaims. And then we embark on the interview itself, during which she displays an eagerness to please combined with a skill in evasion (riding roughshod over interjections) that marks her out as the 'professional' she is. Margaret Thatcher is a *serious* politician and she wants your vote…

Who were your heroes and heroines when *you* were growing up?

I think you've got to remember that I was growing up in wartime when things were very, *very* different. And indeed, if you were growing up in wartime you really

do appreciate peace. It was a time when the bomber force went out most nights and the fighters were about and there were battles and you were losing ships – you just imagine if the Falklands had gone on and on and on – so it was a *very* different time.

But then you had to have all kinds of relaxation and I suppose really our heroes in those days… because we had no television, we had radio and everyone listened to Winston Churchill and everyone listened, for example, to JB Priestley give his talks and Arthur Askey and Tommy Handley – all of those great variety things on radio were very much part of our lives.

And then the other great entertainment in my generation, which one day I hope will come back, was to go to the cinema to see a film. And what did we see? Ginger Rogers, Fred Astaire – fantastic! And these great musical films… and all the Western things – but the point I'm making is that those stars meant as much to us, because it was a life that was way beyond anything we ever imagined and we thought

it was very glamorous. But I suppose things turn out to be less glamorous the closer you get: they were jolly hard working, *jolly* hard working. But we looked to them avidly because it was a kind of escapism from the lives that we led – humdrum lives, sometimes very difficult lives…

So was school difficult and humdrum?

Well, we had another school evacuated to us, so we went in the morning and they went in the afternoon, and so it was very different. Things were much more formal in those days. At primary school we were taught in classes of 40 but, my goodness *me*, by the time we were six or seven we all knew how to read and write, and we knew our arithmetic…

Did you get up to any naughty tricks at school?

I *don't* think I was terribly naughty. I liked the work, I did a certain amount of sport, I tended to be rather serious because they were serious times in which we were living. I was the youngest of the

Paul Rider

Mrs T, ready for *Smash Hits'* Prime Minister's Questions.

family and I very much enjoyed listening to serious discussions – *very* much – and therefore I was thought to be rather a serious child. But it was because I was passionately interested in many of those things – I was interested in debating societies and I was interested in all kinds of things.

I think sometimes, you know, parents try to give their children the things they didn't have. My father left school at the age of 13, and therefore was quite determined that I should have a very good education. My father hadn't had it so he tried to give it to me – *very* much – therefore I did not have a great deal of parties or pleasure. So when I was bringing up my children I wanted them to have more fun times. They were taught to sail. They were taught nearly all of the sports and they had, I hope, a little bit more fun.

Each generation rebels and then only when you become a parent do you realise the wisdom of some of the things your parents were saying.

Did your children rebel? Did Mark grow his hair long?
No. No, he didn't grow his hair long, but he liked motor racing, which worried me *enormously*. But Mark went for the motor racing and he also became a very good golfer. We took them away for holidays. We hired a house, I took them away and my husband came down at weekends, so they learned to sail there. We went to the same place every year so that they had a lot of friends.

Friends are the most important thing in life. They really are. I can't emphasise that enough. And people are friends because you have an interest in common – it may be photography, it may be music. Music gives you a lot of friends. Mark was certainly quite interested in music and Carol had very much her own ideas and still does, and she's a journalist. Young people will have their own ideas as to what they want to do and I think it's a mistake to try to persuade them into a direction into which they don't want to go. On the other hand if they want to do terribly glamorous things which aren't going to give them a living, you've got to say, "Now look, dear,

The Tornadoes: "lovely".

don't you think it would be worthwhile taking some training which will give you a much better chance of earning a basic living?"

So would you have been fed up if your children had formed a pop group?
I wouldn't have been at all upset. I know a *number* of people who are very keen on pop music – jazz in my time – so I shouldn't have been upset at all. I'd have been much more concerned if they didn't do anything. I wouldn't have been at all concerned at a pop group because you meet a lot of people and you're often doing something together and Mark did, as a matter of fact, learn the guitar because he wanted an instrument that you could go around with and get people singing.

Was he any good?
Not particularly. But he had quite a musical sense and they all listened – *heaven* knows we had *all* the latest pop records. There were Beatles in our time, you see, and they're just coming back because their songs were tuneful. I remember "Telestar" – *lovely* song. I absolutely *loved* that. The Tornadoes, yes. And we had Dusty Springfield; The Beatles I remember most of all; Lulu; Dusty Springfield, Dusty Springfield… yes, but they had this thing on all day and it became a part of the background…

They didn't play it too loud?
Good Lord, yes! Ha ha ha! Turn that thing down! Of course they did. Of *course* they did. But far better to be interested in that than not to be interested in anything at all.

How do you react to today's left-wing pop acts – The Housemartins, The Style Council, Billy Bragg – who can't wait to get you out of Number 10?
Can't they? Ha ha ha! Well, I remember when I went down to Limehouse Studios once there was a pop group there who I was told I wouldn't get on with at all well and I was absolutely fascinated because they were rehearsing for television and it is a highly professional business. *Highly* professional. Cameras have to come in on certain shots, they use a fantastic amount of energy… and I've watched Elton John, too, who was highly professional – but I'm so sad that he's having this difficulty with his throat. *Highly* professional. I think it has become much, much more professional in the technique you use now. You just had echo chambers in our time but now it's *much* more professional. You've got to use technology. Don't be frightened of it. It's going to bring fantastic opportunities.

Yes, but about these pop groups that want to get Mrs Thatcher out of Number 10…
I don't mind these… most young people rebel and then gradually they become more realistic. It's very much a part of life, really. And when they want to get Mrs Thatcher out of Number 10 – I've usually not *met* most of them. Ha ha ha! And it really is lovely to have a chance to talk to them – and it's nice they know your name, ha ha ha! But, you see, I'm not up to date with pop music at all, though sometimes I'm told what's the latest thing in the charts and I'm fascinated that

Paul Daniels: "unbelievably skilled".

Elton John: "*highly* professional".

Brotherhood Of Man: "really professional".

some of the older things are right up top – things from the '60s. That one, er, "Love A Woman"? "When A Man Loves A Woman"? Yes, that is *marvellous* and do you know why I think that? Because it's not just noise and rhythm – there's a theme to it and there's melody, and also when you're young so many of the things are either about rhythm or they're really about girl loves boy, boy loves girl. That is the perennial theme and that is absolutely lovely. It's a *lovely* song.

What did you think of Live Aid?
I thought it was *marvellous.* I watched some of it on the Wembley thing and it was absolutely terrific. It was the first time that we'd been able to get

a great body of young people not merely interested in something but actually *doing* something for it and loving doing it. And I watched some of that and one group after another came, and they did a marvellous job. They did a *marvellous* job. I think young people do want to give something; they don't only want to take something but to give too – particularly to other youngsters who just don't have a chance. *Please* believe me – our generation was the same. I wanted when I was young to go and work in India because helping people who are not well off or who are poverty-stricken is very good. And let me say this: you can never judge anyone by their appearance ever. Some of the kindest people have the most

Ma and Pa Thatcher at son Mark's marriage to Diane Burgdorf.

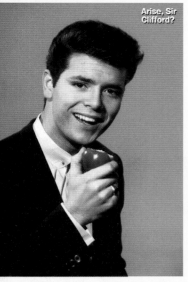
Arise, Sir Clifford?

Adam Faith: "always melodious".

strange appearance. You can't tell their politics by what they look like. You might be able to tell what they've got printed on their T-shirt but not by what they look like.

The Government was widely criticised for not doing enough for Ethiopia and Bob Geldof was rude to you on one occasion…
Was he rude to me? I *met* him. He wasn't *rude* to me. We did talk. Obviously he came up and talked to me about the things that most interested him. But what fascinated me was this: it was not "Why doesn't the Government give more?" but "What can *I* do as a person?" *That* was his approach. And after all, if government took so much away

from young people that they hadn't anything left to give, that wouldn't be much of a life. That would be government substituting their judgement for what people want to do with their own money and that's always been my point.

If you want to take everything away from people in taxes, it's because you don't trust them. Well, I do, and I think they should have some say. Of course we have to have enough for defence, for law and order, for social services, but it's people's earnings and if you left them with nothing with which to give themselves, you'd have a very dull society. And a wrong society. Yes, wrong. Wrong! If government say the money you earn is first mine and I'll decide only what you should have left, I would say that would be… wrong.

What would you say are the worst problems facing young people today? AIDS, unemployment and…
You always wonder what's going to happen to you in the future. I can remember as a teenager some young marrieds I knew… they knew who they'd married, they knew the sort of job they'd got, and it is the tremendous uncertainty and it is both a problem and an excitement and a challenge (*??? – Ed.*).

These days, when it comes to training there are far many more choices than we ever had: we've got the young youth training – YTS – and now we've got another one called Job Training Scheme. There are quite a lot of jobs available for which you can't get people because, in the midst of unemployment, you've got a shortage of people taking the requisite skills. It is problematic when they don't necessarily get the right advice, and that's why I feel that as well as talking to your contemporaries you should have some older people to talk to.

But the future must seem bleak for young people faced with AIDS ads and heroin ads on television?
Yes, I agree. You see, television tells you a lot of things you wouldn't otherwise know but it stops a lot of things because it's

too jolly easy to go home and do your homework and then sit down in front of the television, and the family's sitting down in front of the television and you're not talking to one another.

Television must not be a substitute for doing things you want to do. Alright, it may be going out and belonging to a pop group, it may be that you're keen on going and cheering a football team, it may be that you're keen learning snooker, but do something. Don't just be a spectator. And if families go and do things – they may be interested in model railways – and I think it's marvellous to learn an instrument because music takes you right out of yourself, and we all have gramophones or disc-playing things these days…

Um. Have you ever watched *Spitting Image*?
I did watch one, not with myself, but there were one or two things on about the Royal Family and I didn't like them very much. We are fair game, politicians, but there are certain things I don't like images of and one is the Royal Family, because it is the *monarchy* and I think it's got to be protected. Also I'm told that *Spitting Image* would hurt very much, so I think it's better not to be hurt too much. Like when your youngsters say "I want to get Mrs Thatcher out of Number 10" never having *met* Mrs T.

What do you like on TV?
I adore *Yes, Prime Minister*. It's great fun, isn't it? Sometimes I do watch some of the old films… now, I did watch yesterday one from the First World War called *Dawn Patrol*. It was a very telling film. I just happened to turn on for the news – a Welsh male voice choir – 1000 voices… And I *did* enjoy *Superstore*. I enjoyed it enormously. I didn't know there were things called… TV video? Pop videos? Fantastic!

Paul Daniels I watch. He's fantastic. Marvellous. Really so unbelievably skilled. And the *Eurovision Song Contest*… now we haven't done terribly well recently but when we won we had a group of four and it was a song about a little girl and because

she's only three… Brotherhood Of Man? Lovely! A fantastic young group, really professional and they'd worked out all their actions because in my young day it was Cliff Richard and Adam Faith…

When are you going to knight Cliff Richard?
Cliff Richard has done *wonders*. It was he who got the movement going, really – moving to the music, and Adam Faith came in with a slightly different technique – always melodious and still about… Cliff Richard more than Adam Faith…

So will you put in a word for Sir Clifford?
Always be serious! Alright, ha ha!

You have been called a lot of things in your time, from Margaret Thatcher, Milk Snatcher when you were Education Minister…
Yes, I remember that, too, and it seemed to me one thing that people could purchase – milk for their own children. The important thing is for the state to do things which the state can do but to leave people with money to do things themselves. If people's talents are to develop to their fullest ability, they must have the freedom to do that, so good luck to your pop groups. They do very well for us in exports – they do a fantastic job and if some of them want to have yellow hair, punk hair, short hair, long hair, blue jeans, yellow jeans or, these days, my goodness me we've got some smart ones. Marvellous!

When I go and look at some of the clothes for young people, gosh they are pricey but, really, I think that the sort of informal period has gone. You know, some of the rules are coming back and life is much better when you have rules to live by.

I mean, it's really like playing football, isn't it? If you didn't have any rules, you wouldn't be able to play the game. Of course you'll have the whistle blown sometimes but freedom requires some set of rules to live by to respect other people's freedom, so if we're remembered that way, I think we'll have done a reasonable job for people the world over.

Would you draw a duck, please?

That's what we asked lots of pop stars, so we could see what their doodles revealed about them. Then we got top graphologist Paul Summers to "interpret" the pics – but without telling him who had drawn what...

GEORGE MICHAEL

You can see here the movement strokes of the legs, which means the artist knows they have a large physical presence. It's a baby duck. And that suggests a fear of growing old, of maturing. The duck's mouth is open, which suggests a person who wants to open up and reach out. Also there are no gaps in the duck, so I feel that this is a person who is obsessive about hygiene. I think inside this person there's a very simple character.

JOHN TAYLOR

This looks more like a bee than a duck. I think this person has a close affinity with nature – I can imagine them enjoying camping, but there again it's a very raunchy duck, a very *passionate* duck. There also seems to have been an operation somewhere below the waist. I don't quite know what it is. I feel also that this is a hat person, someone who gets great security from wearing hats. *Look* at that plumage. This is someone who hates people who don't smile. Would they be connected with royalty in any way? I get a very royal feeling from this. Hmmm, I'm getting a strong face here. I feel they like water sports.

TERENCE TRENT D'ARBY

I don't think this person likes ducks very much. I think there is a dislike of animals in general. It's a very esoteric duck – a duck from another planet. If you include water in a duck doodle, that indicates the emotions, and there are very heavy emotions here – there are real waves of water coming up like lava out of a volcano. There's a very strong

mother image in this duck, which may suggest some odd relationship between the artist and their mother. It's a very rebellious and aggressive doodle. Most people draw ducks pointing to the left but this one points to the right, which suggests the artist has a strong ability to visualise images in their head. But it's more like a warship than a duck. It's a battle duck. It's an emotional *tank*. I think what happened here is that the person thought that being asked to draw a duck was a bit stupid. They were

JIM KERR OF SIMPLE MINDS

This duck has four legs. Hmmm. The artist probably hates walking anywhere. It's a very lazy duck. Um, I have feeling that this person got in the music profession by accident, because it seems they can be in the right place at the right time. I feel also that this person might have a weight problem or something – because the duck has a collapsed undercarriage. The legs are detached, which suggests a lack of control – there's a temper coming through. And the space between the legs is ridiculous – that suggests a quirk about time. I suspect this person refuses to wear a watch and is always late. I also feel they may suffer from headaches. There's a certain head tension about this duck.

BEN VOLPELIERE-PIERROT

Oooh dear. This is an *ET* duck. This is a person who is *very* lost with themselves. Notice the rings around the duck's neck – that suggests a rope around the neck, so there's an element of self-pity in this. And the duck is looking up towards the sky – it's a person who hopes to lift themselves out of the position they are in. That neck is a terrible sign. And that is stubble on the duck rather than feathers, so I really feel that if this person wore a paper bag over their head they'd still be able to do what they do. The "qwak" coming out of the beak has no exclamation mark after it, so it's again a drawing that the artist really didn't want to do. They feel it's journalists who have pushed them into a position they don't want to be in.

JANET JACKSON

This is a person who sees people as animals and animals as people. It's a very battered duck and I think it might be a person who feels battered in life. The eyes are very mournful, which shows an almost pathological repression It's very unusual to include the nostrils, the air passages, in a duck doodle – it suggests that the person is feeling claustro-phobic and needs room to breathe. This to me is a very regressed duck, which suggests a desire to get back to childhood. It's going back in time, this duck, almost to a baby, but if you look at it again, it's almost an old man – so there may be some man close to the artist whose health the artist is worried about; it could be a father or a brother.

STAN OF THE HOUSEMARTINS

This person has an android obsession. During childhood they would have enjoyed having little robot toys and watching *Doctor Who* and the Daleks. It's a person who wouldn't join the army, who wouldn't fight for his country. There's a conscious desire here to fight back, an extreme fear of violence. The lips are very enlarged here – and ducks don't even have lips – which suggests this person probably likes kissing. This duck is very symmetrical, which suggest clumsiness. They probably fall over quite a lot.

PHIL COLLINS

A right-hand duck again. Very rare. There is a great desire here to have a baby. It's a person who wants to form a module of themself by creating a new life. This is a person who'd say very little but mean a lot. There's a growing concern about body shape here, and I feel this person may have something wrong with their feet – maybe corns or bunions. There's a really heavy feeling on the feet… It's a person who finds it hard to cry. There may be an interest in aviation as well. There's a desire for flight. Maybe they'll be the next hot-air balloonist.

BOY GEORGE

This duck seems to have a medal, which suggests it's a person who enjoys material rewards and recogni-tion, who wears statements on their clothes. This duck has a very high tail, which is indicative of great pride. There is great energy and presence about the duck – it's a person who's not afraid to speak out. If they do something, they don't feel they have to justify it. There's a great aura around the head too, and I really feel this person is moved by outside forces, spiritual forces, Doris Stokes type things. There's a great belief in karma, a belief in reincarnation. This duck could never die. It's an ongoing duck.

FLUORESCENT HAIRSPRAY AND ZIT CREAM...

...jumbo-sized portable hi-fi systems, punk rock premium-rate phonelines, prehistoric home computers, Prince Charming's calendar and more. All found in the Smash Hits ads of yesteryear.

Have a charmed 1982 with
ADAM and the ANTS™
calendar offer

Great news for Ant People! There are 13 fantastic poster-size (16½" x 11¾") colour pictures in this sensational **1982 OFFICIAL ADAM and the ANTS CALENDAR**. Make a date with the fabulous five each day of the year. Order yours now!

Fill in coupon and send.

£2.99
(inc. P&P & VAT)

Add £1 for each calendar for overseas orders (including Southern Ireland) to: Department Adam, Danilo Promotions Ltd., Bath Street, London EC1. Also available in good record stores.

Delivery within 28 days.
Trade enquiries welcome.

© 1981 MCA Inc. All rights reserved. Adam and the Ants (TM) Trademark of and licensed by MCA Inc.

A12

Name

Address

BLOCK CAPITALS PLEASE   Quantity

Reg. No. 1395823

Department Adam,   Danilo Promotions Ltd.,   Bath Street, London EC1

FIVE EXCLUSIVE COLOUR POSTERS 11½" x 16½" only £2.99 + 76p p&p for 1 or 2, £1.11 3 or more.

DURAN DURAN
FIVE POSTERS

Send away NOW to
DICK WALLIS photography
Duran Duran Offer SS28, PO Box 203, Watford, WD2 4YS.

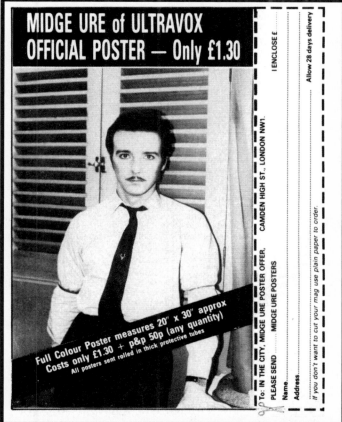

149

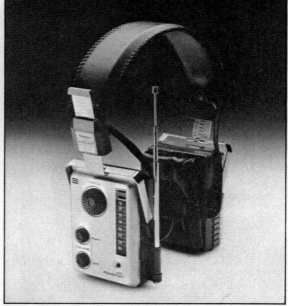
150

THE NEW PIONEER TRANSPORTABLE HI-FI SYSTEM.

The word is out. Something new is happening on and off the streets. A look you've never seen. A sound that the lucky have heard.

The first Transportable stereo Hi-fi System from Pioneer. With technology that makes it more than just a portable. It is everything, in fact, you'd expect of a Pioneer hi-fi.

Features designed for ease of use. Like our one-touch operation and recording with Auto Music Search. And the Pioneer power that'll do wonders for new waves and old faves.

So dust off your jazz slippers. And get on down to your Pioneer dealer now. It's time to dress up with the new street fashion. The Pioneer Transportable Hi-fi System.

It's the sound that's streets ahead.

The unbeatable TI-30 LCD.
You don't become the most popular
in school for nothing.

Popularity has its reasons – whether it's people or calculators.

The TI-30 LCD from Texas Instruments stands out at school like no other calculator does.

And can handle anything you might have to do right up to 'O' level. Without unnecessary gimmicks.

That makes it fool-proof and keeps the price down.

Calculating is dead simple too. Even complicated algebraic problems are put in just the way

they're written – from left to right.

The odd knock on the desk won't damage it either. And you can simply tuck it in your pocket

when you're through.

Try the TI-30 LCD. With so much going for it – including wide approval by teachers everywhere – no wonder it's the most popular calculator in so many schools in so many countries.

TEXAS
INSTRUMENTS
Creating useful products
and services for you.

14

Have you ever wanted green, pink, purple, red, cerise or blue hair for one day or just an evening and have been too frightened to bleach, tint or colour your hair permanently. Well, Jerome Russell Cosmetics Ltd have done it again — their new Ultra Hair Glo washes out of permed, bleached, lightened, tinted and natural hair with complete ease, when desired.

Ultra Hair Glo gives a high degree of fluorescent colour, highlighted by ultra violet lights, as used in discos.

Ultra Hair Glo is terrific for parties, fancy dress, carnivals, dancing schools, etc.

Used sparingly it gives an elegant and subtle effect, used generously it produces a most stunning look.

* ULTRA HAIR GLO IN AN AEROSOL SPRAY. Washes out completely.

* Ultra Hair Glo is available in six vivid fluorescent colours — red, blue, green, pink, purple and cerise.

* Ultra Hair Glo will even cover black hair without the need for bleaching.

This product is manufactured in England.

Jerome Russell Cosmetics Ltd

Ultra Hair Glo Order Form

£2.50 including postage and packing, please allow 28 days for delivery.

Colour	Price	No. of Cans	Total
Red	**2.50**		
Blue	**2.50**		
Green	**2.50**		
Cerise	**2.50**		
Purple	**2.50**		
Pink	**2.50**		
Sub Total			
Total FREE cans (for 5 or more) less **2.50**			
TOTAL			

Please complete, stating number of cans and colours required, DO NOT FORGET to deduct £2.50 per 5 cans.

Name .... Age ....

Address ....

I enclose my cheque/postal order ....

Buy 4 get 1 FREE

Fluorescent Ultra Hair Glo

A new colour craze for hair

10 TO TEENS

Great fashions just for you at Young C&A.

C&A

Where value is always in fashion

Sponsors and supplier British team 1984.

CLOCK HOUSE

RIGHT NOW!

Tie-dye vest. Small, medium, large. £2.99. Ski pants, sizes 8-14. £11.99. Both in 100% cotton. All C&A stores.

C&A

Where value is always in fashion

CLOCK·HOUSE

Paintsplash cotton shirt. S.M.L. £11.99 Capri pants. White, black, pink or grey. Sizes 8-14. £13.50.

TRY·IT·ON!

Check cotton shirt. S.M.L. £11.99. Black stretch canvas ski pants. Sizes 8-14. £14.99.

CLOCK HOUSE

C&A

Where value is always in fashion

All of this.

For the price of this. Only £139.99*

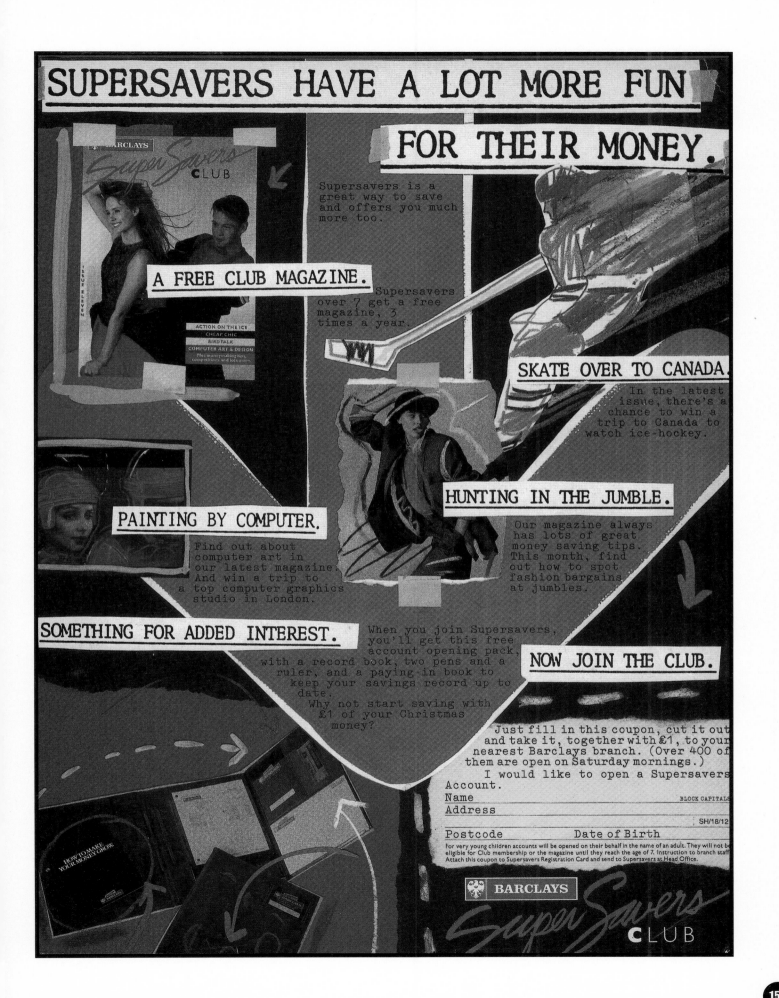

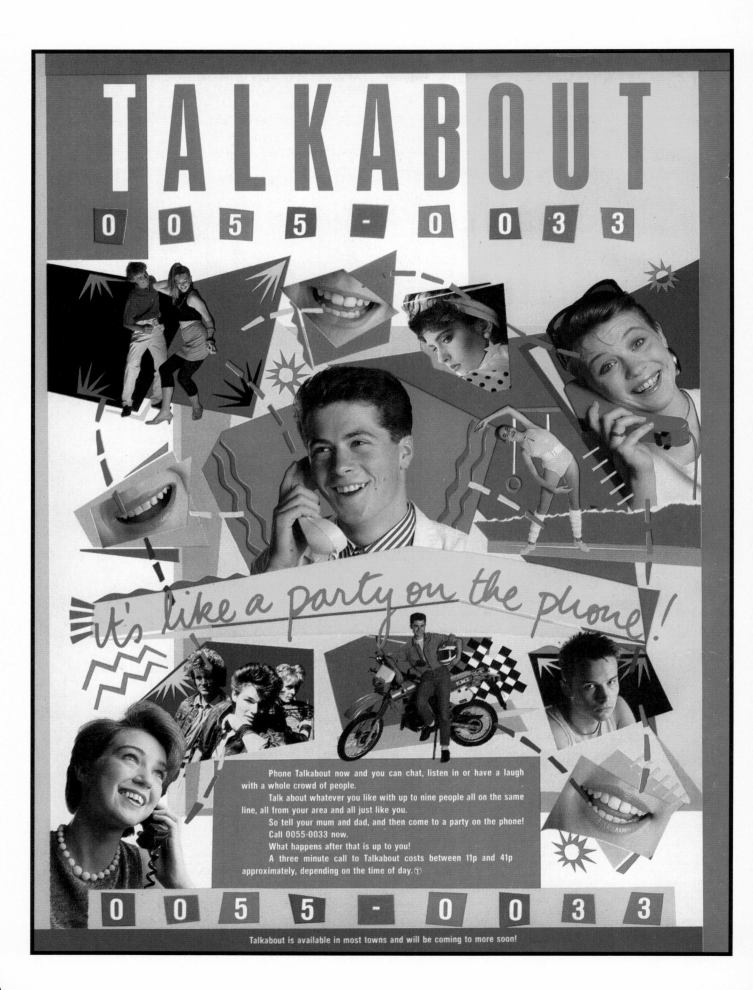

THERE WAS A YOUNG MAN
CALLED TREVOR,
WHO FINANCIALLY WASN'T
TOO CLEVER,
SO HE SAVED WITH 'ON LINE,'
AND IN ALMOST NO TIME,
HE GOT HIMSELF FAR MORE
TOGETHER.

You'll be able to manage your money more effectively with a NatWest On Line account. All you need to open one is a fiver.

Three pounds of that starts you saving. The rest brings you special On Line exclusives like our regular news magazine, packed with pop, fashion, sport and competitions.

You also receive a slimline electronic "continuous memory" calculator in its own stylish wallet.

Just the thing for counting up the cash you'll save with On Line.

TEQUILA London

159

THE NEW ZX SPECTRUM 128
CAN HANDLE HARDER
GAMES. WHETHER YOU CAN
IS A DIFFERENT MATTER.

SLOT A CASSETTE IN AND GET READY FOR A

REAL PASTING. THE NEW SPECTRUM'S 128K

MEMORY WILL SHOW YOU JUST HOW TOUGH IT

IS TO THRASH DALEY THOMPSON AT HIS OWN

GAME. ROUGHLY THREE TIMES AS TOUGH.

OR IT'LL KEEP YOU PINNED TO THE EDGE OF

YOUR SEAT PLAYING A GAME CALLED NEVER

ENDING STORY. IT TAKES THREE TIMES AS

LONG. AND BECAUSE WE WANT YOU TO SEE

JUST HOW BRILL' ITS GRAPHICS ARE, AND

HOW ITS NEW SOUND SYNTHESISER PLAYS

MUSIC AND SPINE CHILLING SOUND EFFECTS,

WE'RE GIVING BOTH TITLES AWAY FREE WHEN

YOU BUY IT. BY THE WAY, THERE ARE

THOUSANDS MORE IF EVER YOU DO BEAT THE

PANTS OFF THOSE TWO.

sinclair

Bros in arms: (from left) Matt Goss, Luke Goss and Craig Logan.

BROS

Paul Rider

THIS IS WHAT YOU DO TO GET ON THE COVER OF SMASH HITS...

It's not just a question of having a huge hit ("When Will I Be Famous?", say) and then standing still for 30 seconds in front of a Woolies Click'n'Presto Happy Snap camera... William Shaw sees Bros prepare for some serious posing.

IT'S 11AM IN south-east London and a black jeep is winding its way at a preposterously fast pace through the traffic to try to make a 12 o'clock appointment in the north of the city. In it are three people who go by the names of Matthew Goss, Luke Goss and Craig Logan, who have showered and spent the morning dressing themselves in readiness for the day ahead. Because, between 12pm when the jeep pulls up at the studio and 4.45pm when they will leave, they'll have around 470 photographs taken of them. Just one of those photos will eventually end up on the cover of *Smash Hits*...

"In the last three months, how many photo sessions have we done?" ponders Matt. "About 20, I reckon. You lose count. But we love the idea of being on magazine covers! We love it! We love it!"

"That's what we're in it for," says Craig. "To be successful."

"This is the first time we've been on the front cover of *Smash Hits*, and this is really doin' it for us," bubbles Luke. "I remember reading *Smash Hits* when I was at school, so now being on the cover of it is really quite weird. It's like being on *Top Of The Pops*."

These days it's all a part of being a pop star, turning up to photo sessions. And to get exactly the right photo for a cover can be a long job.

First comes make-up. When the Bros jeep finally arrives at the studio, they all say their "hullos" to one and all, have a chat with their press officer about the work they've got to do over the next eight days and then disappear, one by one, into the small dressing room where Kate, the make-up woman, awaits with pots of foundation cream, hair gel and powder. Although it might not look like it, by the time a pop star is photographed he is usually covered in layers and layers of make-up, powder and lip gloss.

Kate has to be prepared for anything. For all she knows, a pop star might turn up with the biggest ever spot on his or her nose. "What if they do?" asks Kate. "You just have to hide it by putting on as much make-up as possible." And if they've been out a bit too late last night grooving the night away and come in with bloodshot eyes with massive great bags under them? "Yes, it happens," grins Kate. "Then you have eyedrops – they're a must. You basically have to turn up with everything just in case. It's just a question of making them look as flattering as possible.

"This lot," she adds, indicating the three members of Bros, "I know it sounds really corny – but they're really good. Some pop stars think they know what they want, which can make it really difficult."

Bros already seem perfectly accustomed to being made up. "It's quite relaxing," says Matt. "We don't need much make-up, so it doesn't take very long."

"We don't need that much make-up because we're young," explains Craig.

Paul Rider

165

Making up a pop star takes a while, continues Kate: "If I'm making up a chap it'll take me 20 minutes or half an hour; if it's a girl it'll take an hour."

Which means that it's not till well after one that the photo is taken. Luke has brought his jeep along for the group to be snapped in: it's still his pride and joy. It's a Suzuki Santana and it cost him £7000 last summer; he bought it with the money the record company gave the group when they first got signed. He's already thinking of selling it to buy a Porsche when he gets the money.

He's a bit anxious about the fact that if the jeep's number plate is photographed people will recognise it, so he asks if it can be covered up somehow. A quick phone call to the *Smash Hits* art department and a special "BROS" number plate is on its way by courier to cover the real plate.

Next, the photographer's assistant switches on a wind machine, so that it looks like they're driving along in the jeep and the wind is flowing through their hair. The only problem with this idea is that all three of them have got exceptionally short locks, which don't so much as twitch when the giant fan blows at them. All of a sudden Luke has an "idea". He bounds out of the jeep and attacks the make-up artist, stealing the long grey scarf she's wearing. Before she's had time to protest "Hey, what are you doing?", he's gone and tied it to the aerial, where it flutters in the breeze, making it look like the jeep is zooming along the road.

Now it's time for the session to begin properly (the photographer, Paul, has already been setting up his lighting and cameras for the last three hours). "OK," barks Paul, "Luke, can you lean out of the window a bit more? Stand up a bit, Craig – that's good. Can you grab Matt's jacket? Brilliant!" And the £10,000 worth of camera equipment begins clicking and flashing away furiously.

It's all a bit of a far cry from the first time the three of them had their photo taken as a group. That was when they were 13 and in Luke and Matt's lounge...

"Yeah, with the wallpaper as a backdrop," grins Craig.

This just won't do – they're having a super lark but none of them are looking anywhere *near* the camera...

Luke: "What did it look like? Well, it didn't look too bad at the time, but if anyone found it now I think I'd cry."

"Well, you can't find it," adds Matt. "We burned those photos."

LIKE ALL POP stars, Bros seem to find posing in front of a camera a pretty easy business. "What I do on camera is I just try to relax my face," says Luke. "I don't try and look at the camera."

"We don't really do any of the pouting lips stuff," declares Craig.

"Do we suck our cheeks in?" says Luke. "If we *did* we'd look like skeletons. The thing about having your photo taken is that you gradually learn how to do it."

"You see yourself in one picture and you think, 'Oh God! Shouldn't do that,'" says Matt. "And you learn which is your best side. That's why Craig always wears a paper bag to photo sessions," he adds as a charming afterthought.

So how do they make up their minds what to wear for a photo session like this? "Well," replies Craig, "we've basically only got one set of clothes each..."

Luke: "We always wear 501s, we know that we're all going to wear Doc Martens, so all we've got to decide is the tops to wear."

"I've got loads of T-shirts and stuff, but basically I've got five or six pairs of 501s and two pairs of Docs and I always wear the same," says Matt. "We don't wear sequinned boob tubes or anything."

"We're saving that for the album cover," says Craig.

And what about things like the holes in Matt's trousers? Does he choose pairs specially that have holes in saucy paces, ie his upper thigh? "Ah," answers Matt, "that's an actual hole, worn in genuinely. I don't know how. I'd worry if people could see my underpants through it,

but they can't. Craig," he informs us out of the blue, "doesn't wear underpants. He wears briefs. Bikini briefs."

Meanwhile, Paul the photographer is still snapping bodies into different positions, ordering them to move their arms up a bit, down a bit. Do they mind being bossed around like that?

"Basically," says Matt, "if he tells us to lift up your arm three inches then I worry because Craig doesn't wear deodorant and the result can be quite painful."

Craig looks temporarily aggrieved. "What most people don't realise," says Matt, "is that this is hard work. It's really tiring because there's so much concentration involved."

"It's mental," explains Craig.

"Mental!!!!" they chorus.

And what are the thoughts that pass through their minds as they gaze into the distance while looking dreamy as possible?

Paul Rider

Bros arriving at the studio for the shoot before driving Luke's jeep inside.

Make-up artist Kate slathers the "slap" on Craig...

...before Matt turns the tables!

A courier delivers the bespoke "BROS" number plate – and the shoot can begin.

"We think about our secret language," Craig says. "We think up new words for it."

Now this is a very strange but true fact: the three members of Bros have a secret language of their own. In moments when they don't want other people to understand what they're saying, they utter strange phrases like "Ersh, mersh, nersh" to each other. They explain that they use it to baffle their manager, or to say that they think such and such a woman is good looking, or to decide what time they're all going to leave a certain place without seeming rude. But they refuse to explain the secret of it. Why?

"Because it's a secret," they announce. All that can be deduced is that certain peculiar words represent certain things, or people, or times of day, and by stringing them all together they manage to understand what they're on about. Most odd.

"We invented it about two years ago," they explain, "and we use it all the time now. It's really useful."

Apart from all the photo sessions they've been turning up to, their new-found fame also means that they've been doing billions of interviews all over the place. And they're getting a bit miffed that no one ever seems to get their names right.

"It's simple," says Matt, "Matt's the one who sings, Luke's the one who drums and Craig's the one who plays the bass... Well, *tries* to play the bass."

"I'll master it one day," japes Craig. "And another thing," says Matt. "It's really annoying us some of the things that the newspapers are writing about us. We've got to sort that out. We're *not* gay, we're *not* going out with anyone. These papers are just trying to get us going. Don't believe what you read in the papers. Believe what *Smash Hits* says. We tell the truth to *Smash Hits*. Can you mention this, because we don't want our fans getting the wrong idea about everything?"

IT'S 4.45 AND the very last photograph has been taken. Meanwhile Bros have another appointment to keep with a bloke from Radio One, so they leap back into the jeep, chattering among themselves about some of the pranks they've been getting up to over the last few dizzy weeks.

"Practical jokes?" says Matt. "Yeah, I love them. We were in a hotel the other day and we put itching powder in Craig's bed, so what he did to me was sprayed fart spray in my bedroom and the whole of my floor stunk so badly. In the hotel, me and Mark – our personal manager – pulled Craig out of the room, ripped off his pants and shut the door so he couldn't get back into his room. Mark stuck shaving foam all over him and then called up the hotel porter and said, 'Can you let us back in Craig's room please?' and Craig was standing there in the corner totally naked. So we do joke a bit," Matt finishes.

"God!" blurts Matt as the jeep scuttles through the traffic. "I've just seen the back of an ambulance and now I've got to hold my collar until I see a bird..."

"Or a four-legged animal," interjects Luke.

Matt explains this somewhat baffling chain of events. "It's a Bros superstition. We're really strict with superstitions. That's why we're really successful. We've got loads of them. Like, if you see a magpie on its own you've got to salute it..."

"...and if you drop salt," says Luke as he whizzes his jeep around a bend, "you've got to throw it over your right shoulder."

"...and if you see a dead magpie you've got to spit over your shoulder," adds Matt. "If you pick up a penny you'll have luck, and if you break a mirror you have to break it again and then you'll get seven years good luck."

"Matt did that," Luke says.

"That's because I looked at it," joshes Matt, and with that the jeep finally pulls up at their destination and the three of them bound out. Meanwhile back in the studio, the photographer is packing up his gear and sending 470 photos he's taken off to the processors to be developed.

All that remains now is for the *Smash Hits* Design Editor to choose which is exactly the right one for the cover...

AWWWW... KISSY-KISSY...

Jason Donovan and Kylie Minogue, eh? It's the romance of the millennium, is it not? "Er, no, actually, we're really just good friends," they splutter to Chris "Cupid" Heath…

ROCK'N'ROLL couples – isn't the pop universe just over-flowing with them? There's Madonna and Sean Penn… Carol Decker and Ronnie Rogers… Dave Stewart and Siobhan… Barbra Streisand and Don Johnson… Simon Climie and Rob Fisher (??)… and so on. And now – tara! – it looks as if Kylie Minogue and Jason Donovan have joined this memorable list. Let us look at the impressive evidence:

1. It has been "rumoured" for many aeons that the two of them are in a kiss-up situation and even live together in their native Australia.

2. They've just made a slushy, drippy and utterly romantic duet "Especially For You" (rather brilliant as it happens) all about how "if dreams were wings" they'd fly into each other's arms. Awwww!!

So, can it be true? Have Kylie and Jason truly been skewered by Cupid's arrows? Have they looked at some old tea leaves and seen their destinies inexorably entwined? Er, well, no actually – they won't admit to a ruddy thing.

But are they fibbing? Are they telling the truth? See what you think…

KYLIE MINOGUE IS relaxing back at her hotel preparing for her performance in front of the Queen "Mum" at the Royal Variety Show.

Tim Bauer/Retna, Tim Hall/Redferns

JD ♥ KM...COO-EE!!

She's in slightly fragile spirits, not because the "news"papers keep printing untrue stories about her being horribly snooty and rude and refusing to have anything to do with the *Neighbour*s cast – "The papers don't worry me," she says defiantly – but simply because she's got a wonky throat and speaks in the sort of quiet, crackling voice you hear when you record something off the radio and your cassette player isn't working and the radio wasn't tuned in properly anyway. Nevertheless, even *that* isn't enough to prevent her bravely answering a few queries. For instance – the question that's on everybody's lips – if *your* dreams were wings, would you fly to Jason?

"Oh yeah," she chuckles nervously. "I'd fly over and have dinner with him or something."

Hmmmm. This doesn't sound like someone who is about to confess to any great kiss-up, does it? Isn't making this record together supposed to be the two of you coming into the open about your so-called "romance"?

"Well, no," she says. "That all stemmed from this article in *Woman* or *Woman's Own*."

It's an article which, she insists, wasn't *strictly* true. "If I was going to say something like that," she adds firmly, "I don't think I'd give it to *Woman*."

Quite. But didn't she – as one of the *Smash Hits* staff is sure they heard – appear on the radio recently and tell a phone-in caller that she'd been "dating" Jason for two years? Mysteriously the answer is "no".

"I haven't even been on the radio. Everyone in England is *strange*."

Hmmm. So what, pray tell, is the latest news on the couple's snog-up situation?

"Snog-up situation? What *do* you mean?"

Going "out".

"I don't say anything," she says, in the tone of someone launching into a much-practised speech. "I don't know what Jason says – that's up to him. I just say, 'Maybe we are, maybe we aren't.' I've given up denying that there is any linkage – of course we go out together and see each other, and we've just been working together."

So you don't live together?

"No."

That's a complete fabrication?

"Yes."

And you're not living in a house together in Australia?

"No."

Oh. This is confusing. So how do you feel singing lovey-dovey lyrics to each other?

"Well," she says, "we've been doing the same sort of things for the last three years as Scott and Charlene."

But this *isn't* Scott and Charlene, this is Jason and Kylie.

"Yes," she explains, "but it's the same as if I was doing a duet with someone else, we'd still be singing lovey dovey things. You know, like… er, I can't think of any duets of recent times."

Er… well there *is* Barbra Streisand and Don Johnson, and, spookily enough, there's a bit of a snog-up situation *there*, isn't there?

"Ha ha ha," laughs Kylie, quite amused by this thought. "*Definitely* snogging, I think."

So it does make one wonder, doesn't it?

"What about Dolly Parton and Kenny Rogers?" she asks.

Er… yes. But you must have known that this record would start tongues a-wagging…

"Obviously," Kylie agrees. "I don't know what Jason thought but it was the first thing I thought: 'Oh God, we're going to have to go through the same thing again.' Speaking for myself, I wouldn't have wanted to do it at the start, but the public demand… A rumour went round that we were going to do a record before we'd heard anything about it. The label had an amazing amount of orders for this unknown record, so we just thought, 'OK, we'll do it.' At Christmas time people do seem to do things a little bit different, don't they?"

Indeed. Can Kylie *perhaps* remember that fateful day when she was 11 and she met Jason, who appeared alongside her in an episode of the dreadful Australian TV series *Skyward*s?

"I can *vaguely* remember it," she says.

So what was he like?

The look of love? Jason and Kylie perform their "Especially For You" smasheroonie.

"I don't know," she insists. "At 10 or 11 you're not terribly interested in boys."

What did he *look* like?

"We both looked pretty *terrible*, actually," she admits. "He was really chubby with a bowl haircut and I was really *really* small with long straight blonde hair and big buck teeth."

Gosh. And did they see anything of each other between that meeting and the start of *Neighbours* years later?

"No," she says. "When I joined *Neighbours* I don't think he even remembered me. I said, 'Don't you remember? We did that show together?', because I remembered his name. I had to remind him. I must have made a *really* lasting impression."

Rather *odd* this, as we shall discover when we talk to Jason shortly. Anyway, what, pray Kylie, is Jason's most annoying habit?

"Oh God," she considers. "That would be dobbing him in it [????], wouldn't it?" In the end she plumps for his "perfectionism when acting".

Fair enough. So, if the two of them are not "dating", what do they make of all the stories claiming that they are?

"We have a good laugh about them," she says. "Whenever we're pictured together we are 'together' and when Jason's pictured with another girl I'm always '*terribly upset*'. One of the funniest ones was where I was '*terribly upset*' about

something and I was telling him, 'Grow up, Jason!'. Not *really* the kind of words I'd say to him."

It is true, isn't it, that the two of you did go on holiday together to Bali?

"Yes," she says. "The pressures of *Neighbours* were very great, so it was good just to get away, not to have to get up at six o'clock in the morning." The best, she says, was exploring.

"There's lots of temples, monkey farms, things like that."

Monkey farms?

"It's a place you go," she explains none too clearly, "like a temple."

That's about it then, is it?

"Well, if I *was* going out with Jason," she says finally, "I wouldn't tell *you* anyway."

Thought not…

SO LET US instead talk to Jason Donovan. Jason is not in England, not, as some of the papers suggested, because he wanted to "snub" the Royal Variety Show but because he's filming a mini-series called *The Heroes*. In fact, he is right now on the telephone from Sydney, ringing up at four o'clock *in the morning* Australian time from his apartment. He's just spent two freezing hours filming neck-deep in a river, acting out his part as a naval ratings officer called Huston…

"It's a totally different role to my *Neighbours* character – very serious," he says, "and that's basically the reason I chose to do it."

So what, please tell us, is the best line you have to say?

"My favourite line?" he considers. "'She'll be apples, major!' It's an Australian expression meaning, 'Don't worry, everything will be fine'."

Quite. This, you will be pleased to know, will be aired on British television screens along with other such odd expressions

next April. Meanwhile, though, Jason has this duet out, which inevitably begs none other than the question that's on everybody's lips, ie, if dreams were wings would *you* fly to Kylie?

For some reason this question causes a considerable amount of amused spluttering in Jason's Sydney apartment. After a while, his answer booms – thanks to the miracle of telecommunications – back round the world.

"No comment."

Er, what does *that* mean?

"That's up to the *Smash Hits* readers' imaginations."

So he's not prepared to confess whether he and Kylie are having a snog-up? The record doesn't represent their love affair going public?

"No," he says. "It's *certainly* not the case in real life. It's always been a mystery. The thing is, a lot of people do see us out together and a lot of people also don't understand that we're together because we're friends and there's no more than that, as you may say. It's a funny situation. I would consider Kylie probably my closest friend in terms of that, but not necessarily in a sexual sense. That's the bare facts. She's a good mate and good buddy and I'm sure she considers me the same. It doesn't mean to say we're having a love affair."

The record is going to make even more people suspect the opposite, isn't it?

"Sure it will, but the record is a song and it expresses a friendship… love in the sense of love doesn't necessarily mean being sexually involved in terms of going out with someone. You can love someone without necessarily going to bed with them, for example. And I certainly feel that I've got a very close feeling for and a very close friendship with Kylie, and I think that comes through with the song."

Hmmmm. So can he recall the first time they met?

"I was about 11," Scott answers, "on a television show called *Skyways*."

Here's where the decidedly odd bit comes in…

"We've kept in contact ever since," he says.

Pop's golden couple... *Awww,* ain't they loverly, possums?

"Yeah," he says. "That'd be right. That's true. I just like things to be right. I do expect perfection. I suppose that's me. So many people don't have any goals."

Apart from this duet malarkey and his acting, Jason reveals that he'll be recording an LP with Stock, Aitken & Waterman in January.

He also reveals that he writes songs himself with his mates as well, even though none of them will be on the LP. "I'm still learning as a musician," he says, "but as a lyricist I think I can write quite nice stuff."

He chats away about three of his "self-penned numbers", one called "Hold Me Now", one called "Please Come Back" and one slightly bizarre affair called "The Yellow Cab".

"That was about a trip of mine to New York. It's sort of about a yellow cab that could take you through New York and explore what New York's about, and you can be in the cab, like your thoughts – 'Jeez, I'm in the biggest city in the world, I'm in this cab! Wow!'"

The mind "boggles". Right now though, Jason is looking forward to coming to Britain. One reason is that he wants to feel the excitement of having a hit record while he's here – he wasn't here for the success of "Nothing Can Divide Us" and although it's now at Number 3 in Australia, he explains it's a bit useless because they never play records like his or Kylie's on Australian radio, so it's hard to get excited about it all. The second is that he wants to come over and see a proper British winter.

"I can't wait. I've never had a white Christmas. Do you think it's going to snow for me? *Especially* for me?" he quips.

Oh dear. What a *very* corny thing to say. Jason is delightfully proud of it.

"This record," he repeats, "is especially for you, but could it snow especially for me? That can be my classic comment. You can write that down as the quote."

I *think* we'll just put it at the end, actually...

How *very* strange, for didn't just a few hours before, Kylie state that they'd not met between *Skyways* and *Neighbours*? So you kept in touch in-between?

"Yeah, we kept in contact," confirms Jason. "Not on a regular basis as we did when we were both in *Neighbours* but I guess that's the result of working with people. We used to just phone up to say 'hi', and just have a chat. When I was at school she was just about 20 minutes from my house – I'd just pop round to say 'hi'."

Mmmm. Make of *that* what you will. So how does he remember her on their very first meeting?

"Jeez," he exclaims. "That's going back a long way."

Kylie says that you had a pudding-bowl haircut and were a bit chubby.

This observation serves to spur on his memory. "Oh *yeah*?" he chuckles. "*She* had quite big teeth too. If she's putting one up on me I might as well do the same! 'Pudding-bowl haircut', eh? This is terrible... I suppose her two front teeth were quite prominent, if you want to put it in any shape, way or form. She was," he hurriedly adds, "a very nice person."

So what, now, is her most annoying habit?

"Did you ask this question to her?" he enquires, a little concerned. After thinking for a moment, he answers. "Two things. One, she tends to shake her shoulders sometimes... it's like a twitch... well, not a *twitch*, a mannerism she's picked up. She also tends to pick her lips all the time. That's as far as I'll go. What did she say about me?

Kylie said that you were a terrible perfectionist.

"Mine's a cheese 'n' banana 'n' turnip..."

MATT & LUKE GOSS

"We've got the same favourite – chicken salad on any kind of bread with loads of mayonnaise. And as many sandwiches as possible, please!"

...Berrrlee!! Sandwiches say a lot about one's "personality". Some folk favour cucumber and cress with the crusts cut off. Others go for giant chip butties. But what do the stars prefer?

YAZZ

"Favourite filling? Aw, that's really sweet! [??] Tofu and mayonnaise. Tofu's ab-so-lutely brilliant – honest! You can make sauces with it and all sorts – you can even make it taste like cheese! Then again, there's nothing quite like toast and a nice cup of tea, is there?"

HOLLY JOHNSON

"My perfect sandwich is tuna with mayonnaise and tomato sauce all mixed up together, and then there'll be a few thin slices of cucumber and one slice of tomato, and it'll be an open sandwich on a doorstop-slice of granary bread. Would I have a garnish on top? Mmmm... well maybe an optional green olive, yeah."

Paul Rider, Smash Hits Archive

TIFFANY

"French bread with loads of mustard, thin-sliced smoked turkey, roast beef, lettuce, tomatoes, onions, hot chili peppers, with black olives, and salt and pepper. And the mustard should be spread real thin all over. But not hot mustard – it has to be regular. Real nice!"

DAME DAVID
BROTHER BEYOND

"Tuna fish, coleslaw and mayonnaise in a brown bap."

CARL
BROTHER BEYOND

"Chicken salad and mayonnaise in a wholemeal bap."

NATHAN
BROTHER BEYOND

"Chicken liver paté in a baguette."

MARK SHAW
THEN JERICO

"Sausages. Any kind of sausages. Chipolatas… they're good, pork and beef… mmm… and I'll have that with tomato sauce on lettuce. Actually, I'm not too sure about the lettuce, I don't like green things. I do like carrots but they're not green, are they? Green is obviously the root of the problem…" [??]

MARK MOORE
S'XPRESS

"Well I do like Parma ham and salami sandwiches, but the one I have most is a slice of toasted bread with beans and a slice of Dairylea on top. I usually have four slices of those sitting in the fridge for when I get a bit peckish. Then I take one out, put it under the grill and toast it! And that way I ensure my daily intake of protein. It's my instant meal recipe!!!"

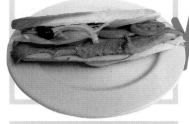

KYLIE MINOGUE

"A chocolate sandwich. That's my favourite food! I try to stay away from things like chocolate but I like things like Flake bars. I don't like too many sweet things generally but I do like chocolate. When I was at school I sort of rationed myself to buy a little chocolate something and I'd nibble it really slowly so it'd last through lunchtime. Have I got any fillings? I haven't got any, actually!"

ROLAND GIFT FINE YOUNG CANNIBALS

"Well, it would be on wafer-thin slices of some sort of stoneground bread. The first slice would have some butter on it, then loads of rashers of bacon, grilled until they're really crispy, then some normal lettuce, some radicchio lettuce, and then some watercress – not that mustard cress crap, the real stuff that looks like spinach leaves. And then on top of all that I'd pile gallons of tomato sauce until it was cascading down the sides, then another slice of bread on top."

10 YEARS... 262 COVERS

Smash Hits greeted 1980 with a pic of New York new wavers Blondie and bade a cheery "tara" to the decade of Thatcherism and padded shoulders with a collage that brought together Bros, Soul II Soul and Axl Rose. In between, our front cover served as an ever-changing window on the giddy world of '80s pop. Which one was *your* favourite?

1980

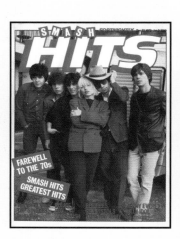

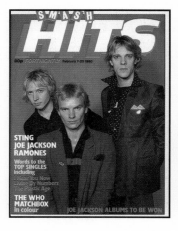

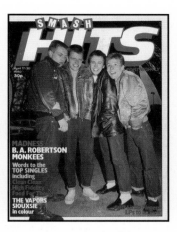

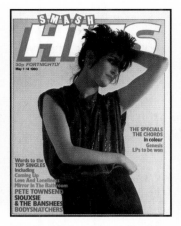

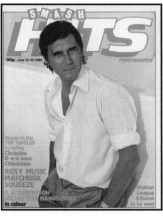

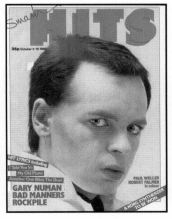

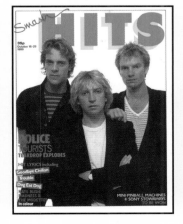

1981

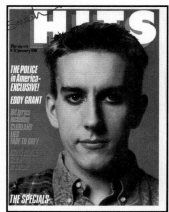

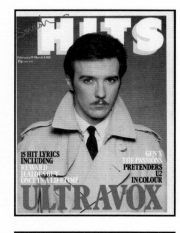

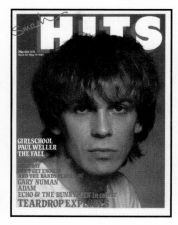

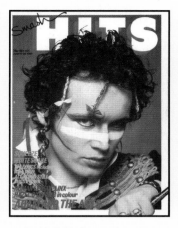

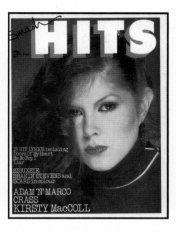

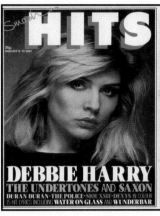

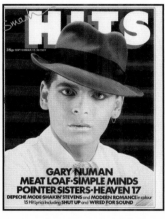

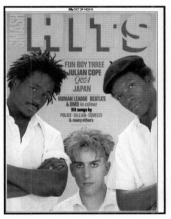

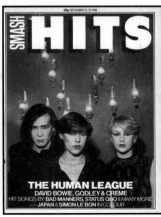

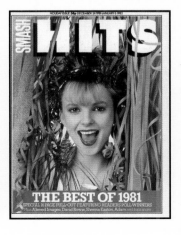

1982

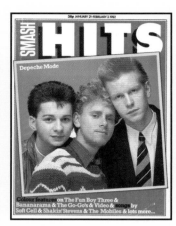

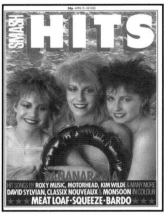

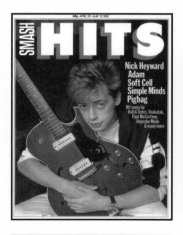

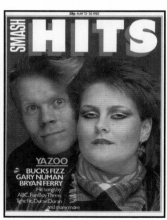

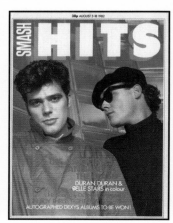

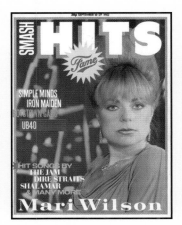

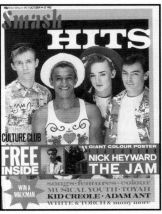

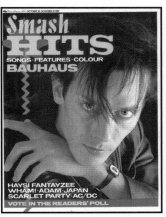

1983

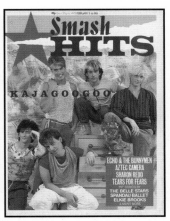

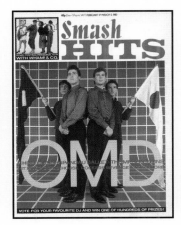

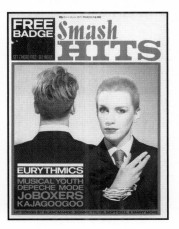

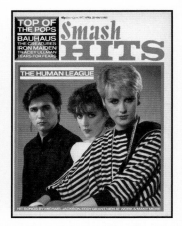

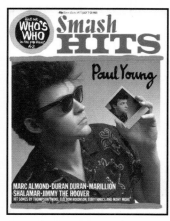

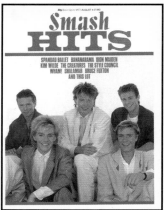

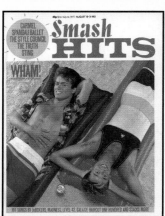

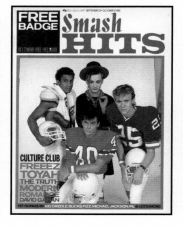

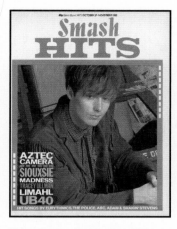

1984

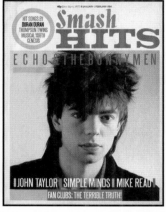

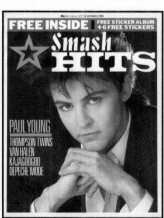

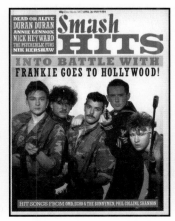

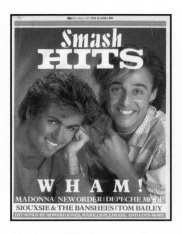

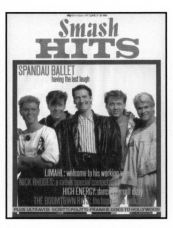

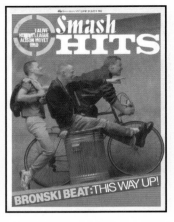

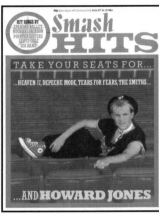

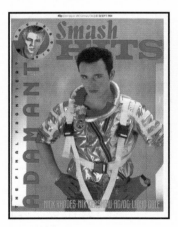

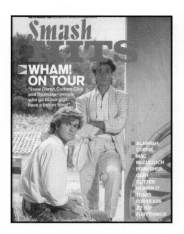

1985

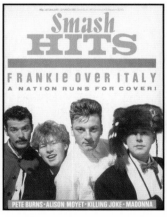

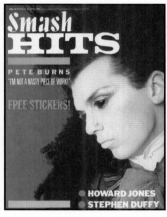

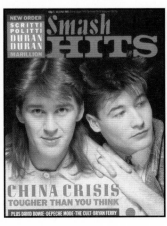

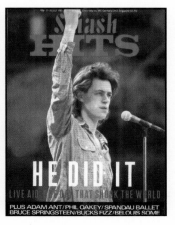

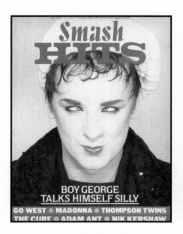

Smash
HITS

BOY GEORGE
TALKS HIMSELF SILLY

GO WEST ● MADONNA ● THOMPSON TWINS
THE CURE ● ADAM ANT ● NIK KERSHAW

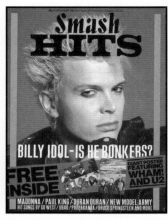

Smash
HITS

BILLY IDOL - IS HE BONKERS?

FREE
INSIDE

GIANT POSTER
FEATURING
WHAM!
AND U2

MADONNA / PAUL KING / DURAN DURAN / NEW MODEL ARMY
HIT SONGS BY GO WEST / UB40 / PROPAGANDA / BRUCE SPRINGSTEEN AND MORE

WHAT IS HAPPENING TO
DURAN DURAN?

+

£2000 WORTH OF PERSONAL STEREOS TO BE WON!

KING / THOMPSON TWINS / KATE BUSH / RED BOX / BANANARAMA
PLUS MADNESS ● THE CARS ● AMAZULU ● MARILLION ● DAVID BOWIE AND MICK JAGGER

SMASH HITS

"Randy Andy!
Arrogant Andy!
Aggressive Andy!
Dribbling Andy!
I just can't win!"

Andrew Ridgeley On
What The Papers Say

Madness
Marc Almond
Tears For Fears
Dream Academy
Stephen Duffy

FREE FLEXI SINGLE!

SMASH HITS

NIK KERSHAW & PAUL YOUNG
THE BEST OF FRIENDS?

MIDGE URE WHAM! BLANCMANGE FREDDIE MERCURY DEAD OR ALIVE

FREE INSIDE
THE SMASH HITS SCRAPBOOK / DIARY

+ MADONNA
4 - PAGE PULL-OUT

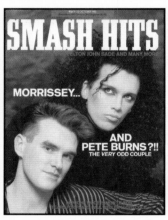

SMASH HITS

MORRISSEY...

AND
PETE BURNS ?!!
THE VERY ODD COUPLE

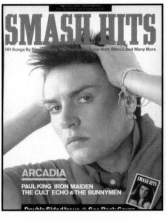

SMASH HITS

ARCADIA

PAUL KING IRON MAIDEN
THE CULT ECHO & THE BUNNYMEN

Double Sided Issue ● See Back Cover

SMASH HITS

SIMPLE MINDS

SIOUXSIE & THE BANSHEES UB40
PAUL HARDCASTLE GO WEST HOWARD JONES

DURAN DURAN: THE FILM

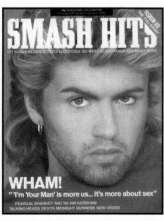

SMASH HITS

WHAM!
" 'I'm Your Man' is more us... it's more about sex"

FEARGAL SHARKEY MAI TAI NIK KERSHAW
TALKING HEADS DEXYS MIDNIGHT RUNNERS NEW ORDER

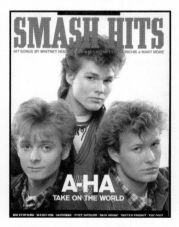

SMASH HITS

A-HA
TAKE ON THE WORLD

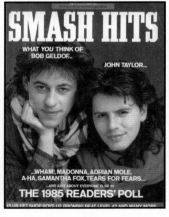

SMASH HITS

WHAT YOU THINK OF
BOB GELDOF...

JOHN TAYLOR...

...WHAM!, MADONNA, ADRIAN MOLE,
A-HA, SAMANTHA FOX, TEARS FOR FEARS...
AND JUST ABOUT EVERYONE ELSE IN
THE 1985 READERS' POLL

PLUS PET SHOP BOYS U2 BRONSKI BEAT LEVEL 42 AND MANY MORE

1986

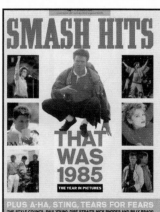

SMASH HITS

THAT
WAS
1985
THE YEAR IN PICTURES

PLUS A-HA, STING, TEARS FOR FEARS
THE STYLE COUNCIL, PAUL YOUNG, DIRE STRAITS, NICK RHODES AND BILLY BRAGG

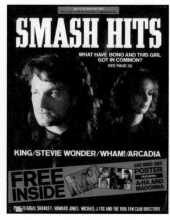

SMASH HITS

WHAT HAVE BONO AND THIS GIRL
GOT IN COMMON?
SEE PAGE 32

KING/STEVIE WONDER/WHAM!/ARCADIA

FREE
INSIDE

GIANT DOUBLE-SIDED
POSTER
FEATURING
A-HA AND
MADONNA

PLUS FEARGAL SHARKEY / HOWARD JONES / MICHAEL J. FOX AND THE 1986 FAN CLUB DIRECTORY

SMASH HITS

THE ALARM
AND THE SPIRIT OF '76

FEARGAL SHARKEY ● FIVE STAR
MR MISTER MADONNA TALK TALK
FINE YOUNG CANNIBALS ● LLOYD COLE

MR & MRS BON

SMASH HITS

LOOK OUT!

HE'S BACK! WHO'S BACK?
SEE PAGE 10

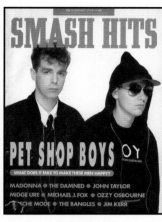

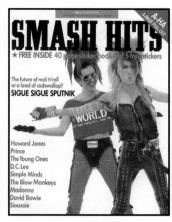

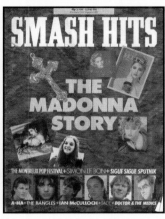

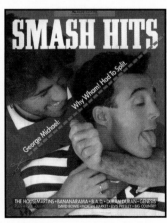

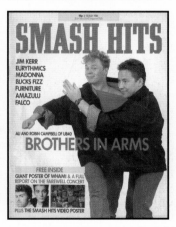

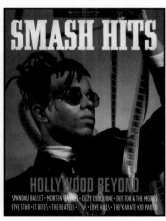

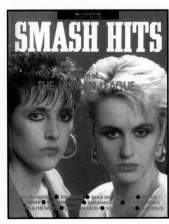

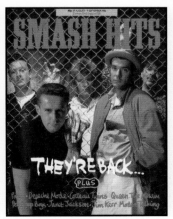

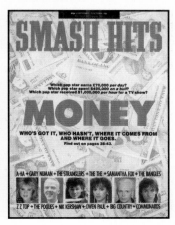

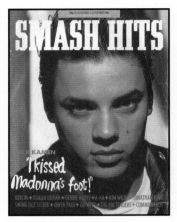
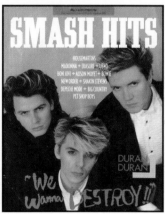

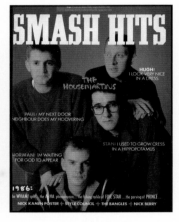

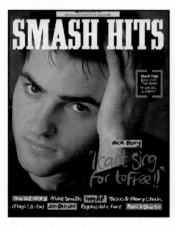

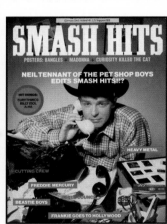
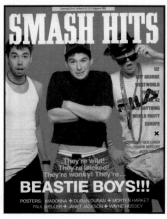

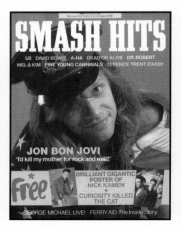

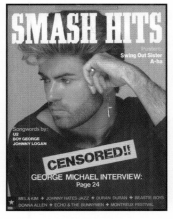

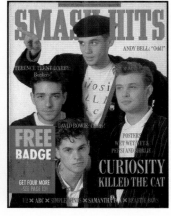

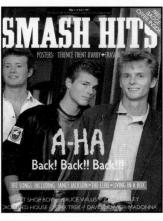

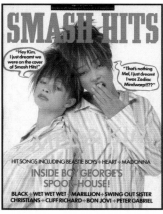

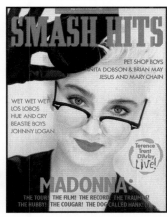

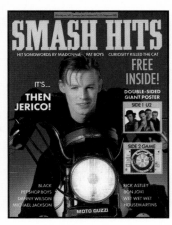

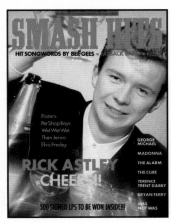

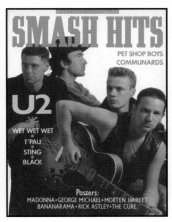

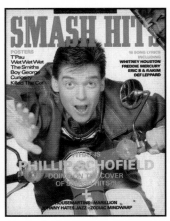

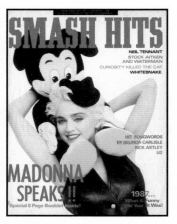

1988

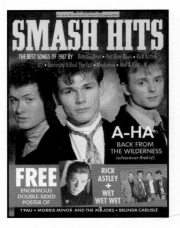

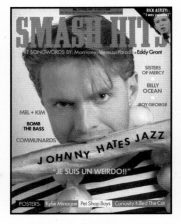

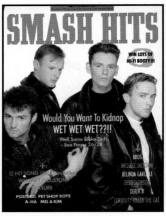

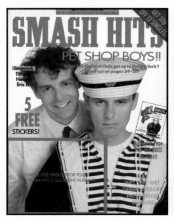

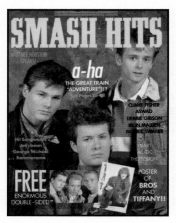

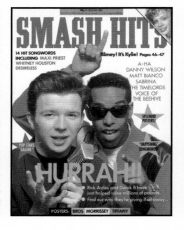

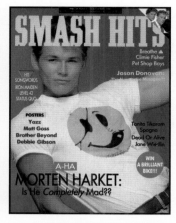

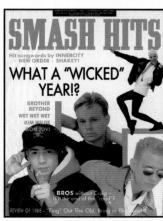

1989

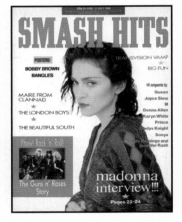

SMASHING STATISTICS

The only '80s pop chart that matters! Appearances on the Smash Hits cover...

15 Duran Duran (including The Power Station, Arcadia)

10 Wham!

8 Bros, Jason Donovan

7 A-Ha, Pet Shop Boys

6 Madonna

5 Culture Club, Frankie Goes To Hollywood, Kylie, Wet Wet Wet

4 ABC, Bob Geldof, Depeche Mode, Howard Jones, Human League, Paul Weller, Paul Young, Rick Astley, Terry Hall, Toyah

3 Altered Images, Blondie, Brother Beyond, Eurythmics, Haircut 100, Japan, John Lydon, Madness, Neneh Cherry, New Kids On The Block, Nik Kershaw, Orchestral Manoeuvres In The Dark, Phillip Schofield, Spandau Ballet, Tears For Fears, The Police

2 Adam Ant, Bananarama, Billy Idol, Curiosity Killed The Cat, Five Star, Gary Numan, Heaven 17, Howard Jones, Marilyn, Morrissey, Pete Burns, Simple Minds, Steve Strange, The Cure, Then Jericho, Thompson Twins, Tiffany, Tracie, Transvision Vamp, U2, Yazz

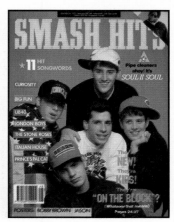

SO, FAREWELL THEN...